RICHARD JEFFERIES

A Critical Study

UNIVERSITY OF TORONTO DEPARTMENT OF ENGLISH
Studies and Texts, No. 13

Richard Jefferies

Title

A CRITICAL
STUDY
BY W. J. KEITH

UNIVERSITY OF TORONTO PRESS
LONDON: OXFORD UNIVERSITY PRESS
1965

Printed and Bound in England by
Hazell Watson and Viney, Ltd., Aylesbury, Bucks

Preface

THIS BOOK is an attempt to define the nature of Richard Jefferies' contribution to English literature, and to isolate the more important and effective qualities of his work. The first chapter provides the basic background material—a brief biographical account and a survey of Jefferies' historical context. The form of subsequent chapters is dictated by the genre of individual books, and not necessarily by chronological order of composition. This is necessary for my particular approach, and the bibliography of Jefferies' books and pamphlets (pp. 170–2) is arranged in order of publication so that the reader should have little difficulty in checking chronology.

I have been assisted in the preparation of this book by many people, and it is a pleasure to acknowledge at least the most obvious debts of gratitude. First and foremost, a serious student of Jefferies must continually be aware of the deep debt he owes to the lifelong research of the late Samuel J. Looker, whose painstaking labours have made so much of Jefferies' previously unpublished or uncollected writings available to the reader. My own debt to Mr. Looker is further increased by his encouraging interest in my work and his readiness to answer queries through several years' correspondence. I would also like to record here that the list of Jefferies' contributions to the *Live Stock Journal*, which Mr. Looker printed at the end of *Field and Farm*, greatly assisted my own check-list of Jefferies' essays and articles. Indeed, it would have been quite impossible to write this book without the benefit of Mr. Looker's work and example, for which I am deeply grateful.

I am also obligated to Mrs. Frances J. Gay, Chairman of the Richard Jefferies Society, Swindon, who has been of incalculable assistance in lending me books and pamphlets, relaying information, checking references, and giving general encouragement.

I would also like to express appreciation to Professor N. J. Endicott of the University of Toronto for helpful criticism and advice during an earlier stage in the writing of this book, and to the Canada Council and the University of Toronto for scholarships that enabled me to engage in lengthy preliminary research. I would also like to record here that a correspondence with Mr. Eric Jones of Oxford helped to clarify some of my ideas concerning Jefferies' agricultural writings.

The publication of this book has been assisted by grants from the Humanities Research Council of Canada and the Publications Fund of the University of Toronto Press. Without the generous support of both these organizations, it is doubtful if this study could have been published. I also owe a particular debt of gratitude to two members of the University of Toronto Press who have been especially helpful: the Editor, Miss Francess Halpenny, for general counsel and encouragement, and Miss M. L. Pearson, for expert advice during the preparation of the manuscript.

Countless others have helped me verbally or by correspondence; their names are too many to be listed individually here, but I hope they will accept this generalized acknowledgment of their services. The inadequacies are my own.

McMaster University
January 1965   W. J. K.

Contents

Abbreviations and References

TO AVOID excessive footnoting, I have used abbreviations in the text when referring to Jefferies' own works. Where possible I have quoted from modern texts that would be more accessible to the reader. A key to the abbreviations and texts is given below. Details of first editions will be found in the bibliography.

AF   *Amaryllis at the Fair.* Everyman edition (with *After London*). London: Dent, 1939.

AL   *After London; or, Wild England.* Everyman edition. *See above.*

AP   *The Amateur Poacher.* World's Classics edition (with *The Gamekeeper at Home*). Oxford: University Press, 1948.

B   *Bevis.* London: Jonathan Cape, 1932.

CH   *Chronicles of the Hedges.* London: Phoenix House, 1948.

DM   *The Dewy Morn.* London: Bentley, 1884. 2 vols.

FF   *Field and Farm.* London: Phoenix House, 1957.

FH   *Field and Hedgerow.* London: Lutterworth Press, 1948.

GFF   *Greene Ferne Farm.* London: Smith Elder, 1880.

GH   *The Gamekeeper at Home.* World's Classics edition. See under *The Amateur Poacher* above.

HM   *Hodge and His Masters.* London: Eyre & Spottiswoode, 1949.

HV   *The Hills and the Vale.* London: Duckworth, 1909.

JL   *Jefferies' Land.* London: Simpkin, Marshall, 1896.

LF   *The Life of the Fields.* London: Lutterworth Press, 1947.

N   *The Nature Diaries and Note-Books of Richard Jefferies.* Edited by Samuel J. Looker. London: Grey Walls Press, 1948.

NNL   *Nature Near London*. London: Chatto & Windus, 1883.

OA   *The Open Air*. London: Eyre & Spottiswoode, 1948.

OHC   *The Old House at Coate*. London: Lutterworth Press, 1948.

RGE   *Round About a Great Estate* (with *Red Deer*). London: Eyre & Spottiswoode, 1948.

RD   *Red Deer* (with *Round About a Great Estate*). See above.

REA   *Reporting, Editing, and Authorship*. London: John Snow, 1873.

RHH   *Restless Human Hearts*. London: Tinsley, 1875. 3 vols.

SH   *The Story of My Heart*. London: Constable, 1947.

SS   *The Scarlet Shawl*. London: Tinsley, 1874.

SY   *The Spring of the Year*. London: Lutterworth Press, 1946.

TF   *The Toilers of the Field*. London: Longmans, 1892.

WL   *Wild Life in a Southern County*. London: Lutterworth Press, 1949.

WM   *Wood Magic*. London: Longmans, 1934.

Acknowledgments

MY CHIEF DEBT of acknowledgment is owed to the late Samuel J. Looker, who has generously allowed me to quote freely from those writings of Jefferies which he was the first to publish and of which he held the copyright. These include *The Nature Diaries and Note-Books of Richard Jefferies*, *The Old House at Coate*, the first draft of *The Story of My Heart*, and the hitherto unpublished material in *Chronicles of the Hedges* and *Field and Farm*.

Acknowledgments are also due to the following: Lutterworth Press and J. M. Dent and Sons for permission to quote from their editions of Richard Jefferies; Penguin Books, Ltd. for the quotations from the *Pelican Guide to English Literature* and Victor Bonham-Carter's *The English Village*; the *Daily Telegraph* (London) for a passage from a review-article by J. H. B. Peel; Q. D. Leavis for passages from her *Scrutiny* article on Jefferies; and Mrs. Edward Thomas and Faber and Faber, Ltd. for permission to quote four lines from Edward Thomas's poem, "Lob."

RICHARD JEFFERIES
A Critical Study

1. Jefferies' Life and Times

THE NAME of Richard Jefferies is often to be found on the periphery of the English literary scene in that indistinct no-man's-land that skirts the boundaries of creative literature, natural history, and rural sociology. Indeed, his neglect can partly be explained as a difficulty of classification, an uncertainty whether he should be considered alongside Thomas Hardy, or Gilbert White, or William Cobbett. He has links with all these, and it may be argued that the range of his interests should serve as a distinction rather than as an encumbrance. He can claim a wider knowledge of rural life than Hardy, a more active imagination than White, a greater intellectul subtlety than Cobbett. This is not to deny that he lacks several of the distinctive qualities of these and other rural writers, but for a comprehensive view of the English countryside at a challenging and decisive moment in its history, there is no more reliable guide than Richard Jefferies.

All this would suggest that, when in search of what is valuable in Jefferies, we should turn to his writings rather than his life, and the emphasis of this book will therefore be more critical than biographical. It may be readily admitted that a knowledge of at least the general tenor of his life is essential for an understanding of his literary output, but the important consideration is not so much the facts of his life as the nature of it. Few writers can have been more influenced by their childhood environment, and the ideals and concerns that underlie his writing were all moulded and governed by his early memories. It is in this sense that we can describe him as an intensely personal writer: his essays are the fruit of an intimate but solitary love for the Wiltshire countryside, his powerful but unequal novels are most successful when most dependent upon his personal knowledge and experience, while *The Story of My Heart*, his spiritual confession, presents the obstinate questionings of a determined, uncompromising, personality. Edward Thomas has already provided us with an excellent biography in *Richard Jefferies: His Life and Work*. Here I am content to give the main facts that are essential as a background to what is for me the more important process of serious discussion and evaluation of Jefferies' work.

Richard Jefferies was born on November 6, 1848, at Coate Farmhouse near Swindon, Wiltshire. His father, the original Iden of *Amaryllis at the Fair*, farmed an area of less than fifty acres, and was destined in later years to fight a losing battle against poverty in an age of increasing agricultural depression. During the years of Jefferies' childhood, however, the family was comfortable enough, and from the earliest years the boy was impressed by the traditional association between his family and the locality in which it had lived and worked for centuries. There is evidence to suggest that Jefferies' family, like Hardy's, had declined in recent generations. Both writers were descended, it seems, from independent yeoman stock which was fast becoming obsolete in the nineteenth-century rural class-structure, and both were affected by the traditions and attitudes of an earlier time. It is helpful at this point to quote from a description by one of Jefferies' cousins, Miss F. C. Hall, of the life at Coate Farm, appreciation of which is vital to an understanding of his general approach to agricultural matters:

James Luckett Jefferies, the father of Richard, has been always placed on a line with the ordinary small tenant farmer, but this is a grave error, as the possession of land in all time has been productive of very different sentiment to that arising from occupancy by tenancy. . . . The farmhouse in which Richard Jefferies was born was the freehold of his father, presented to him on his marriage by his father, John Jefferies, and anyone who ever lived or even visited at the old home, would know how every individual inch of the ground, every sapling tree, every flowering shrub or nest-hiding hedgerow was loved and treasured by its owner. . . . The land was his—a little Naboth's vineyard, much coveted by surrounding landowners.[1]

1. Jefferies Luckett [Miss F. C. Hall], "The Forebears of Richard Jefferies," *Country Life*, March 14, 1908, 375.

When he came to write about farmers and farming, Jefferies continually stressed the importance of a traditional connection with, and love for, the land. "I am a son of the soil," he wrote in a late letter, and added that "my family have been farmers and landowners for nearly three hundred years" (FF, 41).

Jefferies was allowed considerable freedom during his childhood, and has left an idealized picture of his early days in *Bevis*. His formal schooling seems to have been somewhat irregular and unsettled, but this was more than balanced by the natural education that he received in the Wiltshire countryside. It was in the period of boyhood and adolescence that Jefferies developed his loving familiarity with rural things, the material that was later to become the staple of his writing. The few records of his early days that have come down to us bear witness to his shyness and love of solitude. Though he became known in the neighbourhood for his habit of taking long walks on the Downs, he seems to have been somewhat delicate and showed little interest in the more boisterous sports of his fellows. Instead, he was a keen reader and borrowed eagerly from the libraries of relatives and friends. He acquired a reputation as solitary, perhaps even as eccentric, but we can now appreciate that this was a time of accurate observation and learning, a time that laid the firm foundations of his subsequent career as naturalist and writer. When old enough to handle a gun, he adds the role of sportsman to his other achievements, and his friendship with Keeper Haylock of the nearby Burderop estate, the original for *The Gamekeeper at Home*, further increased his rural knowledge. To be set against this, however, is the comment from a local squire: "That young Jefferies is not the sort of fellow you want hanging about in your covers." [2] This need not have been an altogether unjustified suspicion concerning the future author of *The Amateur Poacher*.

His intimate knowledge of the local district was soon to stand him in good stead. Though a loyal countryman, Jefferies had no interest in a career in farming, and at the age of seventeen he obtained a post as reporter on a local newspaper, the *North Wilts Herald*; a little later, he joined the staff of the *Wilts and Gloucestershire Standard*. Provincial journalism may not be the ideal training for a creative writer, but there can be little doubt that it was helpful to Jefferies in giving him plenty of practice in detailed and compact description. Although there are indications that his talents

2. Quoted in Edward Thomas, *Richard Jefferies: His Life and Work* (1909), p. 47.

as reporter were limited, he seems to have taken his work seriously, and his first separate publication was a pamphlet somewhat ironically entitled *Reporting, Editing, and Authorship*. This appeared in 1873, and in it Jefferies draws upon the experiences of these earlier days. "The first object of the reporter," he writes, "should . . . be to acquire an insight into the real state of things, to get behind the scenes, so as to thoroughly comprehend the outward show placed before the public" (*REA*, 3). Jefferies himself reaped the harvest of this advice not as reporter but as essayist, for his success as a literary artist largely depends, as we shall see, on detailed and exhaustive knowledge of his local countryside. A little later in the pamphlet, Jefferies shows how a reporter's knowledge can be applied to more ambitious projects:

The reporter, while going about the country studying as he goes its topography, antiquities, traditions, and general characteristics, will have ample opportunities of amassing materials for original sketches in the paper. . . . He can then write a local history, or, taking an old tradition, or a noted spot, for the centre-piece, weave a short story out of his imagination around it. (*REA*, 27–8)

This is in fact a transcript of his own method. While on the staff of the *North Wilts Herald*, he had written a "History of Malmesbury" and a "History of Swindon," the latter reprinted after his death as *Jefferies' Land*, and a number of early and worthless short stories contributed to the same paper have been collected as *The Early Fiction of Richard Jefferies*. It is clear from the pamphlet that he possessed a soaring ambition which would not long be content with mere provincial reporting.

It was not until 1872 that he attracted attention beyond the immediate limits of Swindon. In November of that year, when agricultural matters were being eagerly debated, *The Times* published three of his letters on the Wiltshire agricultural labourer, and devoted a leading article to the subject which attracted much attention. But at this time Jefferies' ambitions were directed towards fiction and in 1874 he published *The Scarlet Shawl*, the first of three early and unsuccessful novels. Like Hardy's first volumes of fiction, these novels appeared under the imprint of William Tinsley, and Jefferies himself contributed towards costs of publication. In the same year he married Miss Jessie Baden, daughter of a nearby farmer, who was to bear him three children, tend him diligently and faithfully through his years as invalid, and long outlive him.

It has sometimes been argued that Jefferies failed to follow up the *Times* letters, and thereby missed an opportunity to gain a wider reputation, but this is not altogether true. From now on he gradually began contributing to the national magazines. In 1873 "The Future of Farming" appeared, the first of several essays to be printed in *Fraser's Magazine*. The following year, essays appeared in the *Fortnightly Review* and the *New Quarterly*, and in 1875 the *Graphic* and the *Standard* began to accept his work. By 1877 Jefferies felt justified in moving nearer London to take up a literary career, though he could hardly have foreseen that he would never live again in his beloved Wiltshire. He was soon contributing regularly to the *Live Stock Journal* and the *Pall Mall Gazette*, and it was in the latter newspaper that *The Gamekeeper at Home* first appeared. Published as a book in 1878, it was enthusiastically received and ran into four editions by 1880. For the remaining years of his life he continued to write essays on various aspects of the countryside which were subsequently published in book form. These were interspersed with novels and other writings. In 1881 he fell ill with fistula and underwent many painful operations. He was never in full health again, nor was he ever free from financial anxiety. *The Story of My Heart*, which he had been pondering for seventeen years, was published in 1883. But the end was then near; tuberculosis set in, and by 1885 he was a permanent invalid, his last poignant essays being dictated to his ever patient wife. He died at Goring in Sussex on August 14, 1887.

Although within recent years the Victorian age in literature has enjoyed renewed popularity, and many minor writers of the period have been attracting increased attention and appreciation, there seems to have been no general renewal of critical interest in Jefferies' works. This is in many ways surprising. In 1948, the centenary of his birth coincided in England with the popular revival of enthusiasm for the countryside at the end of the Second World War. New cheap editions of his works were issued, commemorative articles appeared in magazines as varied as the *Adelphi*, the *Contemporary Review*, *Country Life*, the *Fortnightly Review*, and *Picture Post*, and the way seemed clear for a renewal of more scholarly attention which never in fact materialized. There are several possible reasons for this neglect at an academic level. One is a belief that Jefferies, as a writer mainly interested in rural life, was more the concern of the naturalist than the literary critic. Another may have been reaction against indiscriminate praise from certain quarters; as C. Henry Warren wrote at the time, "It has been his misfortune to attract the uncritical admiration of a considerable body of what one may call the wind-on-the-heath brethren,"[3] and this may well have aroused the prejudice of the less athletically minded. But whatever the reason may have been, interest cooled; the two publishing companies who announced collected editions have been unable to complete the projects, and apart from the publication by Samuel J. Looker of a book of hitherto uncollected essays, *Field and Farm*, and the recent opening of a Richard Jefferies Museum at his birthplace, his reputation as a literary artist seems to have sunk once more into comparative oblivion.

It is unfortunate that Jefferies should be neglected in this way, for he is one of the most rewarding and interesting of minor nineteenth-century writers. However, from time to time a number of reputable critics have drawn attention to the quality of his work. As early as 1938 Q. D. Leavis, in a detailed review in *Scrutiny*, wrote:

Jefferies was a many-sided and comprehensive genius, not merely a peculiarly English genius but one whose interests, ideas, and temperament associate him with other peculiarly English geniuses: he recalls or embodies now Cobbett, now D. H. Lawrence, now Dickens, now Edward Thomas himself and he had a sensuous nature akin to but more robust than Keats'; he has too a strikingly contemporary aspect as social satirist, and he is in the central and most important tradition of English prose style.[4]

If such praise is justified, and I believe that on the whole it is, there can be no doubt that Jefferies is at present seriously underrated. Mrs. Leavis is also right to stress the extreme variety to be found in his writings; this is not generally acknowledged because most of his readers are content to confine themselves to one particular aspect of his work. Though he can never be said to have been a popular writer, Jefferies has never been without a small but faithful body of admirers. Yet, if we were to ask a cross-section of these to name the book which they considered his masterpiece, there would, I am certain, be a surprisingly large number of different answers. Many would undoubtedly pick one of the books of natural history— either one of the country books or a collection of individual essays; others would unhesitatingly choose *The Story of My Heart*; a third group will

---

3. C. Henry Warren, "Richard Jefferies," *New English Review*, I (Sept. 1948), 25-6.
4. Q. D. Leavis, "Lives and Works of Richard Jefferies," *Scrutiny*, VI (March 1938), 437.

always associate his name with that great classic of boyhood, *Bevis*. Yet we have still to exhaust his range. In *Hodge and His Masters* and *The Toilers of the Field* he was a chronicler as much of rural civilization as of animals and birds, while his later novels can rival those of Thomas Hardy in truth and integrity if not in control and fictional technique.

Despite all this to his credit, the literary histories are generally content to allot him a minor place between Hardy and W. H. Hudson, and the reason seems to lie in the difficulty of establishing his true centre of interest. The problem was conveniently summed up by J. H. B. Peel in his review of *Field and Farm* in the *Daily Telegraph* (Aug. 16, 1957): "The truth is, Jefferies was too vague and too precise for all save the few. He was vague because mystical, and precise because practical. Having set down his intimations *de rerum natura*, he would turn away to analyse the contents of a rook's stomach." It is an argument that often arises when Jefferies is discussed. For my part, I see the combination of the two apparently incompatible ways of looking as a strength rather than a weakness. His "mysticism" (the application of the word to Jefferies is discussed in chapter IV) is to my mind made acceptable by the practical, down-to-earth side of his nature, and his descriptive power is enhanced by his visionary faculty.

We shall be encountering this apparent dichotomy between the reporter and the mystic throughout our discussion, but the two must be appreciated together and not in isolation. For its quality to be fully realized, Jefferies' work must be considered as a whole. Not only will this draw attention to his range, which would be an important result in itself, but it will reveal the essential connections between books which, at first sight, appear unrelated. The unifying element is provided, of course, by the natural environment. Jefferies' distinction lies in his ability to present the countryside on paper in all its variety and complexity, and this variety involves consideration of the human inhabitants as well as of the flora and fauna, matters of opinion and emotion as well as statements of bare fact. Any study of Jefferies will ultimately become a study of the district around Coate Farmhouse, which has become known to English countrylovers as "Jefferies' Land."

In a journal entry for 1853, Thoreau wrote: "I cannot but regard it as a kindness in those who have the steering of me that, by the want of pecuniary wealth, I have been nailed down to this my native region so long and steadily, and made to study and love this spot more and more. What would signify in comparison a thin and diffused love and knowledge of the whole earth instead, got by wandering?"[5] Although circumstances decreed, in Jefferies' case, that he should be parted in his last years from the countryside of his birth, his love and devotion for his "native region" were no less strong than Thoreau's. As he wrote in a notebook, "no one can ever be far from the place where he was born: distance is not separation" (N, 159). The North Wiltshire countryside was the inspiration for all that is best in his writing. "Jefferies' Land," indeed, is as distinctive and as sacred as Hardy's Wessex, and its constant recurrence in description and anecdote throughout his work proves the power of its hold upon his mind. A description at this point would be inappropriate, Jefferies' own essays providing the best possible commentary, but almost a century has passed since Jefferies left Wiltshire, and many profound changes have taken place in the landscape in recent years. Admittedly, much remains the same; it is still possible to follow in Jefferies' footsteps, using his descriptive books as a guide, and see many of the things he saw in the very places where he saw them. None the less, the differences are far-reaching, and Jefferies is now sufficiently distant from ourselves in time for an effort of historical perspective to be necessary.

Moreover, Jefferies was himself impressed by the changes that had taken place during his own tragically short lifetime. Most dramatic was the break in continuity caused by the departure elsewhere of families that had been attached to their particular villages for centuries. The last essay he wrote, or rather dictated, was significantly entitled "My Old Village," and in it he contrasts the village of his childhood with the reports he has heard of its present state:

Almost the first thing I did with pen and ink as a boy was to draw a map of the hamlet with the roads and lanes and paths, and I think some of the ponds, and with each of the houses marked and the occupier's name. Of course it was very roughly done, and not to any scale, yet it was perfectly accurate and full of detail. . . . A map by Ptolemy would bear as much resemblance to the same country in a modern atlas as mine to the present state of that locality. It is all gone—rubbed out. The names against the whole of those houses have been altered, one only excepted, and changes have taken place there. Nothing

5. Odell Shepard (ed.), *The Heart of Thoreau's Journals* (Boston: Houghton Mifflin, 1927), p. 188.

remains. This is not in a century, half a century, or even in a quarter of a century, but in a few ticks of the clock. (*FH*, 359)

It is interesting to note that Thomas Hardy bore witness to a similar trend in his contemporary Dorset. In a letter to Rider Haggard he commented: "I cannot recall a single instance of a labourer who still lives on the farm where he was born, and I can only recall a few who have been five years on their present farms." [6] But the change goes deeper than this, and throughout his writings Jefferies is concerned with the general theme of rural development—changes in agricultural method, in the social structure, in rural life and custom. He was impressed by the changes, and also by the countryside's power to absorb changes into itself—"it is all changed and just the same" (*FH*, 178).

This part of Wiltshire was visited by William Cobbett on several occasions during the period of his *Rural Rides*, and his descriptions give us a vivid portrait of the district in the generation before Jefferies' birth. His first visit, in the autumn of 1821, is of special interest because it describes his first impression of the countryside as seen from the downland, the view that was later to mean so much to the young Jefferies. Cobbett writes:

MARLBOROUGH, which is an ill-looking place enough, is succeeded, on my road to SWINDON, by an extensive and very beautiful down about four miles over. Here nature has flung the earth about in a great variety of shapes. The fine short smooth grass, has about nine inches of mould under it, and then comes the chalk. . . . At the end of this down, the high-country ends. The hill is high and steep, and from it, you look immediately down into a level farming country; a little further on, into the dairy-country, whence the North-Wilts cheese comes; and beyond that, into the vale of Berkshire, and even to Oxford, which lies away to the north-east from this hill. The land continues good, flat, and rather wet, to Swindon, which is a plain country town. [7]

That Cobbett was particularly impressed by this area is evident from a further description of a ride taken five years later:

Swindon is in Wiltshire, and is in the real fat of the land, all being wheat, beans, cheese, or fat meat. . . . There is, in my opinion, no land in England that surpasses this. There is, I suppose, as good in the last three counties, that I have come through [Gloucestershire, Herefordshire, Worcestershire]; but, *better* than this is, I should think, impossible. There is a pasture field, of

6. Quoted in F. E. Hardy, *The Life of Thomas Hardy* (London: Macmillan, 1962), p. 313.
7. William Cobbett, *Rural Rides* [1830]. 2 vols. (London: Reeves and Turner, 1893), I, 20.

about a hundred acres, close to Swindon, belonging to a Mr. Goddard, which, with its cattle and sheep, was a most beautiful sight.[8]

This last sentence points to one significant link between Cobbett's time and Jefferies' in that the land-owning family remained the same, and is thus one obvious example of rural continuity. The young Jefferies was, indeed, commissioned to write a *Memoir of the Goddards* which was privately printed in 1873.

But the most far-reaching change in village life—and one which set in motion the majority of the later changes—had already taken place in the years before Cobbett's rural tours. This was the enclosure of the commons and the open fields which reached a peak in the reign of George III. Jefferies hardly mentions the topic—the process was more or less complete by his time, and he was more concerned with pressing contemporary problems; we must go to a later writer, George Bourne, for an assessment of its consequences. Bourne writes in *Change in the Village*:

To the enclosure of the common more than to any other cause may be traced all the changes that have subsequently passed over the village. It was like knocking the keystone out of an arch. The keystone is not the arch; but, once it is gone, all sorts of forces, previously resisted, begin to operate towards ruin, and gradually the whole structure crumbles down. This fairly illustrates what has happened in the village, in consequence of the loss of the common.[9]

Enclosure was necessary and inevitable; as Victor Bonham-Carter has remarked, it "was indispensable to any improvement in farming technique." It also changed the face of the landscape, and largely created the kind of scene that is now considered typically English—"the countryside resolved itself into a pattern of fields, hedges, and farms much as we know it now." [10] It gave rise, in fact, to the kind of landscape that Jefferies was to describe with such loving care. From a social point of view, however, it deprived the peasant population of grazing-rights and allotment-strips upon which they depended, and created the class of landless agricultural labourers forced to rely completely upon their wages; and this factor in-

8. *Ibid.*, II, 180.
9. George Bourne, *Change in the Village* [1912] (London: Duckworth, 1955), pp. 86–7. Bourne, of course, has a particular Surrey village in mind, but his conclusions are intended to have general relevance.
10. Victor Bonham-Carter, *The English Village* (Harmondsworth: Penguin Books, 1952), pp. 55, 64.

creased the labourers' hardships during the unemployment caused by the later agricultural depression.

The main development in the half century dividing the 1820's of Cobbett and the 1870's when Jefferies emerged as a knowledgeable writer on rural subjects lay in the effect of the Industrial Revolution upon the centuries-old methods of agriculture. The power of steam had completely transformed the ancient methods, and this is a development of which Jefferies is profoundly conscious. A particularly dramatic description of the extent of this change may be found in a passage from *Round About a Great Estate*. Jefferies has been hearing tales of "old Jonathan" who represents the ancient feudal ways, and would have been a contemporary of Cobbett:

Reclining on the sweet short sward under the hawthorn on the Down I looked over the Idover plain, and thought of the olden times. As I gazed I presently observed, far away beside some ricks, the short black funnel of an engine, and made it out to be a steam-plough waiting till the corn should be garnered to tear up the stubble. How much meaning there lay in the presence of that black funnel! There were the same broad open fields, the same beautiful crops of golden wheat, the same green hills, and the same sun ripening the grain. But how strangely changed all human affairs since old Jonathan, in his straight-made shoes, with his pike-staff, and the acorns in his pocket, trudged along the footpaths! (*RGE*, 80)

The point is made pictorially on the cover of the first edition of *Hodge and His Masters*. Each volume is brown with an inlaid gold design; the first volume shows a team of plough-horses, the second an elaborate steam plough.

The introduction of machinery into agriculture was gradual, and at first bitterly resented. In 1830 the agricultural labourers had risen against the use of threshing-machines which, they considered, endangered their livelihood, and there were other local outbreaks of violence in the succeeding years. Again Jefferies has little to say on this subject—there are brief references in *Wild Life in a Southern County* and *The Life of the Fields* —but Alfred Williams, in *Villages of the White Horse*, records disturbances in the neighbouring communities of Liddington and Bishopstone, while stories and reminiscences of this time were collected from the more southerly parts of Wiltshire by W. H. Hudson in *A Shepherd's Life*. But mechanical progress, like enclosure, was inevitable, and the founding of the Royal Agricultural Society in 1840, with the motto "Practice with Science," encouraged the development of modern methods. Increased use of fertilizers, improvements in crop rotation, and widespread ambitious schemes of drainage were only some of the more important ventures encouraged by the Society. Above all, the years of Jefferies' childhood saw the introduction of the steam plough and the general period of agricultural mechanization. The impact of all this is well described in the first part of Jefferies' essay "Notes on Landscape Painting" where the mechanical thresher, reaper, mower, and steam plough are all given their place in the rural picture. The description of the steam plough is memorably vivid—its shares rout up the earth "like the claws of some pre-historic monster," the wheels hold the ground "like a wrestler drawing to him the unwilling opponent." All in all, "this is force—Thor in another form" (*LF*, 156, 157).

Another feature of the times which had a profound effect on agricultural life and methods was the development of the railway system, and this was a factor which Jefferies, born within two miles of Swindon, knew well. If Cobbett had been able to revisit his "plain country town" twenty-five years later, he would have been amazed—and probably appalled. The growth of the great junction and railway workshops transformed both the town and the immediate countryside. Jefferies had related the facts in an early essay, "The Story of Swindon." "Swindon rose as Chicago rose, as if by magic" (*HV*, 107). The railway centre had a double effect on local agriculture: it provided a quick and relatively cheap means of transport for local produce, to which it opened up wide and hitherto undreamt-of markets; on the other hand, it attracted workmen away from the land in search of higher wages. (One might also add that the development of the North American railway system, linking the wheat-growing areas with the Eastern ports, was an immediate cause of the increased imports of American wheat and the consequent depression in England.)

A combination of factors made the middle years of the century (once the "hungry forties" had been passed) a temporarily prosperous period for landowner and farmer, if not for labourer. Even the repeal of the Corn Laws in 1846, greeted by Disraeli with gloomy prognostications of disaster, had little immediate effect. Victor Bonham-Carter has summed up this period neatly and succinctly, and it is a vital background to much of Jefferies' work:

From 1853 to 1874, British agriculture, especially in the south, enjoyed an era of prosperity and progress known to historians and others as the "golden age" or "high farming" or merely the "good old days"! It was due, in part, to a succession of lucky circumstances, whereby (once the Crimean War was over) England was at peace, and free to develop her own industries, while much of the rest of the world was disturbed. Russian trade was suffering from the effects of the Crimea; America, still undeveloped, was torn by the Civil War of 1861–5; Germany was involved in a series of campaigns—with Denmark in 1853, with Austria in 1866, and with France in 1870–1. Each of these events stimulated British exports and diverted the import of foreign food, with the result that home agriculture experienced little competition and prospered exceedingly.[11]

It is at the end of this period that Jefferies begins to write. An early essay entitled "The Future of Farming" shows that he was well aware of the principles involved. He begins by stressing the extent of the development:

The changes which have been crowded into the last half-century have been so numerous and so important that it would be almost reasonable to suppose the limit had been reached for the present, and that the next few generations would be sufficiently occupied in assimilating themselves to the new conditions of existence.

But so far from this being the case, all the facts of the hour point irresistibly to the conclusion that the era of development has but just commenced.[12]

One of the changes, encouraged by the introduction of improved machinery, was a tendency towards larger farms. Jefferies wrote an early essay on this subject, concluding that "the balance of the argument seems to be indisputably in favour of large farms," and estimated the size of "a useful farm" at "250 acres at the lowest."[13] But larger farms depended on greater capital, and required a new, more business-like approach which the traditional small farmer lacked. In "The Future of Farming" Jefferies had written:

The farm was no longer self-supporting. It was necessary to keep account-books, a thing never done before. The words "profit and loss" were introduced and began to be thoroughly understood. To make a "profit" the farm must become a business; a business required a certain amount of speculation; speculation means capital. These men had not got capital. A change, therefore, was imminent.[14]

11. Bonham-Carter, pp. 73–4.
12. "The Future of Farming," *Fraser's Magazine*, Dec. 1873, 687. The essay is uncollected.
13. "The Size of Farms," *New Quarterly*, Oct. 1874, 202, 198. The essay is uncollected.
14. "The Future of Farming," 688.

In *Hodge and His Masters* it is stated categorically that "it was not the least use for a man to go into farming now unless he had got ten thousand pounds" (*HM*, 72). Thus the new type of farming required a new type of farmer, but the man who was in the position to manage a large farm as a business-like proposition was not always the man who knew and understood the men in his employ. He was an outsider, a "foreigner"; farming became necessarily more impersonal, and so the link between master and man, the sense of community which, despite its clumsiness and injustices, characterized the countryside of earlier days, was broken. The Farfraes were destined to replace the Henchards. It was inevitable, and in many ways desirable; yet at the same time there was a loss.

But the prosperity, as I have indicated, was temporary; England was on the brink of an agrarian catastrophe and the Jefferies of "The Future of Farming" was shortly to witness the effects of an agricultural depression which was still continuing at the time of his death fourteen years later. The main causes are obvious enough. Cheap foreign imports, especially American wheat, flooded the markets of the late 1870's, and with no restrictions on such produce, the price of wheat tended to fall. This coincided in England with a series of bad harvests which culminated in what Jefferies described as "the year of rain, 1879, that terrible year which is fresh in the memory of all who have any interest in out-of-door matters" (*NNL*, 72). Not only was the corn crop ruined by the heavy rains, but countless cattle and sheep were destroyed by epidemics of pleuro-pneumonia, foot-and-mouth disease, and liver-rot. "Jefferies' Land" was badly hit. Alfred Williams reports a shepherd from Wroughton, a village three miles from Coate, as saying: "Back in '79 purty nigh every ship an thase downs died, aa, an' hers an' rabbuts, too." [15]

The depression caused considerable agricultural adjustment. There was a steady conversion of arable land to pasture, which was noted by Jefferies as early as 1875; between the years 1871 and 1901 England's wheat acreage declined by about a half, arable acreage as a whole falling by almost two million acres. Sheep-farming also declined, but, once the effects of the 1879 epidemic wore off, cattle-farming expanded, and there was also a considerable increase in market-gardening. The decline in arable farming caused a fall in the demand for labour, and this, linked with the increased movement of unskilled workers towards the towns, explains the

15. Alfred Williams, *Villages of the White Horse* (London: Duckworth, 1913), p. 55.

20 per cent decrease in the number of farm workers during the last thirty years of the century. There was too a noticeable decline in efforts to improve standards, whether of workers' amenities such as housing, or land improvement such as drainage. Landowners were forced to reduce rents, but none the less found it difficult to replace tenants. All classes suffered.

There was a general hardening of attitude. If Science could still be the saviour of agriculture, and many (including Jefferies) still believed that it could, it had to be at a price, and the scientist and practical businessman could not afford to be deterred by sentiment. In the first chapter of *Hodge and His Masters*, Jefferies describes a professor speaking at a farmers' meeting on the subject "Science, the Remedy for Agricultural Depression." And on the question of capital, the speaker makes himself brutally clear: "Of course, continued the professor, it was assumed that the farmer had good substantial buildings and sufficient capital. The first he could get if he chose; and without the second, without capital, he had no business to be farming at all. He was simply stopping the road of a better man, and the sooner he was driven out of the way the better" (*HM*, 20). And it was true. Those who never kept account-books were forced to yield to those who did. But too often, when the poor farmer was driven out, the richer and better man was not forthcoming, and this meant wasted acres for the country and unemployment for the labourer.

The depression was real, but the appearance of the countryside was deceptive. Changes are not always easily visible, as they were in the case of the rise of the Swindon engine-sheds, or the appearance of a steam plough in the meadows. Thus it is probable that, despite the serious economic changes, a casual observer walking in the fields in 1881 would have noticed little difference from the same fields of 1873. I choose 1881 because in August of that year Jefferies published an essay entitled "The State of Farming" which emphasized this very point:

Though tenants quit and farms are to let, the face of the country is not apparently altered. The arable lands are ploughed and sown, and harrowed and rolled; corn is ripening, herds are grazing in the meadows. Farmyards present the same appearance; there are still ricks, and labourers moving about, cart-horses harnessed, and the very barn-door fowls picking among the chaff. It is hard to believe that everything is in such decay. (*FF*, 81–2)

Those who consider Jefferies a mere chronicler of natural history will see little of relevance in the foregoing historical sketch. But it is a mistake to neglect his concern for the human inhabitants of the country, and many of his more straightforward articles on village life provide a mine of information for the social historian. Indeed, their literary interest is secondary, but their matter is of vital importance to a proper understanding of his more purely artistic work. We must now turn to these articles in more detail to make a brief survey of the various classes that go to make up the population of "Jefferies' Land," and, more important, to demonstrate Jefferies' attitude towards them.

It would be easy to over-simplify the rural class-structure of Jefferies' time. Cobbett had claimed that "you are for reducing the community to two classes: *Masters* and *Slaves*," [16] and Disraeli's famous classification of the two nations, the rich and the poor, might encourage a similar division. But when discussing the village social structure, we must be careful to differentiate three distinct classes—landowners, farmers, and labourers. It is not a hard-and-fast division, and it is doubtful if a rigid line could be drawn between the extremities of each adjoining class. Farmers differed greatly in wealth and social standing—Jefferies half sarcastically pointed out that a large farmer "is an agriculturist [while] a small tenant is only a farmer." [17] There is a similar range among labourers, and a distinction needs to be drawn between the regular labourer and the man on piece-work.

The subject is complicated still further by the fact that Jefferies' attitude to the different classes developed and altered with the years, though I doubt if his changes of outlook are as rigidly political as previous commentators have suggested. All his biographers, Walter Besant excepted, have painted a smooth and straightforward picture of Jefferies' inherited conservative viewpoint giving way to a firm and uncompromising radicalism. H. S. Salt, the rationalist and Fabian, has talked of "his socialistic or rather communistic spirit, which is the more remarkable as having developed itself quite spontaneously from his own personality, in direct opposition to all the associations and surroundings of his youth and manhood." [18] Edward Thomas gives a similar, if more guarded picture, and labels much of the early writing as "partisan." It has even been argued that Jefferies

16. Quoted in Raymond Williams, *Culture and Society, 1780–1950* (London: Chatto and Windus, 1958), p. 15.
17. "The Size of Farms," 193.
18. H. S. Salt, *Richard Jefferies: A Study* (1894), pp. 80–1.

maintained a conservative viewpoint after he had abandoned such beliefs in order to continue selling his writings, but there is no real evidence to support this view. In the 1870's and 1880's the agricultural scene was, as I have suggested, in the process of abrupt transition, and it seems more convincing to explain these changes of viewpoint in terms of adjustment to the contemporary situation than of personal change in party-political allegiance.

It is worth noting that Jefferies himself was continually emphasizing his own impartiality. He may have been deceived in this belief, but it is clear enough that he did not look upon himself as a conscious propagandist. Many instances might be cited from all periods of his writing. He ends his essay "The Labourer's Daily Life" with the words: "These are some of the lights and shades of the labourer's daily life impartially presented" (*TF*, 110). This essay was first published in *Fraser's Magazine* as early as 1874, and its sympathetic and faithful presentation of the labourer's hardships is in itself evidence against an early, insensitive toryism. In the preface to *Hodge and His Masters* he insists that "all I claim for the following sketches is that they are written in a fair and impartial spirit" (*HM*, xiii). Finally, in "One of the New Voters" (1885) he specifically denies any attempt to be a propagandist: "I am not trying to make out a case of special hardship; . . . I am simply describing the realities of rural life behind the scenes" (*OA*, 89). He makes similar claims of unbiased delineation with regard to his novels and his descriptions of landscape and natural history. I see no reason to doubt him.

Jefferies himself, as we have seen, belonged to the farming class, and we may take it as a constant rule that he consistently defends and reflects the cause of the farmer throughout his life. This does not contradict his claims of impartiality; it merely indicates where his greatest concerns and experiences lay. Such a rule is useful for our purposes because we shall need some kind of norm against which to measure his varied observations. As we pass from essay to essay, it sometimes appears as if Jefferies is being inconsistent and even contradictory. It is probably this fact which caused the earlier biographers to work out a rough, preconceived theory and then select the quotations which best fitted it. But there are generally some important statements and opinions which refuse to merge into the general pattern. The reason for this is, I think, the very variety and diversity present in the rural scene. It was impossible to portray a typical and representative landowner or farmer or labourer, and hence no generalization is likely to be valid. The good and the bad existed in all classes; there were beneficent and tyrannical landowners, efficient and incompetent farmers, willing and untrustworthy labourers. Thus if Jefferies, in accordance with his claims, painted plainly what he saw, the result in any individual case would be in no sense final.

The whole problem was obscured in Jefferies' own time by his habit of publishing his essays separately, but this should now present no difficulty. In each essay Jefferies described an aspect of the countryside which, though true, was necessarily not the whole truth. Another essay, written from a somewhat different standpoint, would draw attention to other features, and the first essay would thus be qualified. The process may be seen most clearly in *Hodge and His Masters*. The book consists of a collection of short verbal pictures, each describing with detailed particularity the character and approach of a person connected with the land. No single chapter will give us a fair picture of rural society, but taken as a whole the book provides a remarkably comprehensive survey of the agriculture of the time. The other articles on rural life and problems similarly gain in stature and importance if read and considered in bulk. For instance, the articles which Jefferies contributed to *Fraser's Magazine* in 1873 and 1874, though individual and self-contained, bear strict relevance to each other. Thus "The Future of Farming" and "The Farmer at Home" are significantly balanced by "The Labourer's Daily Life" and "John Smith's Shanty." Indeed, I believe that the best approach to Jefferies' agricultural writings is to read them all as if, in their entirety, they formed a complete "canon." If this is done, the effect is impressive. Most of the obvious inconsistencies are easily explained as changes of opinion in the light of changes in the historical situation, and other apparent contradictions will be seen to be, not "partisan" judgments, but differing aspects of an intricately complex situation. "Without Contraries is no progression," as Blake pointed out, and the combination of Jefferies' "aspects" produces not the smooth facilities of generalization, but the detailed complexity of the whole truth.

As far as the landowners are concerned, Jefferies presents us with two extremes in his most vivid delineations of the class. His most critical portrait is Cornleigh Cornleigh in his novel *The Dewy Morn*; his most sympathetic is Squire Thardover in the essay "A King of Acres." Cornleigh has often been cited as a proof of Jefferies' mature political attitude to the landowners, but both novel and essay were originally published in the same year, 1884, and his condemnation of Cornleigh is no more a matter of socialistic principle than his praise of Thardover is conservative prejudice. The essential difference between the two figures can best be understood with reference to a passage in *The Amateur Poacher* where Jefferies speaks of "the keystone of English country life—*i.e.* a master whose heart is in the land" (*AP*, 277). This is precisely where the two men differ: Thardover's heart is in the land, Cornleigh's is not. Jefferies makes an important distinction in "A King of Acres" between "proprietors" and "owners." Thardover "had laid hands, as it were, on every acre. Those who work, own. There are many who receive rent who do not own; they are proprietors, not owners; like receiving dividends on stock, which stock is never seen or handled. Their rights are legal only; his right was the right of labour." (*HV*, 85) On these terms Cornleigh is decidedly a proprietor, and the word is actually used of him. Jefferies refers, moreover, to "his absolute lack of interest in the place which belonged to him" (*DM*, II, 75). Again, there is a living relationship between Thardover and the men he employs: "There was not an acre on the property which he had not personally visited. The farm-houses and farm-buildings were all known to him. He rode from tenancy to tenancy; he visited the men at plough, and stood among the reapers. Neither the summer heat nor the winds of March prevented him from seeing with his own eyes." (*HV*, 91) In contrast, Cornleigh is well known for never seeing anything; he leaves everything to his steward, and never goes among his employees. As his gamekeeper is made to remark: "I have been with him nineteen year, and he have never said a word to I" (*DM*, II, 72). Old Abner Brown emphasizes the difference when he says, with a profound simplicity: "Yer grandfeyther used to come round to us folk" (*DM*, II, 106).

Any generalization about Jefferies' view of the landowners must take both Cornleigh and Thardover into consideration. He has nothing but contempt for the village tyrant, and is appalled at the power which the landlord was legally able to wield. There are times when he suspects that there are far too many Cornleighs maintaining feudal sway over the English villages, but at others he looks to the landlords as the countryside's leading hope in a decade of depression. In an unfinished discourse on "The Squire and the Land," which appears by internal evidence to have been written around the year 1881, he sarcastically denies the charge that "to be a landowner is to be the bodily presentment of ignorance and anti-civilization" (*OHC*, 160). And he is always aware of the responsibilities that the landlords carry. Even in "The Wiltshire Labourer" (1883), which is usually quoted in support of Jefferies' later championing of the labourer against the establishment, he remarks that "it is always the landowner who has to bear the burden in the end" (*HV*, 262).

I have already pointed out that the farming class is that to which Jefferies himself belonged, and it is the farmers' cause that he is continually representing and defending. This is as true of his last essays as of his first. It is already explicit in his 1872 letters to *The Times*, where in his second letter on the Wiltshire labourer he challenges critical statements which "I feel bound to resent on the part of the farmers of this county" (*TF*, 233). It is still implicit in his last work of fiction, *Amaryllis at the Fair* (1887), where the character of Iden, weak and impractical as he is, becomes a memorable figure recorded with sympathy and love.

The tenant farmer of the Victorian period may be conveniently viewed as a mean between the rich land-owning class on the one side and the poor labouring class on the other. More often than not the farmer combines the role of master and servant, of landlord and tenant, and the farming class itself includes a wide variety of standards. At the one extreme he may approach the social level of the landowner; at the other he may appear indistinguishable from the labourer in the fields. Although the prosperity of the "high farming" period allowed the farmer to raise his living standards, and thereby to weaken the traditional links with the labouring class, both extremes still existed in Jefferies' time, and the varying vignettes that go to make up *Hodge and His Masters* sufficiently illustrate this variety. None the less, the contemporary conception of the farmer seemed to take in the lower rather than the upper grades of this division. In "The Farmer at Home" Jefferies describes them as "a remarkably observant race, and as a rule peculiarly well-informed. This is contrary to the popular belief, which represents the farmer as rude and ignorant, a pot-bellied beer-drinker, and nothing more." (*TF*, 38) This general ignorance of the farmers' nature was one of the reasons why Jefferies considered it incumbent upon him to defend them as a class. He does not, of course, claim a high standard of education and awareness in all farmers—indeed, he admits the ignorance and prejudice of many occupiers of smaller farms—but none the less asserts that "the typical agriculturist of the day is a man who knows books as well as bullocks, science as well as sheep." [19]

In the second *Times* letter he goes so far as to say that "a harder-working class of man does not exist than the Wiltshire farmers" (*TF*, 247). This was in 1872, at the close of the "high farming" period. Eleven years later, the only difference seems to be that there is no longer even the smallest reward for his labour. Jefferies remarks in "A Southdown Shepherd" that "there is nothing, in fact, in this country so carefully provided against as the possibility of an English farmer becoming wealthy" (*NNL*, 223). All these themes—intelligence, hard work, and financial difficulty—are eloquently summed up in a comment on Iden of Coombe Oaks: "Always at work, and he could talk so cleverly, too, and knew everything, and yet they were so short of money" (*AF*, 206).

I have already enumerated the most important changes that overtook agriculture during this period, and the tragedy of the situation was that the traditional English farmer, by his very nature and despite his real intelligence, was incapable of making the changes that were becoming necessary. This is true of many of the farmers in *Hodge and His Masters*, and particularly of Iden, but it is also a theme present in Jefferies' earliest writings on the subject. He was himself in favour of progress—"my sympathies and hopes are with the light of the future" (*RGE*, xvi)—and he lamented the traditional farmers' inability to adapt to the new situation. In "The Farmer at Home" he notes "a stubborn unchangeableness, a dislike and hatred of all things new and unfamiliar, a nervous dread of reform" (*TF*, 42). But the old farmers had Jefferies' sympathy because, like his model landowner James Thardover, they genuinely loved the land. "Of all other men," he wrote in *Wild Life in a Southern County*, "the farmer is the most deeply attached to the labour by which he lives, and loves the earth on which he walks like a true autochthon. He will not leave it unless he is suffering severely." (*WL*, 151) What criticism he levels at farmers is generally concerned with the new "businessman," or with the younger generation which had lost its satisfaction with a hardworking

---

19. "The Spirit of Modern Agriculture," *New Quarterly*, July 1876, 308. The essay is uncollected.

rural life, and was attempting to rival the landowner in social grace and style. This again was a significant development in Victorian rural life, which widened the breach between employer and employed.

Jefferies' best-known studies of the agricultural labourer are the *Times* letters, which represent his first published work outside the Swindon area and thus show him under the disadvantage of inexperience. They were also intended to state the neglected farmers' case and consequently they have sometimes been cited to show that Jefferies was unsympathetic towards the labourers' claims. He confines himself to an account of the Wiltshire labourers, of whom alone he was competent to speak, and he gives a detailed and dispassionate report on their physical appearance, their wages, their houses, their food, their habits. The letters are coldly analytical, and it is true that they are not without a tinge of complacency and condescension. His qualified satisfaction with labouring conditions is unlikely to meet the standards of our own century, but it would be a mistake to confuse his objective, journalistic manner with a personal lack of sympathy. Two years later, in "The Labourer's Daily Life," he shows that, even at this early period, he has a full comprehension of the labourers' hardships. There is nothing of the false pastoral about his picture. "In the life of the English agricultural labourers," he writes, "there is absolutely no poetry, no colour," and he remarks sarcastically that "there are few persons who could long remain poetical on bread and cheese" (*TF*, 97, 93). He demonstrates how the hard work and conditions lead to "the blunting of all the finer feelings, the total erasure of sensitiveness" (*TF*, 95). At the same time, Jefferies has high hopes concerning the potentiality of the class, and attacks the idea of the unthinking, ignorant labourer as he had attacked that of the unthinking, ignorant farmer. "He is not a fool," he writes in a notebook (April 1880), "he is grit stuff" (*N*, 94), and in *The Life of the Fields* he insists that "nothing is so contrary to fact as the common opinion that the agricultural labourer and his family are stupid and unintelligent" (*LF*, 235).

The earlier essays refer to pre-depression conditions but "The Wiltshire Labourer," published in *Longman's Magazine* in 1883 as a companion-piece to Thomas Hardy's "The Dorsetshire Labourer" which had appeared in the same magazine four months earlier, analyses the effect of the depression on the labouring class. Jefferies differs from the agricultural historians in finding the farm labourer decidedly worse off in the eighties than in the previous decade. Although wages had continued to rise in most areas, this was more than counterbalanced by decreased employment and consequent lack of security. The change in tone is obvious from the opening sentence: "Ten years have passed away, and the Wiltshire labourers have only moved in two things—education and discontent" (*HV*, 247). Like Hardy, he laments "a drifting about of the agricultural population"; he detects restlessness and insecurity, and consequently "the fixed population may be said to decline every year" (*HV*, 255, 257). He blames neither landowner nor farmer, but finds the root of the trouble in the fact that the labourer has no fixity of tenure. The essay ends, however, with an assertion of faith and a gleam of hope: "I say that such a race of men are not to be despised; I say that they are the very foundation of a nation's stability. I say that in common justice they deserve settled homes; and further, that as a matter of sound policy they should be provided with them." (*HV*, 269)

Labourers appear in his novels from time to time, and are presented in characteristic variety. In *The Dewy Morn* there is old Abner Brown who is evicted from his tied-cottage by Cornleigh, and, as if to restore the balance, in *Amaryllis at the Fair* there is "Jearje" who enjoys consideration and contentment under Iden, and of whom it is recorded that "a more willing fellow never lived" (*AF*, 299). And Jefferies makes a characteristic and important comment on him:

There are such as George still among the labourer class, in despite of the change of circumstance and sentiment, men who would be as faithful as the faithfullest retainer who ever accompanied a knight of old time to the Crusade. But, observe, for a good man there must be a good master. Proud Iden was a good master, who never forgot that his man was not a piece of mechanism, but flesh and blood and feelings. (*AF*, 299–300)

It is this essential connection between master and man that Jefferies continually supports, though he wisely does not exaggerate the point which, when over-stated, sentimentalizes a by no means perfect relationship. As he wrote in "The Power of the Farmers" (1874): "Without laying much stress on the oft-talked of sympathy and good feeling between master and man, now broken for ever, there still remained bonds which it is a mistake to have severed." [20] From this early period down to the final work of

20. "The Power of the Farmers," *Fortnightly Review*, June 1874, 808. The essay is uncollected.

fiction published in the year of his death, Jefferies continues to maintain that the real interests of landowner, farmer, and labourer are not opposed but identical. The problem is, of course, to distinguish between real interests and those that are disguised selfishnesses. The masters who concern themselves with this second category are roundly condemned by Jefferies, as are reform-fearing farmers and irresponsible labourers. But for those members of all three groups who carry out their tasks competently and fairly he has nothing but praise, and alongside the praise goes an unemphatic but none the less genuine interest and sympathy.

I should perhaps make it clear that I am not denying a change in Jefferies' later attitude to life and labour, though I suspect that it was a development rather than a reversal of his earlier position. The changes of viewpoint seem not so much the result of a change in political theory as the practical reaction to a fluctuating situation. The picture of a gradual but steady progression from uninformed conservative to enlightened radical is both inaccurate and unnecessary. It assumes that conservatism and radicalism are mutually exclusive, the falsity of which assumption is readily demonstrable by reference to Cobbett. Indeed, were I required to "place" Jefferies as far as his political ideas were concerned, I should set him in the tradition of Langland and Cobbett, both of whom, though hailed as early socialists, were in fact reactionary in their general attitudes. Piers Plowman's vision is of all classes cultivating God's half-acre, the earth, according to their station and skill, recognizing each other as necessary and worthy parts of a complete process. And Cobbett's ideal rural society consisted, in the words of a recent biographer, of "a beneficent landowner, a sturdy peasantry, a village community self-supporting and static." [21] Jefferies, while welcoming the promise of the future, possessed at the same time a warm vision of an idealized *status quo* in which the evil and injustice would be cut away, leaving only the good and the true. It is, at bottom, a simple, unexceptional, perhaps even ingenuous position, but it is reconcilable with a sturdy independence and a humane sensitivity. Indeed, the development of Jefferies' ideas is best interpreted not as an increasing radicalism, but as a broadening humanitarianism. Artistically

21. W. Baring Pemberton, *William Cobbett* (Harmondsworth: Penguin Books, 1949), p. 139.

(and it is with Jefferies as literary artist that we are primarily and henceforward concerned) his position mingles well with accurate observation and honest commentary. A passing comment in one of his late essays applies just as happily to his political concerns as to his literary aims—"I do but delineate" (*FH*, 227).

ii. The Rural Vision: From Article to Essay

JEFFERIES WAS much more than a reporter, and had higher literary ambitions even in the first years of his writing career. For all their faults, the three early novels, written between 1874 and 1877, demonstrate at least that Jefferies considered himself a creative writer. He continued persistently writing novels while contributing topical articles to the agricultural journals in order to earn his daily bread. These worlds are admittedly far apart, yet it would be strange indeed if the two sides of his writing life did not overlap at some point. It is commonly noted with surprise that his early novels and short stories often portrayed the high life of London society with which Jefferies himself was unfamiliar. It would have been reasonable to suppose that a man of Jefferies' interests might have explored the possibilities of the regional novel, yet it was not until 1880, after the success of the country books, that he combined his experience with his ambition to produce the fictional country idyll of *Greene Ferne Farm*. It would be wrong, however, to equate in Jefferies creative and non-creative with fiction and non-fiction. The combination of commercial and creative writing had been achieved at an earlier stage in some of the more ambitious essays.

There is an important distinction to be drawn between the journalistic, factual articles, and his artistic presentations of the rural scene, essays in the true sense of the word, which deserve separate treatment. Jefferies seems to have decided that the complexities of the rural situation could be conveyed with more success by a kind of writing that strengthened pure description with literary devices and artistic form. This kind of writing is more common in his later years, particularly in the essay "One of the

New Voters," but there are various examples in the earlier work, including "A True Tale of the Wiltshire Labourer," "John Smith's Shanty," "The Midsummer Hum," and "Gaudy as a Garden." In *Hodge and His Masters* the two methods intermingle, though the most effective chapters are supreme in their elaborate but inconspicuous subtlety.

"John Smith's Shanty" (1874) lies somewhere between the short story and the descriptive essay. There is no tightly knit plot; the centre of interest lies in the doubts and uncertainties in the mind of the labourer John Smith. Jefferies' primary intention is not to tell an interesting story, but to give, in the words of the conclusion, "an uncompromising picture of things as they are" (*TF*, 210).

The narrative opens with an impressionistic portrait of Smith himself. He is a middle-aged hedger, at present engaged in chopping down an elm tree. Jefferies focuses our attention on a close-up of his work-moulded hands:

The continuous outdoor labour, the beating of innumerable storms, and the hard, coarse fare, had dried up all the original moisture of the hand, till it was rough, firm, and cracked or chapped like a piece of wood exposed to the sun and weather. The natural oil of the skin, which gives to the hand its beautiful suppleness and delicate sense of touch, was gone like the sap in the tree he was felling, for it was early in the winter. (*TF*, 175)

There is obviously a different—a more literary—approach here than in, say, "The Labourer's Daily Life." The concentration on the detail, the hand, by means of which we learn of Smith's life and circumstances, the carefully chosen similes which place him firmly in his natural environment, both these effects are primarily artistic, adding to our understanding of the scene and of Smith at the same time. Jefferies goes on to stress his physical features: "His chest was open to the north wind, which whistled through the bare branches of the tall elm overhead as if they were the cordage of a ship, and came in sudden blasts through the gaps in the hedge, blowing his shirt back, and exposing the immense breadth of bone, and rough dark skin tanned to a red-brown by the summer sun while mowing." (*TF*, 176) He hastens to add, however, that the man is by no means a rural Hercules. He lacks what Jefferies describes as "the grace of strength" (*TF*, 177), and what strength he possessed was without beauty. Jefferies succeeds in resolving in his description one of the many paradoxes concerning the agricultural labourer of the period—his great strength of physique on the one hand, and his inadequate diet on the other. From the full account of Smith we accept both aspects as part of a single picture, and the resolution has been made not directly, not even intellectually, but artistically. We are told nothing of Smith's character, only of his physical appearance. The inner picture is left blank, for the reader to fill in later as he will.

We are now introduced to two of Smith's acquaintances: first, an elderly ditcher, and later a young navvy. Although we are never told so explicitly, it becomes clear that these represent the older and younger generations. There is certainly no toning down of the hardships of the ditcher's pro-fession. He is presented as black with mud and wet:

"Thee's bin in main deep," said John, after a slow survey of the other's appearance.
The fellow stamped his boot on the ground, and the slime and slush oozed out of it and formed a puddle. "That's pretty stuff to stand in for a man of sixty-four, yent it, John?" (*TF*, 181)

He goes on to complain bitterly of his lot—of the long hours, the wretched conditions, the bad weather and his increasing rheumatism. When Smith mentions his conveniently situated cottage, the old man begins to complain about its bad position, its poor materials, and its in-adequate size. " 'Thee built 'un thee-self, didn't 'ee?' said John, in his slow way" (*TF*, 184). With this simple remark we learn a good deal about John Smith and about Jim the ditcher. Jefferies had commented in the *Times* letters on the difference in quality between the houses constructed by the landowners and those built by the labourers themselves; here the context makes it far more meaningful than in the earlier, direct argument. We realize that Jim's complaints cannot all be laid at the door of his "masters"; we also appreciate that Smith possesses a quiet shrewdness and subtlety which is not to be forgotten.

When Jim continues his list of complaints, we submit his arguments to a closer scrutiny. At the end we are told that Smith "was too well ac-quainted with the private life of the orator" (*TF*, 189) to take his argu-ments at their face value. None the less, the old man's speech contains cer-tain truths, some of which are expressed with a vivid and pungent wit, like the following assessment of female philanthropy:

He minded when that sharp old Miss —— was always coming round with tracts and blankets, like taking some straw to a lot of pigs, and lecturing his "missis" about economy. What a fuss she made, and scolded his wife as if she was a thief for having that fifteenth boy! His "missis" turned on her at last, and said, "Lor, miss, that's all the pleasure me an' my old man got." (*TF*, 187–88)

The broad humour underlines rather than obscures the terrible social hardships behind that last remark.

Jefferies himself does not analyse the speech in any detail, though he points out that it contains both contradictions and at the same time a substratum of stern truth. Instead, he portrays Smith's analysis of it, according to his knowledge of Jim's character. Thus the artistic presentation allows Jefferies to portray the complexities and incongruities by showing them as Smith sees them. In one respect, this makes the narrative even more objective in that the commentary comes from a character who is within the framework, but it also serves to give him greater freedom of manipulation, for Smith's judgment does not need to be profound nor even valid. This is not to say that Jefferies is shirking his responsibilities as social commentator, for there was probably no complete answer to the difficulties and any attempt to give one would lead, as it does in some of Jefferies' own articles, to an oversimplification. It cannot be stressed too forcefully that Jefferies' aim is to present not a solution, but a full statement of the problems. Smith is not convinced by the exaggerations of Jim's complaints; none the less, the meeting has an effect upon him because he sees in Jim a possible image of his own old age: "He had felt a certain rude pleasure in opening his broad chest to the winter wind. But now he involuntarily closed his shirt and buttoned it. He did not feel so confident in his own power of meeting all the contingencies of the future." (*TF*, 191)

Smith's second acquaintance is a young navvy who tells him with pride that he has just found promising employment on the new railway. He talks enthusiastically of the higher wages and the possibilities of further rise, and causes Smith to weigh the pros and cons of the rural life. Perhaps he too should have joined the ever increasing band of countrymen who were deserting the land. The point is a doubtful one, but the aspiring confidence of the youth contrasts with Smith's plodding staidness. This second meeting is shorter and less important than the first, but it too has its effect in leading up to Smith's return in the evening to his "shanty."

The scene is not, perhaps, one that we expect. Smith's shrewdness and general attitude have suggested that he would occupy a comparatively high position among his fellow-labourers, but we are presented with a picture of slovenliness, of overcrowding, of poverty, above all, of unhappiness. His wife turns on him, complaining of the lack of money and her consequent inability to feed the three children properly. Her complaint is not against inadequate pay, but against Smith's spending a large percentage of his meagre earnings at the "pot-house." It is a dismal homecoming, and Smith turns to go out. " 'Ay, thee bist agoing to the liquor again', were the last words he heard as he shut the door" (*TF*, 199). Martha is right in her suspicions, and he does not come home that night but falls asleep drunk in a ditch. Yet Jefferies does not condemn him; instead, he tries to understand, and to convey this understanding to the reader. He does not need to labour the paradox—the vicious circle that causes Smith to go to the ale-house to escape from the visible evidence of his having gone there too often in the past. No sensitive reader can fail to grasp the point, although it is not directly stated by the author. Such an effect would be impossible in a straightforward discussion; the situation requires imaginative creation, not merely accurate description, to give it its force.

The climax comes in the morning when, after a few harsh words from his wife, Smith strikes her, and later finds himself in the magistrates' court facing a charge of assault. It is a vivid description culminating in a long but stammering speech from Smith in which he tells of his responsibilities and his insufficient wages, his worries, and his weakness. It reaches a height of poignant simplicity when he refers to his drinking: "I knows I drinks beer, and so would anybody in my place—it makes me kinder stupid, as I don't feel nothing then" (*TF*, 208). In view of his general good character, and the plea of an elderly magistrate who puts in a word on his behalf, he receives only half the maximum penalty, and the fine is later paid by an unknown hand (presumably, the same elder magistrate), but he has to endure the second part of the sentence—a fortnight's imprisonment. And so his wife and children are forced into the workhouse.

Jefferies ends with the words: "This is no fiction, but an uncompromising picture of things as they are. Who is to blame for them?" (*TF*, 210) The question does not, I think, expect an answer—Jefferies himself does not know who is to blame. Certainly there seems no real blame that can be attached to the landowner, the farmer, or to Smith. The elderly magistrate seems to be the landowner, and has done his best in the courtroom;

the farmer, we are told, cannot afford to give higher wages, and Smith himself is condoned on account of the conditions in which he is forced to live. "John Smith's Shanty" is not propaganda for reform nor a defence of the *status quo*; it is an artistic presentation of the facts which reveals the complexities and difficulties as they exist, and blends the motifs to bring out the full force of the intricate situation.

The literary effect present in the first chapter of *Hodge and His Masters* (1880) is even more telling. Indeed, it is not too much to say that here Jefferies presents the agricultural situation in terms which verge on the symbolic. The difference lies not in the choice of an ordinary scene sufficiently typical to give the reader a convincing picture of "things as they are," but in the artistic selection and combination of particular details which are suggestive of far deeper significances than they represent in themselves. The first chapter, "The Farmers' Parliament," is a good example of the process. It opens with a description of the town of Woolbury on market-day. It is a typical country town, and Jefferies concentrates on the narrow streets, insufficient pavements, and general lack of planning:

Had the spot been in the most crowded district of the busiest part of the metropolis, where every inch of ground is worth an enormous sum, the buildings could not have been more jammed together, nor the inconvenience greater. Yet the little town was in the very midst of one of the most purely agricultural counties, where land, to all appearance, was plentiful, and where there was ample room and "verge enough" to build fifty such places. (*HM*, 15)

Here the illogicality of the district, its clumsiness and bad management, the inability of the inhabitants to make the necessary improvements to increase efficiency, and therefore prosperity, is stressed. This is a theme that is to emerge much more clearly later in the chapter. The time is the late nineteenth century, but for generations nothing has changed. Customs and habit are fixed and definite:

The trade of a country market-town, especially when that market-town, like Woolbury, dates from the earliest days of English history, is hereditary. It flows to the same store and to the same shop year after year, generation after generation, century after century. The farmer who walks into the saddler's here goes in because his father went there before him. His father went in because his father dealt there, and so on farther back than memory can trace. (*HM*, 16)

Such is the character of the rural countryside. It is against this background that the debate between science and traditional agriculture is to be waged.

The precise location of the farmers' meeting is an upper room in the Jason Inn. (The ironical allusion to the Golden Fleece is an example of Jefferies' unemphatic subtlety which, if my own reaction is at all typical, only reveals itself after several readings.) Arrival is impeded by the jostling crowds and narrow ways, but the resultant delay is unimportant:

A maid-servant comes tripping down, and in answer to inquiry replies that that is the way up, and the room is ready, but she adds with a smile that there is no one there yet. It is three-quarters of an hour after the time fixed for the reading of a most important paper before a meeting specially convened, before the assembled Parliament of Hodge's masters, and you thought you would be too late. (*HM*, 18)

Time is apparently of no consequence here, and the room is still deserted. It provides a dramatic and meaningful contrast with the bustle and sound of the street outside—"noise of man and animal below; above, here in the chamber of science, vacancy and silence" (*HM*, 18). The room is described briefly; it is plain and unadorned, possessing few distinctive details, yet Jefferies, ever sensitive to rural anomalies, discovers a significant feature even in this ordinary scene. He describes the class-structure by reference to the different kinds of chairs provided—an armchair for the president, two lesser chairs for the secretary and his clerk, plain chairs for the tenant-farmers, and then: "Last of all are two long forms as if for Hodge, if Hodge chooses to come" (*HM*, 18). The ambiguity here is beautifully presented; Hodge rarely attends such gatherings, but we are left uncertain whether his absence is the result of his poor treatment ("two low forms," "last of all"), or whether this scanty provision is made for the valid reason that Hodge is uninterested and never comes.

Gradually the room fills, the meeting begins, and the professor proceeds to read his paper, entitled "Science, the Remedy for Agricultural Depression." His are the conventional arguments of "high farming." He blames the farmers for their lack of initiative, their refusal to act upon the recommendations of science and so take advantage of the technological improvements made in the realms of agricultural development. He laments the lack of progress in drainage, the refusal to use new machinery and artificial manures. With up-to-date scientific equipment, he claims, the farmer could defy the weather; if science had been heeded in the past, there need have been no agricultural depression. Much of the criticism is no doubt justified; indeed, Jefferies himself had made the same points in various early essays, such as "The Size of Farms" and many of his contributions to the *Live Stock Journal*. He now realizes, however, that there is more to the problem than conversion from manpower to steam. The irony of this whole chapter works in two distinct ways. The very fact of the professor reading his plea for increased efficiency to an audience that has arrived an hour late is ironical in itself, justifying some of his arguments, but demonstrating the unlikelihood of his words producing much effect. On the other hand, the rest of the book, with its detailed miniatures of different types of farmer and countryman, together with subtle analysis of their difficulties, suggests that it is much more than a mere clash between ignorance and enlightenment.

Question time provides an opportunity for the farmers to defend their cause. Their spokesman talks for some time, but his speech is a brilliant study in amateur argument. He is obviously offended by the criticisms levelled against the farmers, but his retorts are quite inadequate as logical debate. None the less, they have their effect in emphasizing, albeit unconsciously, the human element which the lecturer has ignored, and they serve to underline the gap between scientific inventions and the persons expected to make use of them. The fundamental problems of communication and education are conveyed indirectly through the clash of personalities. The farmer ends by challenging the lecturer to give the name of a single farmer who has prospered through scientific means. Without waiting for an answer, he leaves along with several of his colleagues. It is partly because he does not intend to hear an answer, indicating that the strain between the two outlooks is by no means one-sided, but partly because "the rain was already splashing against the window-panes" (*HM*, 23)—the first sign of an approaching storm. While science is theorizing, the weather beats down the crops. The speaker rises to reply, but never finishes, for the storm gathers force and the meeting hurriedly breaks up. Thus the speaker never answers the challenge because a greater challenge is at hand.

The chapter ends as it began with the scene outside, which, as we now realize, has considerable connections with the meeting inside:

The place was darkened by the overhanging clouds, the atmosphere thick and close with the smoke and the crush. Flashes of brilliant lightning seemed to sweep down the narrow street, which ran like a brook with the storm-water; the thunder seemed to descend and shake the solid walls. "It's rather hard on the professor," said one farmer to another. "What would science do in a thunderstorm!" He had hardly spoken when the hail suddenly came down, and the round white globules, rebounding from the pavement, rolled in at the open door. Each paused as he lifted his glass and thought of the harvest. As for Hodge, who was reaping, he had to take shelter how he might in the open fields. Boom! flash! boom!—splash and hiss, as the hail rushed along the narrow street. (*HM*, 24)

It would be legitimate to praise this passage for its vivid directness, its faithful presentation of the scene, its skilful combination of visual and auditory suggestion to build up a complex picture. But I would stress rather the heightened effect conveyed by the breaking storm. I hesitate to use the word "symbolic," but there is a sense in which the storm is more than a meteorological phenomenon. At one level, it is Nature's answer to both farmer and scientist—it proves by its very existence the futility of the preceding discussion. The farmers realize its power, but they can do nothing; they sit drinking, and think of the harvest. The scientist claims that the weather can be defied and the depression halted, but the storm gives him his answer. In another sense, however, I would go so far as to suggest that the storm *is* the agricultural depression, that it represents in its metaphorical function the uneasy times that lie ahead, times that can in some ways be seen as immanent in the failure of communication between the two outlooks with which the whole chapter is concerned. This clash, indeed, forms the foundation of the book, for the rest deals with the contemporary state of agriculture in all its bewildering complexity. The final reference to Hodge is a brilliant detail. He had failed to attend the meeting, and we now know why. It has sometimes been objected that Jefferies, despite his title, gives a disproportionate amount of space to the "masters," and tends to ignore Hodge. But such things cannot be measured in lines on the page; it is the whole effect that is important, and here, as in the book as a whole, it is Hodge who gets the last word. As far as Hodge's welfare is concerned, agricultural science, for all its fine words, seems powerless, and the storm of depression, as an ill omen for the future, symbolizes that Hodge too will suffer.

The chapter can stand by itself as an admirable piece of description and

is also a fine introduction to the book as a whole. It presents all the major
themes of which the later vignettes of farmers, landowners, labourers,
will provide corroborative detail. Here Jefferies has fused his specialized
knowledge with his artistic imagination; descriptive reporting has transcended its own bounds and has emerged as creative literature.

An interesting late study of the labourer is to be found in "One of the
New Voters," an essay collected in the volume *The Open Air* (1885). In
some ways, it may be seen as a later reworking of the matter which formed
the basis of both "John Smith's Shanty" and "The Labourer's Daily Life."
I shall be dealing with the artistry of the maturer essays in a later chapter,
but it will be as well to consider this one here, because of the common
interest in subject-matter.

These later essays, when most successful, are generally built, for all
their apparent ease and artlessness, upon some particular literary effect
which provides the artistic framework for what might otherwise be random observation. In the case of "One of the New Voters," which presents
a whole day in the life of Roger the reaper, the essay depends upon the
startling contrast between the beauty of the countryside golden with the
ripening wheat, and the sordid realities in the lives of the people who live
and work in these picturesque surroundings. The essay opens with a description of an early August morning with a thick mist covering the corn-
fields and meadows, a day promising heat and sunshine. Against this is
set our first glimpse of Roger :

Roger, the reaper, had slept all night in the cow-house, lying on the raised
platform of narrow planks put up for cleanliness when the cattle were there.
. . . Roger did not so much as take off his boots, but flung himself on the
boards crash, curled himself up hedgehog fashion with some old sacks, and
immediately began to breathe heavily. He had no difficulty in sleeping, first
because his muscles had been tried to the utmost, and next because his skin
was full to the brim, not of jolly "good ale and old," but of the very smallest
and poorest of wish-washy beer. In his own words, it "blowed him up till he
very nigh bust." (*OA*, 78)

Thus the essay develops naturally and without a sense of strain into a discussion of the beer supplied to labourers during the harvest season. Jefferies
condemns it as "the vilest drink in the world," demonstrates its bad effect
upon the labourers, and points the contrast we have already noted by

commenting: "Upon this abominable mess the golden harvest of English fields is gathered in" (*OA*, 79).

It must not be supposed, however, that Jefferies is taking up a temperance line. Far from it; he has no sympathy with those who try to discontinue the custom of harvest beer, or substitute something less alcoholic ("The spectacle of John Bull—jovial John Bull—offering his men a bucket of oatmeal liquor is not a pleasant one" [*OA*, 79]); he has far too much knowledge of the facts of farmwork to underestimate its importance. No, what he is complaining about is the quality of the drink offered. Indeed, he maintains that "those who really wish well to the labourer cannot do better than see that he really has beer to drink—real beer, genuine brew of malt and hops, a moderate quantity of which will supply force to his thews and sinews, and will not intoxicate or injure" (*OA*, 80). Nor does Jefferies blame Roger himself for his excess; the very aim of the essay is to look more deeply into the matter before any judgment is made. "Roger had indeed gone supperless, as usual; his supper he had swilled and not eaten. His own fault; he should have exercised self-control. Well, I don't know; let us consider further before we judge" (*OA*, 80).

The evidence required for this judgment is now offered. In a more extended description of the August morning, Jefferies notes the birds and butterflies, the trees and flowers that go to make up the natural scene beside Roger's path to work. But the description is not given merely for the sake of description (a charge that can be legitimately brought against some of Jefferies' less successful writings); instead he is deliberately chronicling the features of the landscape which Roger fails to notice. For Roger, like Peter Bell at the beginning of Wordsworth's poem, has no interest in these things; he is perhaps in a worse state than Peter Bell in that he would probably never have noticed even the existence of the "primrose by the river's brim." But again Jefferies does not blame him for this lack of interest or sensitivity. Instead he explains:

His life was work without skill or thought, the work of the horse, of the crane that lifts stones and timber. His food was rough, his drink rougher, his lodging dry planks. His books were—none; his picture-gallery a coloured print at the ale-house—a dog, dead, by a barrel, "Trust is dead; Bad Pay killed him." Of thought he thought nothing; of hope his idea was a shilling a week more wages; of any future for himself of comfort such as even a good cottage can give—of any future whatever—he had no more conception than the horse in the shafts of the waggon. A human animal simply in all this, yet if you reckoned upon him as simply an animal—as has been done these centuries—you would now be mistaken. But why should he note the colour of the butterfly, the bright light of the sun, the hue of the wheat? This loveliness gave him no cheese for breakfast; of beauty in itself, for itself, he had no idea. How should he? To many of us the harvest—the summer—is a time of joy in light and colour; to him it was a time for adding yet another crust of hardness to the thick skin of his hands. (*OA*, 82–3)

Once again, we see Jefferies' characteristic attitude to the labourer: a refusal to idealize him, yet at the same time a refusal to treat him merely as an animal. Throughout the essay there are remarks and comments which could be extracted from context and quoted as evidence of his social ideas. A little later, he defends Roger's action when, work being over for the day, he proceeds to the public house to drink away the evening:

Had Roger been a horse he would have hastened to borrow some food, and, having eaten that, would have cast himself at once upon his rude bed. Not being an animal, though his life and work were animal, he went with his friends to talk. Let none unjustly condemn him as a blackguard for that—no, not even though they had seen him at ten o'clock unsteadily walking to his shed, and guiding himself occasionally with his hands to save himself from stumbling. (*AO*, 87)

There is obviously considerable social relevance in these lines; but they are more than this, for they have been transformed to the level of art. It spoils these passages to detach them from their context, and this in itself suggests that there is an artistry present in the essay which was absent from, say, "The Labourer's Daily Life." I am not denying, of course, that Jefferies' social conscience is at work in this later writing; rather, the literary effect strengthens it and at the same time transcends it. Jefferies is now an essayist in the strict sense of the word, and has graduated, as it were, from the lower grade of descriptive writer.

The remainder of the essay covers Roger's daily work. With the vivid particularity of which only Jefferies is capable, we appreciate the intense heat in the cornfield, and feel the aching labours of the toilers in the fields. And so the days continue with a deadening sameness. Jefferies can only differentiate them by the reapers' varying capacity for drink—"now a little less beer, now a little more" (*OA*, 87) until harvest is gathered. But by the time the season is over, despite all the extra harvest payment,

Roger's only profit is thirty shillings, two thirds of which is spent upon a new pair of boots. The rest has gone on evening beer, and although he does not labour the point, Jefferies draws an implicit contrast between the remaining half-sovereign and the golden wheat that he has helped to harvest. Nor, again, does he blame Roger for his lack of thrift—"this life of animal labour does not grow the spirit of economy" (*OA*, 89).

And Jefferies ends where he began with an eloquent contrast between two pictures—that of the harvest, and that of the harvester:

The golden harvest is the first scene; the golden wheat, glorious under the summer sun. Bright poppies flower in its depths, and convolvulus climbs the stalks. Butterflies float slowly over the yellow surface as they might over a lake of colour. To linger by it, to visit it day by day, at even to watch the sunset by it, and see it pale under the changing light, is a delight to the thoughtful mind. There is so much in the wheat, there are books of meditation in it, it is dear to the heart. Behind these beautiful aspects comes the reality of human labour—hours upon hours of heat and strain; there comes the reality of a rude life, and in the end little enough of gain. The wheat is beautiful, but human life is labour. (*OA*, 89-90)

The last sentence, beautiful in its simplicity and depth, sums up the whole of the essay, thus performing a similar function to the title, the double irony of which has not, so far as I know, been pointed out. *The Open Air* was first published in 1885, just before the agricultural labourer first exercized his newly won suffrage. "One of the New Voters" would have been an appropriate title for a straightforward account of rural political trends (an article, for instance, like Jefferies' own "After the County Franchise" published the previous year), but this essay contains no word of voting or pure politics. Any comment is implicit, and has to be drawn out by the reader. It invites, I think, two different reactions, as paradoxical as the two contrasted visions of the beautiful wheat and the labouring life. One is that this particular voter, Roger the reaper, has no knowledge to make his vote (if, as is doubtful, he cares to use it) of any value beyond a single unit in the count. The other turns the responsibility upon society as a whole, and shows this new voter as a challenge to the moral conscience, as a man (not an animal) whose burden must be lightened. This ability to see both sides of the question, and to present them in all their complexity without any attempt to judge between them except to plead for a practical humanity, may be seen as a prime feature of Jefferies' best work. Above all, this later work possesses a greater richness and eloquence, and must be read in its entirety for the complete effect to be realized. The clarity and precision of earlier days were admirable qualities in themselves, but they required something more to qualify as a permanent contribution to the art of letters. Here, matter and expression are fused into an artistic whole which carries complete conviction. It is the harvest of the earlier writing, and would not have been possible without it. Not only has description turned into art, but observation has been transformed into vision.

III. The Country Books

"THERE ARE NO COUNTRIES IN THE WORLD," wrote George Borrow in the preface to *Lavengro*, "less known by the British than these self-same British Islands." [1] The realization of this truth, together with a desire to remedy the situation, was one of the significant aesthetic trends of the later nineteenth century, though Borrow's remark, made at the turn of the half-century, was just as applicable to the late seventies when Jefferies was coming into prominence. There are many reasons why an appreciation of the English countryside should have developed as a popular taste at this time. Scientific progress, formerly confined to the pioneering expert, was now arousing the interest and excitement of the man in the street. Natural history, geology, archaeology, all gained a new following. Stuffed specimens of wild life were displayed not merely as trophies of the hunting-field or the shooting-expedition, but as exhibits of scientific interest and significance. Thanks mainly to the enthusiasm of Charles Kingsley, numerous natural history societies were formed; the assembling of a herbarium and a rock collection became fashionable pursuits, and the study of history and pre-history intensified as experts made more and more detailed discoveries about the nature of the past. In literature, too, the viewpoints and attitudes of Romanticism had gradually filtered through into "popular" culture. The Victorian public was laid once more "on the cool flowery lap of earth." Wordsworth was firmly enthroned as the bard of nature, and Tennyson was following in his footsteps with his famous rural notebook. Moreover, to turn to more practical considera-

1. George Borrow, *Lavengro: Scholar, Gipsy, Priest* [1851] (London: John Murray, 1907), p. vii.

tions, the improved methods of transportation, especially the railway system, had brought rural nature into more familiar contact with the town. The countryside was no longer, in the eyes of city-dwellers, a remote outpost of the nation; instead, it was the varying scenery observed from the train window. Its wildness, its mystery and "romance," may have diminished, but it became on the other hand an object of increased curiosity.

But the main factor in the change was undoubtedly, and ironically, the decline of the countryside. Not only were the two brought into closer contact, but the town spread over the countryside and, where it did not actually destroy it, brought significant, inevitable, and by no means wholly undesirable changes. The old ways of rural life were gradually but surely passing away, and thus became, to the cultured mind, interesting. At the beginning of the century, England was predominantly a rural civilization; by its close the Industrial Revolution had had its effect, and the majority of the population was urban in outlook. As D. H. Lawrence was to express it, "even the farm-labourer today is psychologically a town-bird."[2] In earlier times, the holiday season involved a movement towards the town, to London or Bath, and fashionable life was found to be of absorbing literary interest; when positions were reversed, and families (including an ever increasing number of middle-class families) flocked from the workaday world of the town to the fresh and invigorating country air, the rural scene became a focus of literary attention. But this change in taste reminds us of the important and significant fact that the literature of the countryside, though produced by countrymen, was written primarily with an urban audience in mind.

It is not surprising that the contemporary countrymen with literary aspirations, of whom Jefferies was one, should have taken some time to realize their opportunity. The countryside was all they knew, it was the scene in which they had grown up, and they did not realize that what to them was familiar and commonplace might be new and exciting to a stranger. Jefferies himself began with a series of incredibly inept short stories dealing with adventures in countries and social milieux of which he knew nothing. His early novels, with the partial exception of *Restless Human Hearts*, took place in an urban setting to which he was an outsider. He found some of his true gifts, as we have seen, almost by chance with the *Times* letters and the subsequent agricultural essays. But it was

2. D. H. Lawrence, *Phoenix* (London: Heinemann, 1936), p. 139.

not until he moved into an urban atmosphere (to Surbiton in 1877) that he realized the full literary possibilities not only of his knowledge of the rural social scene, but of his unique rural lore in general. With *The Gamekeeper at Home* (1878) he achieved success, if only temporarily, and much of his reputation to this day depends upon those books where he talks frankly and easily about the hundred-and-one varied details of the country scene. His contribution was to bring back to the public a sense of nature, as opposed to isolated natural objects. "Where," Thoreau had asked, "is the proper herbarium, the true cabinet of shells, and the museum of skeletons, but in the meadow where the flower bloomed, by the seaside where the tide cast up the fish, and on the hills and in the valleys where the beast laid down his life and the skeleton of the traveller reposes on the grass?" [3] Jefferies, who had probably never read Thoreau, none the less thought along the same lines, and rose to the challenge. In these country books—*The Gamekeeper at Home, Wild Life in a Southern County, The Amateur Poacher*, and *Round About a Great Estate*, to which we may add for convenience the later *Red Deer*—the stuffed birds and pressed flowers were shown alive in their true environment, the countless species which science had subdivided and analysed were replaced in their rightful context, and the minute details of the rural scene, half observed and soon forgotten by the country-loving townsman, were evoked with a precision and ease which combined nostalgia with a hard sense of reality.

The qualities which the townsman asked of the rural writer are suggested in an interesting essay by Leslie Stephen entitled "Country Books," first published in the *Cornhill Magazine* in December 1880 and collected in the later editions of *Hours in a Library*. Contemporary with Jefferies' rural writings, though not alluding to them, Stephen's essay is an unusual mixture of the flippant and the sincere. It is obviously the product of an unrepentant townsman, as can be seen from the tone of the opening passage, where he makes the important point that rural literature presents us with nature at second hand—the pleasures without the discomforts:

A love of the country is taken, I know not why, to indicate the presence of all the cardinal virtues. It is one of those outlying qualities which are not exactly meritorious, but which, for that very reason, are the more provocative of a

3. Quoted in Joseph Wood Krutch, *Henry David Thoreau* (London: Methuen, n.d.), pp. 182–3.

pleasing self-complacency. People pride themselves upon it as upon early rising, or upon answering letters by return of post. . . . We assert a taste for fresh and innocent pleasures, and an indifference to the feverish excitements of artificial society. I, too, love the country—if such a statement can be received after such an exordium; but I confess—to be duly modest—that I love it best in books. In real life I have remarked that it is frequently damp and rheumatic, and most hated by those who know it best.[4]

He then lists the requirements for the best country books:

Who are the most potent weavers of that delightful magic? Clearly, in the first place, those who have been themselves in contact with rural sights and sounds. The echo of an echo loses all sharpness of definition; our guide may save us the trouble of stumbling through farmyards and across ploughed fields, but he must have gone through it himself till his very voice has a twang of the true country accent.[5]

This is certainly Jefferies' best qualification, and one of which he is well aware. In the preface to *The Gamekeeper at Home* he emphasizes that "the facts here collected are really entirely derived from original observation" (*GH*, 3), and similar remarks may be found scattered throughout his writings.

Revealing a definite Wordsworthian influence, Stephen continues by noting that the country writer must recreate within us some of the magic which we felt in childhood, but which has since been lost. He makes the good point that such a writer's art must appear to be artless—"he must have the art—the less conscious the better—of placing us at his own point of view"[6]—and goes on to suggest that he should also be something of an eccentric. The essay deals specifically with Izaak Walton, Gilbert White, William Cobbett, and George Borrow, so his personal taste is clear enough. For all its wit, and a generous helping of blunt good sense, there is an underlying complacency in his attitude. To Stephen, the rustic is a "character," an eccentric, lacking in the sophistication which we claim to deplore but upon which we actually rely. Jefferies is eager to stress that the countryman, whether landowner, farmer, or labourer, is neither a yokel nor a lout, neither boorish nor simple-minded. On this point he differs from Stephen, and his books fully justify his position. In his later writings he realized the need for what Stephen called "supplying the magic," but both

4. Leslie Stephen, *Hours in a Library* (3 vols.; enlarged ed.; London: Smith Elder, 1899), III, 175.
5. *Ibid*., III, 177.   6. *Ibid*., III, 182.

the circumstances and the means he took to combat them were very different, and will be discussed in a later chapter.

But Stephen has a final point, which is shrewd and noteworthy. We want an account, he says, of the country as it is now, which implies not only descriptions of wild nature and picturesque ruins, but a complete survey of nature and man, country and countryman:

But nature, as I have said, is not the country. We are not in search of the country which appears now as it appeared in the remote days when painted savages managed to raise a granite block upon its supports for the amusement of future antiquaries. We want the country which bears the impress of some characteristic social growth; which has been moulded by its inhabitants as the inhabitants by it, till one is as much adapted to the other as the lichen to the rock on which it grows.[7]

There is no need to illustrate this aspect of Jefferies' work. It is the principle which distinguishes him from chroniclers of wild nature like Gilbert White or Thoreau, or his successor Edward Thomas. Thus his concern with the rural population is consciously present in *The Gamekeeper at Home*, as can be seen from the sub title: "Sketches of Natural History and Rural Life."

An important ingredient which Stephen neglects to mention, but which Jefferies successfully provides, is the element of pure instruction. It is not merely a matter of evocation, of description, of nature without tears. Jefferies relates pieces of information, which are interesting in themselves, and also gives pieces of advice, which the reader can use with profit. Stephen's position on this point may be gauged from his treatment of Walton. The advice given in *The Compleat Angler* on how to fish is, he claims, dubious, but this does not matter because Walton's chief claim to fame is his quaintness. But Jefferies' advice, on such subjects as choosing a gun, observing wild life, even (in *The Amateur Poacher*) on how to lay an illegal wire, is essentially practical. He knows what he is talking about, and is read as an authority. This, of course, is not necessarily an advantage for a country writer—not when he is judged by purely literary standards. As T. Michael Pope has written: "Jefferies demands from his reader an interest in his subject-matter almost as keen as his own. Without that interest he will infallibly prove dull, tedious, and uninspired."[8] A

7. *Ibid.*, III, 197.
8. T. Michael Pope, "Richard Jefferies," *Academy*, LXXIV (March 28, 1908, 617).

more personal writer like W. H. Hudson might conceivably be enjoyed by a reader who had no particular interest in the countryside about which he was writing, but such a reader would find Jefferies merely boring. His descriptions are too lovingly minute, too much concerned with detailed accounts of the commonplace and apparently trivial. Because, as we have noticed before, Jefferies revolts from the conception of the eccentric countryman, he makes no concessions to the Leslie Stephens of this world, and the reader must find what he writes about interesting for its own sake. Without this original interest on the part of the reader, no writer, however talented, could succeed with this kind of book.

A question which inevitably arises with regard to these country books is: are they an original contribution to rural literature? Had anyone else brought quite the same knowledge and approach to the genre? There had, of course, been many books on various aspects of the countryside, but there had been little attempt to weld these into a comprehensive study. There was, for example, the literature that had grown up around hunting, from the factual anecdotes of Charles St. John to the fictional adventures of Surtees' Sponge and Jorrocks. Different aspects of rural life and natural history had attracted such diverse personalities as Izaak Walton, Charles Waterton, William Cobbett, and George Borrow. There had been the natural historians, like Gilbert White, the botanists, like the eccentric Culpeper and the scientific Linnaeus, and the antiquaries, like Stukeley and Aubrey. Jefferies was capable of writing on all these topics. There are essays on shooting and guns, on fishing, on gipsies, on flora and fauna, and his local articles posthumously gathered together in the volume entitled *Jefferies' Land* demonstrate his determined, if somewhat laboured, attempts to chronicle local history. But in volumes like *The Gamekeeper at Home*, he offered all this and more besides within the covers of a single book. He gives us not merely aspects of the countryside, as in the rural articles, but the countryside itself in all its variety of detail. Before Jefferies no one had combined the detailed knowledge and experience with the requisite literary instinct and ability to present the essence of the country in words.

How familiar Jefferies was with the "predecessors" that I have already mentioned is by no means clear. He knew Culpeper, and probably Walton. He knew Aubrey, but used him for the most part only as a source for his own local history. He also knew Linnaeus, and his comment on his *Tour of Lapland* demonstrates so clearly Jefferies' own tastes in country books that it must be quoted:

The best book he wrote to read now is the delightful "Tour of Lapland", with its quaint pen-and-ink sketches, so realistically vivid, as if the thing sketched had been banged on the paper and so left its impress. I have read it three times, and I still cherish the old yellow pages; it is the best botanical book, written by the greatest of botanists, specially sent on a botanical expedition, and it contains nothing about botany. It tells you about the canoes, and the hard cheese, and the Laplander's warehouse on top of a pole, like a pigeon-house; and the innocent way in which the maiden helped the traveller in his bath, and how the aged men ran so fast that the devil could not catch them. . . . (*FH*, 45)

Linnaeus caught the real countryside in his book, while his collection of specimens and scientific discoveries gave only the bare skeleton. Although Jefferies welcomed and practised the scientific method of careful and accurate observation, he wrote creative literature, not text-books.

Two writers with whom we know him to have been acquainted are Gilbert White and Charles St. John, and brief reference to their work may help to isolate Jefferies' distinctive gifts. *The Natural History of Selborne* is the naturalist's bible, and subsequent biological higher criticism, while qualifying many of its findings, can do nothing to lessen its essential appeal. Our appreciation of White is, however, sharply divided between the man and his work. We praise him first, in the words White himself used of James Thomson, as "a nice observer of natural occurrences" [9]— a patient collector of facts about the wild life in his district. But what makes the book of perennial interest is the character of the man behind the writing, his enthusiasm, his curiosity, his humility—in short, his humanity. And Jefferies, in his introduction to the book, stressed his directness of style and simplicity of manner: "His mind was free and his eye open" (*SY*, 56). None the less, there is none of the feeling for nature in White that we can find in Jefferies himself. White is a collector of facts, and they are interesting and useful facts, for which we respect him. But the "magic" is lacking as Jefferies must have been aware, though he treats White as a pioneer naturalist without criticizing him for something he did not at-

9. Gilbert White, *The Natural History of Selborne* [1789] (London: Arrowsmith, n.d.), p. 34.

tempt. His only regret, as has often been noted, is that White did not pay a similar attention to "a natural history of the people of his day" (*SY*, 59) —a significant and legitimate qualification. It reminds us that White's qualities are the foundations upon which Jefferies builds; the latter's work depends upon White's earlier achievement, but surpasses it in scope.

The work of Charles St. John (1809–56) is closer to Jefferies in intention, if not in execution. His best-known work is *Short Sketches of the Wild Sports and Natural History of the Highlands* (1845). A reference in one of Jefferies' essays ("Outside London") makes it clear that he knew this work. Though he paints himself as primarily a sportsman, St. John was a naturalist of considerable standing, and he also reacted with feeling to the landscape into which his sport and observation took him. His book is a pleasing, leisurely account of his life in Scotland, and includes some amusing anecdotes concerning the shepherds and poachers whom he knew and befriended. There are differences, of course; St. John is more interested in "the habits of the wilder and rarer birds and beasts," [10] while Jefferies is content with the humbler, commoner species which we may meet every day. None the less, the book contains something of the variety and detail which we associate with Jefferies' best work. Unfortunately, St. John's style and attitudes are fairly conventional and commonplace; his work lacks Jefferies' richness and spontaneity. His effects are laboured, and he falls too often into a Victorian pomposity. The difference is particularly obvious in his treatment of the countrymen and it is significantly the Highlanders and their love of nature that Jefferies mentions in his reference to the book. St. John's anecdotes are interesting enough, but he lacks the power to catch a character in a phrase. When in *The Amateur Poacher* Jefferies records Little John's rebuke to him for failing to secure a net during a rabbit-hunting expedition—"Us must be main careful how us fixes our nets, you" (*AP*, 325)—he conveys more in a single sentence than St. John tells us about Donald or Malcolm in his whole book. It is probably Jefferies' experience as a novelist that gives him the advantage in this respect. He is more subtle than St. John, and altogether more natural. St. John's descriptions are conscious set-pieces; Jefferies' arise easily and fully from his mood.

10. Charles St. John, *Short Sketches of the Wild Sports and Natural History of the Highlands* [1845] (London: John Murray, 1893), p. 4.

A perennial difficulty with a book of this kind—and one particularly germane to a critical discussion of its effect—is the problem of form. There is always the danger that the book will deteriorate into a collection of disjointed anecdotes. On the other hand, a consciously imposed form will destroy the feeling of spontaneity which is an indispensable ingredient in such writing. It is a part of Jefferies' effect, however, to portray the natural world in all its variety, to present the fascination which is part of our appreciation of the countryside. Just as we never quite know what may meet us round the next hedge or the next bend in the bridle-path, so in Jefferies' writings we are never quite sure what will confront us over the page. There must be some unity and form, but it should be both slight and inconspicuous.

I suspect that Jefferies was acutely conscious of this difficulty, and considered the matter carefully before embarking upon a new book. The evidence for this may be seen in the prefaces to the various volumes where he draws attention to his general aim. It is interesting, too, that each of the books uses a different method to get round the problem, a different general framework upon which to weave the varied strands of material.

In *The Gamekeeper at Home*, as the title suggests, it is a particular personage who is the centre of attention. The wide range of the keeper's work in the fields and woods gives Jefferies an admirable excuse to include any detail which could conceivably come in a gamekeeper's way. The underlying plan may be gathered from the preface, where he writes:

The Gamekeeper forms, indeed, so prominent a figure in rural life as almost to demand some biographical record of his work and ways. From the man to the territories over which he bears sway—the meadows, woods, and streams—and to his subjects, their furred and feathered inhabitants, is a natural transition. The enemies against whom he wages incessant warfare—vermin, poachers, and trespassers—must, of course, be included in such a survey. (*GH*, 3)

The various elements can be checked off against the chapter headings. Furthermore, Jefferies concentrates upon one particular gamekeeper, in real life Haylock of Burderop estate; as he writes a few lines later, "the character of a particular Keeper has been used as a nucleus about which to arrange materials that would otherwise have lacked a connecting link" (*GH*, 3). This last phrase is important. To my mind, Jefferies was wise to map out the rough plan of his book in the preface; the reader thus knows what to expect from the start, and accepts what would otherwise require an awkward intrusion of comment in the text itself. It is interesting to note that this particular plan is practically identical with that used by Hudson in *A Shepherd's Life*, where the diversity of the shepherd's work is presented through the experience of a single shepherd, Caleb Bawcombe. It seems obvious to me that Hudson consciously modelled his book upon *The Gamekeeper at Home*; this would explain why it is the most reminiscent of Jefferies of all his works.

It must be admitted, however, that some critics have considered the result of Jefferies' plan not altogether satisfactory. The portrait of Haylock has been found inflated and uncritical. To Edward Thomas he is "a policeman god," [11] and to David Ascoli "Haylock, a veritable monarch of all he surveys, is grossly overdrawn" (*GH*, xvi). Jefferies' attitude to gamekeepers in general was certainly far more favourable than that of most naturalists and nature-lovers. St. John talks of "so opinionated and conceited a personage (as most keepers are)," [12] and Hudson refers to "that rare being, an intelligent gamekeeper." [13] Rare being or not, Keeper Haylock seems to have had much of the stature that Jefferies gives him, and Alfred Williams, while gathering material for his *Villages of the White Horse*, heard stories about him from the local population a quarter of a century after Jefferies' death. Jefferies realizes that Haylock is somewhat exceptional, and tells his readers so in the first chapter: "I am at present delineating the upright keeper, such as are in existence still, notwithstanding the abuse lavished upon them as a class—often, it is to be feared, too well deserved" (*GH,* 13). And in the last chapter he restores the balance by devoting a section to "Black Sheep." Personally, I find his portrait of Haylock acceptable. His speech has the ring of truth, and in fact he is less prominent in the book as a whole than some critics have suggested. The over-all plan taking in his territories and subjects, his assistants and enemies, is in itself a safeguard against too limited a concentration on the man himself.

Wild Life in a Southern County is built around a very different scheme. Again Jefferies is careful to explain what he is doing in a preface:

A difficulty confronts the explorer who would carry away a note of what he has seen, because nature is not cut and dried to hand, nor easily classified, each

11. Edward Thomas, *Richard Jefferies: His Life and Work* (1909), p. 128.
12. St. John, p. 107.
13. W. H. Hudson, *A Shepherd's Life* [1910] (London: Dent, 1923), p. 108.

subject shading gradually into another. In studying the ways, for instance, of so common a bird as the starling it cannot be separated from the farmhouse in the thatch of which it often breeds, the rooks with whom it associates, or the friendly sheep upon whose backs it sometimes rides. Since the subjects are so closely connected, it is best, perhaps, to take the places they prefer for the convenience of division, and group them as far as possible in the districts they usually frequent. (*WL*, 21)

Consequently, the book is arranged topographically. It begins with a description of the downland, then follows a small stream down into a valley, past village, hamlet, and farmhouse, chronicling each locality as it comes, finishing with an orchard and lake in the vale. It is an interesting scheme, but does not quite succeed. It is the least successful of the books at present under consideration. There are many fine passages, and the information about various species of wild life is often fascinating, but as a whole it tends to be rather dull. One reason for this may be that it contains less about the human inhabitants of the county than any other Jefferies book. John Burroughs, the American naturalist, accurately describes it as "a kind of field newspaper." [14] It is often loose and desultory in execution, and this is the part of Jefferies where the reader has to meet him more than half way. Here some of W. E. Henley's strictures are justified; even the most fervid admirer must admit that there are passages where we "clamour for a breath of inspiration while he is bent upon emptying his notebook in decent English." [15]

I shall be considering *The Amateur Poacher* in some detail a little later, so at this point I need only mention it in passing. It is, in my opinion, easily the best of the country books, and this judgment would not, I think, be disputed by most readers. The subject-matter is identical with that of *The Gamekeeper at Home*; the difference, as its title suggests, is that it is told from the other side of the fence—literally and metaphorically. It might be expected, then, that the form would follow that of the earlier book, but this is not the case. Instead Jefferies chooses a chronological arrangement. "The following pages," as he writes in the preface, "are arranged somewhat in the order of time" (*AP*, 171). In this way he is enabled to fall back upon his earlier memories, to write with a controlled

14. John Burroughs, *Riverby* [1894] (Boston: Houghton Mifflin, 1904), p. 224.
15. W. E. Henley, *Views and Reviews* (1890), p. 180.

nostalgia which in its vivid unsentimentality is perhaps Jefferies' greatest contribution to Victorian letters.

Round About a Great Estate has a different theme, though the chronological element is still important. Jefferies is acutely conscious here of profound changes in the life of the countryside; he sees the approach of new situations and problems, and the evolution of a new type of country-man. "The cottager," he writes, "is no longer ignorant, and his child is well grounded in rudimentary education, reads and writes with facility, and is not without knowledge of the higher sort" (*RGE*, xv). Change is inevitable. It is the end of an era, and the aim of *Round About a Great Estate* is to catch the impression of this vanishing era before it is too late. Again Jefferies is using his childhood memories, and mingling them with observations from his notebooks. It is a delightful record of a way of life told with ease and economy. But it must not be imagined that the book is in any way reactionary. Jefferies is recording the passing of an age that he loved, but he does not mourn its demise. He shows us its strengths, its appeal, its beauty, but he does not fall back into a vague yearning for the "good old days." He is careful to make his attitude clear in the preface: "In this book some notes have been made of the former state of things before it passes away entirely. But I would not have it therefore thought that I wish it to continue or return. My sympathies and hopes are with the light of the future, only I should like it to come from nature. The clock should be read by the sunshine, not the sun timed by the clock." (*RGE*, xvi) Altogether it is perhaps the freshest of his books, packed with delightful vignettes of country folk which look forward to his later novels, humorous anecdote, sensitive pictures which build up an unforgettable impression of mid-Victorian rural life. As the title indicates, there is also a geographical form to the book in that the incidents are for the most part confined to a single district—Okebourne Chace.

Red Deer, the last of the five that I shall discuss here, is something of an exception. While the books which we have already mentioned, together with *Hodge and His Masters*, were written in a remarkably short space of time, between 1878 and 1880, *Red Deer* was not written until 1883 and not published till the following year. Meanwhile, Jefferies had proceeded to other things. His rural descriptions now took the form of separate essays rather than full-length books, and these were later printed as collections of essays, like *Nature Near London* and *The Life of the Fields*. Besides, he had returned to fiction, following up *Greene Ferne Farm*, which also belongs to the same period as the main country books, with *The Dewy Morn* and also with the two books of boyhood, *Wood Magic* and *Bevis*. And to add to all this, he had also produced *The Story of My Heart*.

But almost immediately after completing the latter work in May 1883, he visited Exmoor for two or three weeks, and had completed *Red Deer* within six weeks of his return. The main difference between this book and its predecessors is that Jefferies is here dealing with a countryside which is unfamiliar to him. The earlier books had portrayed a scene which he had known intimately since childhood, which had entered into his very being and become a part of him as he was a part of it. Here he faced a new scenery and new countrymen, yet *Red Deer* reads with such authority and confidence that it is hard to believe that it was not written by a native. He must have steeped himself in Exmoor's "spirit of place" throughout his brief visit, and it was no doubt vital that it should be written immediately on his return, while the details were still fresh in his mind. None the less, it is a remarkable achievement, and shows Jefferies' powers of observation and selection at their keenest.

Because of this unusual quality about *Red Deer*, it can be profitably compared with the English books of W. H. Hudson. Indeed, the most significant difference between the two writers is that Jefferies is normally inside the subject he is describing whereas Hudson, when writing of England, is a sensitive and sympathetic stranger. In *Nature in Downland*, for instance, Hudson takes a particular stretch of country and travels within it reporting his experiences in a quiet and forthright manner, and Jefferies, sixteen years earlier, is doing the same thing in *Red Deer*. This is especially true of the first half of the book, where Jefferies describes with freshness and clarity his wanderings in search of the deer. He conveys the landscape, which is, as he says, "instinct with the presence of the wild deer" (*RD*, 140), with a remarkable economy and truth. Moreover, he sets the deer in the landscape, subject and object, deer and background, perfectly balanced and equally in focus. The following passage is widely known, but well illustrates Jefferies' beautifully modulated prose at its best:

There is no more beautiful creature than a stag in his pride of antler, his coat of ruddy gold, his grace of form and motion. He seems the natural owner of the ferny coombes, the oak woods, the broad slopes of heather. They belong to him, and he steps upon the sward in lordly mastership. The land is his and the hills, the sweet streams and rocky glens. . . . He is as natural as an oak, or a fern, or a rock itself. He is earth-born—autochthon—and holds possession by descent. . . .

The branching antlers accord so well with the deep shadowy boughs and the broad fronds of the brake; the golden red of his coat fits to the foxglove, the purple heather, and later on to the orange and red of the beech; his easy bounding motion springs from the elastic sward; his limbs climb the steep hill as if it were level; his speed covers the distances, and he goes from place to place as the wind. He not only lives in the wild, wild woods and moors—he grows out of them, as the oak grows from the ground. The noble stag in his pride of antler is lord and monarch of all the creatures left to us in English forests and on English hills. (RD, 161-2)

At this point, it is necessary to clarify Jefferies' position with regard to the vexed question of hunting. In all these books, but particularly in those concerned with gamekeepers and poachers, hunting and shooting provide a constant background. Jefferies' general attitude to such sport is therefore of some importance, and especially so because it has been misunderstood in the past. The reason for the confusion stems no doubt from the fact that Jefferies' attitude to sport, like his attitude to gamekeepers, differed somewhat from those of his fellow nature writers. We realize this most forcibly when we read in Hudson's *A Shepherd's Life* the statement that "the curse of the pheasant is on . . . all the woods and forests in Wiltshire."[16] Had Jefferies looked at the matter in this way, it is obvious that *The Gamekeeper at Home* and *The Amateur Poacher* could never have been written. Yet many of Jefferies' admirers have been disturbed by his apparent approval of blood sports, and H. S. Salt was particularly concerned. He wrote: "His early books are disfigured by many revolting details of the seamy side of sportsmanship, which are intolerable to any reader in whom either the humane or artistic instinct is well developed."[17] It soon becomes clear that Salt's dislike of this interest is related to his dislike of Jefferies' early politics, and that his disapproval is as much of the class who do the shooting as of the shooting itself. Salt's tactics here resemble his earlier political argument—he tries to show another progres-

16. Hudson, p. 282.
17. H. S. Salt, *Richard Jefferies: A Study* (1894), pp. 36–7.

sion in Jefferies from an insensitive predatory sportsman to an enlightened precursor of the Anti-Cruel-Sports-League. However, the theory is no closer to the facts in this case than in the other. He forgets that in *Red Deer*, published as late as 1884, Jefferies had referred to stag-hunting as "the noblest sport of all" (*RD*, 168), and since Salt wrote, other essays have come to light which go against his thesis. For instance, in one essay entitled "Shooting Poachers," which appeared in the *Pall Mall Gazette* in December 1884, Jefferies goes so far as to proclaim himself "a champion of sport, a true believer in sport" (*CH*, 236). Even more interesting is a long essay called "A Defence of Sport," published in the *National Review* in the previous year. It begins with the revealing sentence: "I do not think that any one ever walked through a field with a gun, or by water with a rod, without being the better for it" (*CH*, 250). His attitude is logical enough, it is at one with his emphasis on the tangible and the real. "I claim for sport in its general sense that it brings the mind in contact with the facts of life, and imparts the higher education which is independent of and superior to mere literary knowledge" (*CH*, 250). I agree with Samuel J. Looker that the essay "is not entirely free from an element of speciousness and special pleading" (*CH*, 18); there is, indeed, a faint suggestion that the battle of Waterloo was won upon the English hunting fields. But facts are facts, and there can be no doubt that Jefferies never renounced his love of sport, though it is true that he participated less in his later years. The obvious reasons for this, however, are his residence in London, pressure of work, and his subsequent ill-health rather than any change of heart. All in all, Jefferies' position resembles that of Pierce Lestrange in *Restless Human Hearts*, of whom he writes: "With one of those singular inconsistencies which mark human nature, Pierce, the protector of the timid creatures in his garden—the human and the gentle—was passionately fond of field-sports, be it hunting, shooting, or fishing" (*RHH*, II, 9).

But it must be emphasized that Jefferies was never a fanatical sportsman; it would be strange indeed if he had ever been a wholesale destroyer of wild creatures. He has nothing but contempt for the organized battue, and deplores the so-called sportsmen who wantonly exterminate any form of natural life. He was well aware, however, how much his intimate knowledge of natural history owed to his boyhood days when he carried a gun or a fishing-line around the Coate countryside. He would have agreed with Thoreau when he wrote: "Fishermen, hunters, woodchoppers, and others, spending their lives in the fields and woods, in a peculiar sense a part of Nature themselves, are often in a more favourable mood for observing her, in the intervals of their pursuits, than philosophers or poets even, who approach her with expectation." [18] Thoreau considered that hunting was "one of the best parts of my education," [19] and both writers probably owe to this aspect of their youth their refreshingly unsentimental appreciation of wild nature.

Jefferies followed men like Cobbett and St. John as far as his hunting instincts were concerned. The latter had written:

I have much more satisfaction in killing a moderate quantity of birds, in a wide and varied range of hill, with my single brace of dogs, and wandering in any direction that fancy leads me, than in having my day's beat laid out for me, with relays of dogs and keepers, and all the means of killing the grouse on easy walking ground, where they are so numerous that one has only to load and fire. [20]

In other words, the sport is in the challenge and the difficulty, in the pitting of one's skill against the prey. Jefferies objects to the perfection of modern guns, which are designed merely for slaughter, and destroy the balance to man's advantage. Salt rightly quotes the passage from *The Amateur Poacher* where Jefferies tells how he was about to shoot a pheasant, but paused to watch its beauty, and continues:

That watching so often stayed the shot that at last it grew to be a habit: the mere simple pleasure of seeing birds and animals, when they were quite unconscious that they were observed, being too great to be spoiled by the discharge. . . . I have entered many woods just for the pleasure of creeping through the brake and the thickets. Destruction in itself was not the motive; it was an overpowering instinct for woods and fields. Yet woods and fields lose half their interest without a gun—I like the power to shoot, even though I may not use it. (*AP*, 349-50)

To be scrupulously fair, however, he ought to have continued his quotation a little further:

There could be no greater pleasure to me than to wander with a match-lock through one of the great forests or wild tracts that still remain in England. A hare a day, a brace of partridges, or a wild duck would be ample in the way

18. Henry David Thoreau, *Walden, or Life in the Woods* [1854] (Boston: Houghton Mifflin, 1888), p. 227.
19. *Ibid.*, p. 228.   20. St. John, p. 29.

of actual shooting. The weapon itself, whether match-lock, wheel-lock, or even a cross-bow, would be a delight. .... The consciousness that everything depends upon your own personal skill, and that you have no second resource if that fails you, gives the real zest to sport. (*AP*, 350-1)

The sport for Jefferies does not reside in the amount of game killed, but in the excitement, the skill, and, above all, the insight which it provides into the ways of Nature. His may not be a simple position, but it is not, fundamentally, inconsistent. It is the precise attitude of that other Wiltshireman in Edward Thomas' poem "Lob":

> He was a squire's son
> Who loved wild bird and beast, and dog and gun
> For killing them. He had loved them from his birth,
> One with another, as he loved the earth.[21]

I choose *The Amateur Poacher* for more extended discussion, not only because I believe it to be the best of the country books, but because it is as interesting for its anticipations of later successes as for its own intrinsic merits. It is, in fact, something of a microcosm of Jefferies' whole corpus; there is a general widening of horizons, the realization of whole new fields of experience still to be explored and portrayed. *The Gamekeeper at Home* had revealed a writer of specialized interests with a stylistic gift for communicating his particular knowledge to the reader, but it gave little suggestion that the author was more than "a reporter of genius." But *The Amateur Poacher* bubbles over with new ideas and possibilities. It is, I would say, the great turning-point in Jefferies' career; it sets him firmly upon his true course, and is almost a guarantee of later development.

There are four different themes running through the book, all of them typical of Jefferies at some stage of his writing, three of them looking forward to his later and maturer work. First, there is the Bevis theme, concerning itself with his personal autobiographical account of childhood pursuits; second is the country theme, common to all the books of this period, but presented here with an exceptional vividness and directness; third is the social or human theme, which anticipates *Hodge and His Masters* and the later fiction; finally, there are occasional but noteworthy passages which point toward the visionary theme that is to come to full flower in *The Story*

21. Edward Thomas, *Collected Poems* (London: Faber, 1956), p. 55.

of My Heart and the late essays. But far from being a mere *pot-pourri* of disconnected fragments into which Jefferies subsequently dipped when in need of a new subject or approach, the book possesses a unity of its own. It is yet another, and particularly dramatic, example of the close connection in Jefferies between the reporter and the mystic, between the naturalist and the artist.

The first four chapters cover the period of Jefferies' boyhood and his youthful initiation into the poacher's art. The distinctive tone of the later *Bevis* is here caught for the first time; the details and the setting are plainly recognizable, and Orion is an early portrait of Mark. The book begins abruptly with a confident note which we have not met before:

They burned the old gun that used to stand in the dark corner up in the garret, close to the stuffed fox that always grinned so fiercely. Perhaps the reason why he seemed in such a ghastly rage was that he did not come by his death fairly. Otherwise his pelt would not have been so perfect. And why else was he put up there out of sight?—and so magnificent a brush as he had too. But there he stood, and mounted guard over the old flintlock that was so powerful a magnet to us in those days. (*AP*, 173)

We are conveyed immediately into a boy's world. The garret, the gun, the equivocal fox with its fierce grin, all combine to communicate the maximum of effect in the minimum space. The language is clear, direct, and colloquial, picking up an occasional boyish intonation ("a ghastly rage," "and so magnificent a brush as he had too") as the childhood mood is recalled, and intensifies in both writer and reader. Not only are the material objects brought vividly before us but the mood of boyish excitement in which they were first examined and treasured is conveyed as well. The details that Jefferies gives us are not the conventional "childish things" that can be relied upon to produce a facile stock response. Instead, he chooses the random, trivial sights and sounds, meaningless and unmemorable in themselves, but all helping to produce a genuine recreation of experience. We are told of old women munching crusts at luncheon time, the rustle of pear tree boughs against a window, the noise of the worm-eaten planks of an old staircase springing back into place just as they had been forgotten, a rusty cannonball found among the rafters.

The predominant mood is one of enthusiasm and carefree adventure. There are, for instance, moments recalling a humorous boyish make-believe: "We had determined to sail that lovely day to visit the island of

Calypso, and had got all our arms and munitions of war aboard, besides being provisioned and carrying some fruit for fear of scurvy" (*AP*, 186). But Jefferies does not limit his description to unalloyed happiness, and there are the occasional childhood tragedies, as when, returning at last to his original subject, he relates the disaster of the burning of the gun :

But, however that may be, one day, as we came in unexpectedly from a voyage in the punt, something was discovered burning among the logs on the kitchen hearth; and, though a desperate rescue was attempted, nothing was left but the barrel of our precious gun and some crooked iron representing the remains of the lock. There are things that are never entirely forgiven, though the impression may become fainter as years go by. The sense of the cruel injustice of that act will never quite depart. (*AP*, 176)

Here for a moment the hint of a harsh outer world penetrates the childhood paradise.

But the cloud passes, and later, when his parents permit him to carry a single-barrel gun, we are given graphic accounts of the early morning shooting expeditions, with the trials and errors, the advice of friends, and all the excitement of the first kill. It is at this point that the matter of poaching first arises. The two boys embark upon it for a very definite and practical reason—not for any love of destruction, but in order to earn enough money to buy a boat with a keel. The ruse is suggested by Ikey the blacksmith, who agrees to purchase any rabbits they may catch at sixpence apiece. Ikey, however, is no fool; while putting the idea into their heads, he professes ignorance about the methods to be adopted. The boys decide to find out for themselves, and their experiments with wires—"turnpikes," as they call them—form the matter of an absorbing chapter. The interest is twofold. It is not merely in the initiative and intelligence displayed by the two boys as they learn from their mistakes and gradually master the requisite skills; equally important and interesting are the insights which they gain from this close, if illegal, contact with wild nature. Slowly they learn to recognize the rabbits' favourite runs, to adjust the wire to the exact height above the ground, to avoid all chances of leaving a human scent on the trap. The sport, as in more legal methods of hunting, consists of the battle of wits between boy and animal; it lies in the ingenuity and care required to outwit the opponent, in the adventure and the slight element of danger. Later they resort to more varied and ambitious methods. Shooting from trees is attempted, and catching fish by means of wire, the latter method being employed when trespassing on a strictly guarded local preserve. And so the childhood recollections develop smoothly and naturally into the second theme, that of hunting in general.

This part of the book may be seen, of course, in relation to *The Game-keeper at Home*, and in some respects the two books ought to be considered together. Both cover the same aspects of the countryside from opposing points of view, and each side is given its due in its respective book, though it is true that *The Amateur Poacher* seems not to have been conceived until after *The Gamekeeper at Home* was completed. None the less, it is not altogether fair to criticize Jefferies' attitude to Haylock in the earlier book without taking the latter into consideration. In the one, Haylock puts the case of the gamekeeper; in the other, the poacher has his revenge. Indeed, the poacher gets the best of the bargain, for by the time Jefferies comes to present his case, he has himself progressed in literary ability and experience. The very title carries a suggestion of carefree bravado. W. H. Hudson, who, as we have seen, did not share Jefferies' tolerance for the gamekeeper, is also less charitable towards the poacher. While distingish-ing between the casual and the professional offender, he remarks in *A Shepherd's Life* that "the village poacher as a rule is an idle, dissolute fellow";[22] Jefferies, if forced to a generalized moral judgment, might have agreed, but his treatment in the book under consideration is sympathetic in its sheer richness of presentation. He knew both sides intimately, as Hudson did not. Because the youth who roamed with Haylock around the Burderop estate was the same boy who had set up his own poaching wires and trespassed on the neighbouring preserves, he was in an ideal position to see the arguments of both sides. It was almost certainly wisdom rather than class interest that discouraged him from making an unequivocal com-parative judgment.

Be that as it may, we now follow him into the fascinating but disreput-able company of the poachers. Orion temporarily disappears from the narrative and is replaced by Dickon, the village inn-keeper of Sarsen. Sarsen is, it seems, a village of poachers, a devil-may-care community where the game laws are ignored and every man fends for himself. Jefferies records it all with a loving minuteness that turns the balance on the reporter's impartiality:

22. Hudson, p. 91.

The reason of these things is that Sarsen has no great landlord. There are fifty small proprietors, and not a single resident magistrate. Besides the small farmers, there are scores of cottage owners, every one of whom is perfectly independent. Nobody cares for anybody. It is a republic without even the semblance of a Government. It is liberty, equality, and swearing. As it is just within the limit of a borough, almost all the cottagers have votes, and are not to be trifled with. The proximity of horse-racing establishments adds to the general atmosphere of dissipation. Betting, card-playing, ferret-breeding and dog-fancying, poaching and politics, are the occupations of the populace. A little illicit badger-baiting is varied by a little vicar-baiting; the mass of the inhabitants are the reddest of Reds. Que voulez-vous? (*AP*, 247)

The scene is thus set for the next stage of Jefferies' education. "They are full of knowledge of a certain sort," he writes, "and you may learn anything, from the best way to hang a dog upwards" (*AP*, 248). It is in this company, along with a renegade keeper who thus presents the necessary contrast to Haylock, that Jefferies gets much of his unauthorized shooting. And the excuse, as in his boyish days, is sheer excitement and high spirits—"there was plenty of shooting to be got elsewhere, but the spice of naughtiness about this was alluring" (*AP*, 253).

It is the details of this kind of sport to which such people as H. S. Salt object. I have already alluded to his disgust at scenes which he finds intolerable to anyone possessing "the humane or artistic instinct," but the example which he cites of such a passage is noteworthy, and may be quoted. It concerns Little John, the stoutly built labourer who assists at a rabbit-hunt:

It was always a sight to see Little John's keen delight in "wristing" their necks. He affected utter unconsciousness of what he was doing, looked you in the face, and spoke about some indifferent subject. But all the while he was feeling the rabbit's muscles stretch before the terrible grasp of his hands, and an expression of complacent satisfaction flitted over his features as the neck gave with a sudden looseness, and in a moment what had been a living straining creature became limp. (*AP*, 327)

"This," comments Salt, "is scarcely a worthy theme for the artist," [23] but to an unbiased reader the passage is, for sheer artistry, one of the most brilliant in the book. The prose itself is wonderfully varied and modulated, but the main effect arises out of a clash of sympathies. There is the striking

23. Salt, p. 37.

contrast between Little John's expression and his action, between his "keen delight" and the death which he is causing. But there is also a clash of attitudes in the writer, an ambivalent reaction which is communicated to the responsive reader. We admire the rabbit as "a living straining creature," but on the other hand we cannot help admiring the labourer's skill and power. Furthermore, there is a comparison, even a connection, implied between "the rabbit's muscles" and "the terrible grasp of his hands," almost a tie of blood that fuses the contrasted attitudes into a single experience. Indeed, the phrase that suggests itself is D. H. Lawrence's "blood-intimacy," the link between man and nature which he describes so memorably in the first chapter of *The Rainbow*. Lawrence even uses a related image to drive home his point: "It was enough that they helped the cow in labour, or ferreted the rats from under the barn, or broke the back of a rabbit with a sharp knock of the hand." [24] The "life" of the man in its teeming strength and the death of the rabbit are, at this level, one.

The irony that man in nature must perforce lead to man against nature, that the more "natural" the life, the greater the need and lust for blood, is one which lies at the heart of Jefferies' country writings. There are many examples of this "blood-intimacy," but none more effective than the pheasant-shooting sequence, where the excitement and heat and delight in slaughter combine in a passage of unparalleled power:

Every now and then Dickon's shot when he fired high cut the twigs out of the ash by me. Then came the distant noise of the beaters' sticks, and the pheasants, at last thoroughly disturbed, flew out in twos and threes at a time. Now the firing grew fierce, and the roll of the volleys ceaseless. It was impossible to jam the cartridges fast enough in the breech.

A subtle flavour of sulphur filled the mouth, and the lips became dry. Sunshine and gleaming leaves and sky and grass seemed to all disappear in the fever of the moment. The gun burned the hands, all blackened by the powder; the metal got hotter and hotter; the sward was poached and trampled and dotted with cases; shots hissed through the air and pattered in showers on the opposite plantation; the eyes, bleared and bloodshot with the smoke, could scarce see to point the tube. Pheasants fell, and no one heeded; pheasants escaped, and none noticed it; pheasants were but just winged and ran wounded

24. D. H. Lawrence, *The Rainbow* [1915] (Modern Library ed.; New York: Random House, n.d.), p. 3.

into the distant hedges; pheasants were blown out of all living shape and could hardly be gathered up. Not a word spoken; a breathless haste to load and blaze; a storm of shot and smoke and slaughter. (*AP*, 256)

No commentary could do justice to such a passage. It is perfect in its complete and unflinching communication of the scene. The effect upon every sense is noted and conveyed—the smell and taste of the sulphur, the scorching heat of the gun-metal, the sight of the empty cases scattered heedlessly on the grass. The penultimate sentence, with its cumulative piling of balanced clauses, conjures a hypnotic effect in which all reactions beyond the enjoyment of the moment are excluded. He admits openly that the pleasure is in the destruction, a primitive urge to kill which is Man's inevitable inheritance from nature. We cannot but admire Jefferies' truth and honesty in presenting such a scene with complete fidelity, in refusing to ignore the "baser" motives. It demonstrates an insight into human behaviour, an acceptance of crude facts, which sets him far above the "sensibility" of his more squeamish critics.

Hardly less impressive are the character sketches which Jefferies gives of the local disreputables—of Oby the moucher, whom he finds one night drunk in a road and drags from the path of the mailcart, or Luke the rabbit contractor, who so successfully plays on everyone's interest that he can break almost any law with impunity. The analysis of rural motives and situations is masterly, and when a character is allowed to tell his story in his own words, we are given as genuine a "twang of the true country accent" as Leslie Stephen could desire. Oby's account of one of his numerous appearances before the bench is unforgettable: "Last time the chairman said to I, 'So you be here again, Oby; we hear a good deal about you.' I says, 'Yes, my lard, I be here agen, but people never don't hear nothing about *you*.' That shut the old duffer up." (*AP*, 263)

Best of all, perhaps, is the extended description of another of Oby's courtroom appearances, this time charged with trespassing in pursuit of game. Here the treatment and tone resemble the rural vignettes which Jefferies later collected into the volume *Hodge and His Masters*; indeed, there is a similar, though somewhat inferior, courtroom scene in the later book. Jefferies succeeds in catching on the one hand the sleepy, unhurried atmosphere of the country court with its humble attempts at ceremony, and on the other the vigorous life of the participants, ignorant and contemptuous of official procedure. Once again, Oby's tongue does not desert him when he is called upon to defend himself—he is never without an excuse:

"All as I did, I know I walked up the hedge to look for mushrooms. I saw one of them things"—meaning the wires on the table—"and I just stooped down, to see what it was, 'cos I didn't know. I never seed one afore; and I was just going to pick it up and look at it" (the magistrates glance at each other, and cannot suppress a smile at this profound innocence), "when this fellow jumped out and frightened me. I never seed no rabbit." (*AP*, 285)

He is eventually fined two pounds with costs, which Oby claims he cannot pay, and he is consequently led off to gaol. Just before the court rises, however, his wife returns and throws down the money out of a bag half-full of coin, and Oby is released. The final paragraph sets the whole incident in context:

Half an hour afterwards, two of the magistrates riding away from the town pass a small tavern on the outskirts. A travelling van is outside, and from the chimney on its roof thin smoke arises. There is a little group at the doorway, and among them stands the late prisoner. Oby holds a foaming tankard in one hand, and touches his battered hat, as the magistrates go by, with a gesture of sly humility. (*AP*, 287)

It is in phrases such as "sly humility" that Jefferies displays his keen but unostentatious feeling for words. And it is in paragraphs such as this that he succeeds in setting his sketches into a framework which gives them an increased subtlety. What would have been an amusing but inconsequential scene is raised into a significant and valid comment on rural life and behaviour.

The visionary theme, though less emphatic than the others, and occupying far less space in terms of lines on the page, is none the less an important element in the book, and, be it noted, is allowed the honour of the last word. Though the physical pleasures of shooting and hunting are stressed, the pleasures of the mind are not forgotten, and hold their place in the total scheme. The game-park is not merely the abode of fox and pheasant, but a sanctuary for the solitary dreamer:

It was a lovely spot, too, for dreaming on a summer's day, reclining on the turf, with the harebells swinging in the faint breeze. The extreme solitude was its charm: no lanes or tracks other than those purely pastoral came near. There were woods on either hand; in the fir plantations the jays chattered unceasingly. The broad landscape stretched out to the illimitable distance, till the power of the eye failed and could trace it no further. But if the gaze was lifted it looked into blue space—the azure heaven not only overhead, but, as it seemed, all around. (*AP*, 250-1)

Here the natural world is viewed not with the microscopic detail which is the general approach of these books; rather, it is seen through—Jefferies is going beyond Nature, searching for a higher reality, and anticipating the tone of much of his later work.

"As for myself," he writes, "a mere dreamy lad, I could go into the woods and wander as I liked, which was sufficient" (*AP*, 251). This may be considered an odd statement coming, as it does, within a few pages of the pheasant-shooting episode, but it is perhaps appropriate that the book which displays the most dramatic examples in Jefferies of "blood-intimacy" should also contain strong hints of a higher, spiritual yearning. In the final paragraphs of the book, immediately following the discussion of the related delights of shooting and natural observation, this element springs forth with a new eloquence which affords an effective and memorable climax:

Let us be always out of doors among trees and grass, and rain and wind and sun. There the breeze comes and strikes the cheek and sets it aglow: the gale increases and the trees creak and roar, but it is only a ruder music. A calm follows, the sun shines in the sky, and it is the time to sit under an oak, leaning against the bark, while the birds sing and the air is soft and sweet. By night the stars shine, and there is no fathoming the dark spaces between those brilliant points, nor the thoughts that come as it were between the fixed stars and landmarks of the mind.

Or it is the morning on the hills, when hope is as wide as the world; or it is the evening on the shore. A red sun sinks, and the foam-tipped waves are crested with crimson; the booming surge breaks, and the spray flies afar, sprinkling the face watching under the pale cliffs. Let us get out of these indoor narrow modern ways, whose twelve hours somehow have become shortened, into the sunlight and the pure wind. A something that the ancients called divine can be found and felt there still. (*AP*, 351-2)

There is a symphonic nobility about these last lines, though they are less a summing-up of the book's thematic structure than the herald of new potentiality and a new beginning. The book which opened with recollections of the past closes with a plea for the future and the promise of greater achievement. In effect, Jefferies is bidding farewell to the frenzied life of rural pleasures, though this is not renounced, but rather transcended. Instead, he passes into a new sphere and a new realm of experience. Sight must take second place to vision, and in his subsequent work he will endeavour to speculate more broadly about this "something that the ancients called divine."

IV. *The Story of My Heart*

The Story of My Heart is a spiritual confession, a personal philosophy and a record of religious belief all in one. It is doubtless an unexpected book to come from the pen of the young man who, seventeen years earlier, had begun his literary career as a provincial reporter, though Jefferies tells us that his first impressive but disturbing preternatural experiences, to which the book bears impassioned witness, occurred at precisely that time. It is best to state at the outset that *The Story of My Heart* is a paradox—in its inception, in its argument, in its effect. It reveals Jefferies at his most profound and at his most naïve; it reflects both a practical radicalism and a dreamy idealism; at one moment he seems to believe nothing, at another everything. There is one quality, however, that is constant throughout, that no one, sympathetic or hostile, would deny him: he is always passionately sincere.

As a child Jefferies inherited a mild, unchallenged Anglicanism. Edward Thomas notes that his father was an irregular church-goer, and it is evident that the religious atmosphere around Coate Farmhouse was by no means strong. None the less, the boy seems to have gone through periods of devout enthusiasm, and a sermon written in his youth is still extant. By the time he came to write *The Story of My Heart*, however, he had become, like so many of his contemporaries, an honest doubter. His spiritual progress was neither wholly original nor wholly conventional, but an interesting individual version of a common Victorian pattern. Though Jefferies disliked (and fought hard against accepting) the Darwinian hypothesis, the scientific arguments that led towards it helped to undermine his faith in an orthodox god and a traditional system of belief. And like so many other honest doubters, Jefferies found himself obliged to work out for himself an acceptable and credible world view. It is as if he were anticipating Hardy's statement: "Let every man make a philosophy for himself out of his own experience." [1] The outcome was *The Story of My Heart*—the philosophy of a non-philosopher, fragmentary and imperfect, but none the less interesting for that. Jefferies was a man who wanted to believe but could not, who found the empirical approach of science as unsatisfactory as the "high Priori Road" of revealed religion, who considered atheism as illogical as conventional Christianity but was unable to find peace in a vaguely sceptical agnosticism. But although the impulse of the book stems from his own experience, Jefferies is nothing if not eclectic, and he is anxious to find in earlier thinkers and writers evidence to suggest that his own conclusions had more than a merely personal validity. His method is to sift the findings of other systems with which he is acquainted and, after discarding what he finds unacceptable, to forge the rest into a unity. The result is necessarily a patchwork in which elements from such diverse sources as Platonic philosophy and Lamarckian biology are invoked to support the records of Jefferies' own intuitive experience. And this is communicated in a prose which takes on a heightened eloquence from the sublime possibilities of the subject-matter.

To summarize the theme of *The Story of My Heart* in a few sentences is almost impossible; Jefferies himself was asked to perform the task by his publisher, C. J. Longman, and observed that "to describe it properly would need another book." [2] It begins by describing the deep effect, even from early youth, that natural phenomena such as sea, sun, sky, and downland had upon his innermost feelings, and Jefferies takes great pains to convey to his readers something of the nature and depth of his emotion and the intellectual problems which it provoked. For he was not content merely with a feeling of exaltation and renewed joy. The passage of the seasons confronted him with the problems of birth and rebirth, and the prehistoric tumuli on the hills opened his mind to the mysteries of death and possible immortality. After much hard thought, he fails to find anything in nature which is not completely indifferent to Man's existence, and is forced to

1. F. E. Hardy, *The Life of Thomas Hardy* (London: Macmillan, 1962), p. 310.

2. Letter to C. J. Longman dated November 3, 1883, and reproduced in the Preface to the Second Edition. Quoted from the Uniform edition of *The Story of My Heart* (London: Eyre & Spottiswoode, 1949), p. xx.

RICHARD JEFFERIES: A CRITICAL STUDY

reject the concept of a benevolent god. The idea of God is insufficient; Jefferies yearns for "a Fourth Idea" over and above the concepts of soul, immortality, and deity, which he considered to be the only discoveries "of that which concerns the inner consciousness since before written history began" (*SH*, 46). Eventually he appeals towards "the unutterable existence infinitely higher than deity" (*SH*, 21). This "Superdeo" (*SH*, 161) is in fact the "Fourth Idea" to which Jefferies lays claim: "The very idea that there is another idea is something gained" (*SH*, 48). The final chapters are more negative, and come as an anticlimax. He laments the lack of progress towards the perfection of which he believes Man to be capable, and ends on a plea which is repeatedly stressed for the increased exercise and education of the soul.

It can readily be understood why *The Story of My Heart* is the most controversial of Jefferies' books. To some critics it is the peak of his achievement; to others it is a painful, embarrassing production which is best ignored. For myself, without wishing to associate fully with either extreme, I must insist that, whatever its ultimate value to literature or thought, it is the central document in Jefferies' work, and must be considered in detail. There can be no doubt that Jefferies himself placed great importance upon it; he states categorically that it contains "my most serious convictions" (*SH*, 125). We may well feel that its broad, unqualified generalizations and its seemingly wilful eccentricity are very real barriers to understanding and acceptance, yet around it almost all Jefferies' books, early or late, seem to revolve. It is generally acknowledged, of course, that the later essays such as "Nature in the Louvre" and "Nature and Eternity" are closely connected with *The Story of My Heart*; similarly its influence can be found throughout *The Dewy Morn*. I have drawn attention in the previous chapter to the anticipations of *The Story of My Heart* in *The Amateur Poacher*, and the fifth chapter will discuss the even more dramatic anticipations in *Wood Magic* and *Bevis*. But even in the first three novels, usually dismissed as worthless, we can find passages which prove Jefferies' statement that he had been planning the book years before putting pen to paper. In *The Scarlet Shawl* the hero "really thought that it was his mission to instruct mankind. All the books of religion were wearing out; the Vedas, the Koran etc. etc. were out of date. He began to seriously contemplate writing a modern Koran." (*SS*, 177) Edward

Thomas notes here "a faint foretaste of 'The Story of My Heart'," [3] but there is surely more than this in *Restless Human Hearts*. For one instance among many, we may quote the following description of a walk taken by the heroine, Heloise: "She climbed up the steep-sided downs, and, choosing a hollow sheltered from the wind, lay down upon the soft thymy turf, while the bees flew overhead and the lark sang high above her, and dreamt day-dreams, not of heaven, but of something—she knew not what; of a state of existence all and every hour of which should be light and joy and life" (*RHH*, I, 33). The connection with *The Story of My Heart* is obvious. It is both misleading and unscholarly to regard the latter as an imaginative freak. As Peter Coveney has written: "it is the frame into which Jefferies' other works, the child-books, the novels, and the essays, fit." [4]

The Story of My Heart took shape as a result of various preternatural experiences which Jefferies had known from his youth, and any discussion must begin with a consideration of this mystical element. The closing pages of the book provide a convenient introductory account:

I was not more than eighteen when an inner and esoteric meaning began to come to me from all the visible universe, and indefinable aspirations filled me. I found them in the grass fields, under the trees, on the hill-tops, at sunrise, and in the night. There was a deeper meaning everywhere. . . .

I was sensitive to all things, to the earth under, and the star-hollow round about; to the least blade of grass, to the largest oak. They seemed like exterior nerves and veins for the conveyance of feeling to me. Sometimes a very ecstasy of exquisite enjoyment of the entire visible universe filled me. I was aware that in reality the feeling and the thought were in me, and not in the earth or sun; yet I was more conscious of it when in company with these. (*SH*, 125)

This is Jefferies' most sober and straightforward account, and with the exception of the interesting qualification in the last sentence (to which I shall return), it differs in no important respect from the experience of other sensitive observers. This is the Animism which W. H. Hudson discusses in *Far Away and Long Ago*, though the word has various meanings, and it must be understood that the term is used here according to Hudson's own definition as the "sense of the supernatural in natural things." [5] It is

3. Edward Thomas, *Richard Jefferies: His Life and Work* (1909), p. 93.
4. Peter Coveney, *Poor Monkey: The Child in Literature* (1957), p. 186.
5. W. H. Hudson, *Far Away and Long Ago* [1918] (London: Dent, 1923), p. 237.

certain that Jefferies retained this Animism, which Hudson believed generally faded as one grew older, with no apparent diminution throughout his life. "Everything around is supernatural," he wrote; "everything so full of unexplained meaning" (*SH*, 47). There are countless references throughout *The Story of My Heart* and the kindred essays which support this statement.

But there are other passages in which Jefferies claims a more significant experience, and in these, I am convinced, he goes far beyond Animism. The following professes to describe an early occasion, but its expression reveals an advance in profundity:

I looked at the hills, at the dewy grass, and then up through the elm branches to the sky. In a moment all that was behind me, the house, the people, the sounds, seemed to disappear, and to leave me alone. Involuntarily I drew a long breath, then I breathed slowly. My thought, or inner consciousness, went up through the illumined sky, and I was lost in the moment of exaltation. This only lasted a very short time, perhaps only part of a second, and while it lasted there was no formulated wish. I was absorbed; I drank the beauty of the morning; I was exalted. (*SH*, 58–9)

Here Jefferies is eloquent but at the same time simple and, what is more, natural. There is besides a feeling of exultant joy, and his prose is positive and assured. Indeed, so confident and certain is this passage that we can understand the temptation of some commentators to liken his experience to those of the orthodox and accepted mystics. But it is important that we acknowledge a vital difference: Jefferies gives no indication that it is in any sense a religious experience. There is no reference to a god or an absolute. The phrase "I was absorbed" should be noted; there is no suggestion of absorption into a supreme deity. It is true that we are told in another context that he was "absorbed into the being and existence of the universe" (*SH*, 23), but this too implies no personal god. It is an "at-one-ment," but the suggestion is rather that outward phenomena are at one with Jefferies than that Jefferies is at one with anything outside himself. It is here that his remark noted earlier is important—"I was aware that in reality the feeling and the thought were in me, and not in the earth or sun." Jefferies, if we like to put it that way, is his own absolute.

But his most significant statement, ironically enough, is not an account of his transports on Liddington Hill or in Badbury Coombe, but a supreme moment on London Bridge. He begins with an eloquent and detailed description of the view from the bridge, and continues:

Burning on, the great sun stood in the sky, heating the parapet, glowing steadfastly upon me as when I rested in the narrow valley grooved out in prehistoric times. Burning on steadfast, and ever present as my thought. Lighting the broad river, the broad walls; lighting the least speck of dust; lighting the great heaven; gleaming on my finger-nail. The fixed point of day—the sun. I was intensely conscious of it; I felt it; I felt the presence of the immense powers of the universe; I felt out into the depths of the ether. So intensely conscious of the sun, the sky, the limitless space, I felt in the midst of eternity then, in the midst of the supernatural, among the immortal, and the greatness of the material realised the spirit. By these I saw my soul; by these I knew the supernatural to be more intensely real than the sun. I touched the supernatural, the immortal, there that moment. (*SH*, 64)

This account, though it has not received much attention from critics, is in fact the climax of Jefferies' mystical experience; yet even in this passage it is doubtful whether there is any truly religious ingredient. It is significant that what Jefferies sees is not a vision of God but "my soul." It seems as if the feeling and the thought are still within him, that there is no contact with an exterior Reality. True, he says "I touched the supernatural," and this is perhaps the most tantalizing phrase in the whole book, but the verb is obviously a metaphor, and we cannot assume that it implies anything more than an extreme feeling of what Wordsworth called "possible sublimity," a feeling that the distinction between the natural and the supernatural is meaningless, a confidence that "there is so much beyond all that has ever yet been imagined" (*SH*, 47). Jefferies certainly acknowledged a Beyond; he even accepted an all-embracing Absolute which is so much beyond the world as to be completely independent of it. He satisfies himself (not without a struggle) that such a Force exists, but never in fact gains contact with it. His experience persuades him, however, that such contact is possible.

The scholars of mysticism are for the most part agreed that, while experiencing with a peculiar intensity a lower stage of the Mystic Way (to use the orthodox terminology), Jefferies failed to attain a complete mystical experience. In the words of Evelyn Underhill, "Jefferies stood, as so many mystically minded men have done, upon the verge of such a transcendental life. The 'heavenly door,' as Rolle calls it, was ajar but not pushed wide. He peeped through it to the greater world beyond; but, unable to escape from the bonds of his selfhood, he did not pass through to live upon the independent spiritual plane." [6] With this analysis one feels bound to agree. Jefferies prayed in the first chapter that he might "touch to the unutterable existence infinitely higher than deity," but there is no definite evidence that the prayer was answered. At best he remains, in his own words, "on the margin of life illimitable" (SH, 47); the final experience is lacking.

It has often been maintained that Jefferies was a pantheist, but, if we accept the strict definition of that term as one who believes that God is present in all and all in God, this can be rebutted easily enough by direct quotation. Discussing the indifference of Nature and the almost tragic uniqueness of Man, he concludes: "There being nothing human in nature or the universe, and all things being ultra-human and without design, shape, or purpose, I conclude that no deity has anything to do with nature. There is no god in nature, nor in any matter anywhere, either in the clods on the earth or in the composition of the stars." (SH, 55) This passage answers such objections once and for all, but at the same time raises another, and perhaps greater, problem. To be fair to the critics, it must be remembered that the natural world occupies as central a position in The Story of My Heart as in the rest of Jefferies' work. It is therefore reasonable to ask why this is so if "there is no god in nature." Why, if the earth and the stars are indifferent and without design, did Jefferies throw himself on to the earth at Liddington, or lie in meditation on summer evenings looking up at the stars from the garden of Coate Farmhouse? Not, surely, just to make the discovery that they contained no god. Part of the answer is that Jefferies is fully aware that his "soul-life" comes from within. As R. C. Zaehner writes in his Mysticism, Sacred and Profane: "it is not the physical object with which he communes, but its 'inner meaning', the idea or essence that man projects into it, or which he draws out of it." [7] The world of nature was at first a necessity because it encouraged his feelings of immortality and aspiration. At this time he needed to get away from the humdrum routines of ordinary existence before his soul-life could manifest itself. Gradually, however, as the principles behind his thought develop and clarify, so the need for the positive stimulus of nature

6. Evelyn Underhill, Mysticism [1911] (London: Methuen, 1952), p. 193.

7. R. C. Zaehner, Mysticism, Sacred and Profane (Oxford: Clarendon Press, 1957), p. 47. Zaehner's discussion of Jefferies has considerably influenced my argument in this and the succeeding paragraph.

grows less. Soon not only nature but a piece of beautiful sculpture can give the same feeling. When he gets to London, he finds the city no less congenial to the thought, and his supreme experience is felt on London Bridge. In the end, he does not need to seek the prayer—instead the prayer seeks him: "The same prayer comes to me at this very hour. It is now less solely associated with the sun and sea, hills, woods, or beauteous human shape. It is always within." (*SH*, 33) In the last moving notebooks, when Jefferies is bedridden and dying, it is the creative soul of man which is uppermost in his mind, and Nature takes a backward place. The following notes, extracted from the entries for the beginning of May 1887, tell their own story: "No good except from man. I have been through nature, I am weary of nature, nothing there. . . . I hate nature. I turn my back on it. Works of man greater than nature. . . . Finding no mind in nature leads to the dread and mistake lest no mind elsewhere. Analyse away the soul: the soul returns." (*N*, 258–9) It is evident from these jottings that Nature is not a *sine qua non* in his scheme.

Jefferies is quite clear about the natural world. It is controlled, he says, by "a force without a mind," by "something more subtle than electricity," something which "is certainly not the higher than deity of whom I have written" (*SH*, 55). Nature, then, is animated, but not by a soul, and it is *because* nature is soul-less that the individual soul can expand and contain it. It is a challenge to which the soul is equal—more than equal; without it, the soul would be unable to realize its potentialities. Thus in Jefferies the material and the spiritual are not merely of equal importance, but mutually dependent. As he observed concerning the moment on London Bridge, "the greatness of the material realised the spirit." The material is the means by which the spiritual may be attained, or, in Jefferies' own words from "The Life of the Soul," "we can only get at the immaterial through the material" (*OHC*, 192). Indeed, in "Hours of Spring" he goes so far as to say that "the chief use of matter is to demonstrate to us the existence of the soul" (*FH*, 25). It is this connection which explains Jefferies' separation from the more orthodox ways of mysticism. The self depends on the material to realize its possibilities, and it is this self which creates the prayer. Hence, as Miss Underhill noted, Jefferies was "unable to escape from the bonds of his selfhood," because this selfhood was an essential part of his scheme.

But underlying the contrasts and connections between the spiritual and the material is a central paradox in which the abstract and the concrete seem to be distinguished and associated at the same time. The point is important because the prose style, in its vivid directness, is here in admirable harmony with the ideas presented. As we shall see when we come to consider the more specifically literary qualities of *The Story of My Heart*, the natural images used to convey the argument are notably tangible objects; indeed, it is likely that we shall first notice Jefferies' preoccupation with the sense of touch as an effective literary device. The following passage is a useful and important example:

Then, returning, I prayed by the sweet thyme, whose little flowers I *touched* with my hand; by the slender grass; by the crumble of dry chalky earth I took up and let fall through my fingers. *Touching* the crumble of earth, the blade of grass, the thyme flower, breathing the earth-encircling air, thinking of the sea and the sky, holding out my hand for the sunbeams to *touch* it, prone on the sward in token of deep reverence, thus I prayed that I might *touch* to the unutterable existence infinitely higher than deity. (*SH*, 21 [my italics])

Only with the last, unexpected use of the word do we become aware of the earlier usages. There are many other examples of Jefferies' concern with the sense of touch. It is a characteristic carried over to Felise in *The Dewy Morn* ("She liked to touch all things" [*DM*, I, 11]), who makes a similar pilgrimage to the hills. It is true too of the well-known passage from the essay "On the Downs": "Stoop and touch the earth, and receive its influence; touch the flower, and feel its life" (*HV*, 273). Indeed, Jefferies' whole conception of matter and spirit can be seen in its clearest form in such passages. Perhaps the best comment comes from "The Old House at Coate": "It is very curious to touch anything; it is as if the soul thereby ascertained the existence of matter" (*OHC*, 41). The soul, we notice, not the body. Again, in *The Story of My Heart* we get the statement: "Matter is beyond understanding, mysterious, impenetrable; I touch it easily, comprehend it, no" (*SH*, 42); and a little later he complains that "immortality is not tangible" (*SH*, 49). A notebook entry carries on the same idea: "Transcendental excitement of the soul (by prayer for instance) no good; it should repose in touch" (*N*, 284). Jefferies is suspicious of the purely abstract—even of his own more transcendental ideas. He wants these feelings (the very word is significant) to be verified by the tactile sense before he can be sure of their existence. When this is not possible, he demands intuitive perceptions so strong that they really seem tangible. Thus, "I grasp death firmly in conception as I can grasp this bleached bone" (*SH*, 49). Here the simile has all the accuracy and rightness that we expect from the highest poetry. By touching the bone which was once living, Jefferies argues, one can in fact touch death.

It is with this kind of perception, which seems to lie half-way between philosophic reasoning and poetic logic, that he finally satisfies himself on the vexed question of immortality. It is not true to say, as has sometimes been stated, that Jefferies' views on this subject were naïvely confident. In fact, there are passages in the book which prove that he laboured under no delusions. The following paragraph is typical:

That there is no knowing, in the sense of written reasons, whether the soul lives on or not, I am fully aware. I do not hope or fear. At least while I am living I have enjoyed the idea of immortality, and the idea of my own soul. If then, after death, I am resolved without exception into earth, air, and water, and the spirit goes out like a flame, still I shall have had the glory of that thought. (*SH*, 39)

The clue to his general feelings on the matter may be gleaned from another passage in "The Old House at Coate": "If, while thinking of other things, I chanced to see a sunbeam on the wall: if I see it now, it instantly recalls the same feeling. Put your hand on it—you touch the sun; and know that you are as much in the ether, in space, as the sun itself" (*OHC*, 38). Jefferies touched everything he could in order to ascertain the existence of reality. But when, by touching the sunbeam on the wall, he felt not only the wall but the warmth from the sunbeam, this gave him the confidence he needed that the invisible can be *felt* as well as the tangible, and therefore exists. The climax comes, as we noted earlier, when on London Bridge in a supreme moment he can say: "I touched the supernatural, the immortal, there that moment."

From the philosophical viewpoint, *The Story of My Heart* is, as I have suggested, a patchwork. Here, in order to clarify our understanding of the book, it is only necessary to notice two of the more important influences on Jefferies' thinking. At the same time it is necessary to insist that, however odd Jefferies' combination of disparate traditions may seem, the individual ideas are mainly derived from respectable sources and cannot be ignored.

In "Nature and Books" Jefferies declares that "it took me a long time to read Plato, and I have had to unlearn much of him" (*FH*, 54), and although one must acknowledge the qualification, there can be no doubt that Plato was a major influence on his earlier thought. Philosophic (rather than religious) arguments for the immortality of the soul, the relation between Time and Eternity, the existence of a transcendent reality beyond the world of experience—all these exert an influence upon *The Story of My Heart* which is none the less significant for being, in certain cases, severely qualified by Jefferies' intuitive individualism. Even the notorious statement about "the unutterable existence infinitely higher than deity" (*SH*, 21) is readily explicable in Platonic terms. The difficulty here is rather verbal than intellectual. "Deity" for Jefferies means a beneficent, anthropomorphic being, the existence of which he rejects as untenable in fact and unworthy in conception; his "unutterable existence" resembles the Platonic "Form of Good" which is, in A. E. Taylor's words, "the transcendent source of all the reality and intelligibility of everything other than itself" and is therefore "distinct from and transcendent of the whole system of its effects or manifestations."[8] It is, to quote Paul Friedländer, "beyond being,"[9] and this phrase excellently sums up Jefferies' belief as well as Plato's. But perhaps the best gloss on the whole phrase, especially on the word "unutterable," is the remark from Plato's *Phaedrus* (274c): "But of the heaven which is above the heavens, what earthly poet ever did or ever will sing worthily?"

The Platonic conception of the universe provides Jefferies with a world of appearance and a transcendental, independent world of reality beyond. But this is not in itself sufficient, and *The Story of My Heart* was originally written because of a need for a more soundly based faith. Plato's explanations of the existence of Evil were such as Jefferies could not accept—this was part of what he had to "unlearn." None the less, he finds an excuse for optimism in his acceptance of a life-source which evidently derives from the Lamarckian theories of evolution. (The anti-Darwinian paragraphs which mar *The Story of My Heart* for modern readers are partly explained by Jefferies' evident disposition to find the rival theory more congenial.) The concept of a life-force enables him to believe

8. A. E. Taylor, *Plato, the Man and his Work* [1926] (New York: Meridian Books, 1956), p. 289.
9. Paul Friedländer, *Plato, I; An Introduction*, trans. Hans Meyerhoff (New York: Pantheon, 1958), p. 363.

that Man will indeed achieve the high destiny of which he believes him capable. It is a force common to all nature which in Man takes the form of intellect. In a notebook for 1887 he talks of "our intelligence something in us propelling—prompting—driving us on as plants are driven with adaptations" (*N*, 249). It is the innate impulse which makes development and progress possible. It is the driving-force behind all life, comparable with Nietzsche's life-will and Bergson's *élan vital*, which Jefferies insists is a perfectly natural and not a mysterious principle. "Life-force," he wrote, "is not a secret, inviolable and sacred thing: it is as ordinary and common as water; and water is sacred, holy, and beautiful—a marvel and a miracle" (*OHC*, 55). And this power which directs development is one which Man can turn to his own advantage, the means by which he will be able to penetrate into the unknown.

As Jefferies realized, the fact of Man's intellectual and spiritual powers cuts him off dramatically from the rest of the animal kingdom. As T. H. Huxley had argued, Man has developed, perhaps evolved, the power to influence the course of evolution, including his own, and may therefore be said to have freed himself from absolute dependence upon the process out of which he originated. In other words, evolution in Man can become creative, and for Jefferies this was a source of hope.

It would be a mistake, however, to treat *The Story of My Heart* merely as a text for exegesis and interpretation. Equally important to our study are the literary and stylistic features of the book. After all, Jefferies, though an amateur philosopher, is primarily a writer; his prose is the prose of a professional writer and must be judged as such. We have already seen how important are the literary methods by which he communicates the truth of the agricultural scene, and the same is true here of the presentation of his theories and ideas.

The first point that needs to be emphasized is the extreme care with which Jefferies expressed his thoughts. It has sometimes been suggested that *The Story of My Heart* was written in a rush of creative inspiration, that it is a haphazard outpouring of random thoughts and ideas, but Jefferies himself continually argues that the book was the result of long and continued meditation. The stylistic expression was similarly a matter that had been pondered long and thoughtfully. Jefferies wrote of the extreme difficulty that he had encountered, and how he made numerous unsuccessful attempts to express his ideas on paper. In a letter to C. J. Longman, the eventual publisher, he wrote: "I have just finished writing a book about which I have been meditating seventeen years. . . . After so much thinking it only makes one small volume—there are no words wasted in it."[10] In the book itself there are several references to its composition, of which the most informative occurs in the last chapter:

I began to make efforts to express these thoughts in writing, but could not succeed to my liking. Time went on, and harder experiences, and the pressure of labour came, but in no degree abated the fire of first thought. Again and again I made resolutions that I would write it, in some way or other, and as often failed. I could express any other idea with ease, but not this. (*SH*, 125)

The evidence of the early drafts and notebooks bears out this statement. But the choice of style is as important as the choice of individual words, for *The Story of My Heart* explicitly appeals to the emotions even more than to the intellect. Jefferies' arguments depend first and last upon feeling, and the right feeling can only be stimulated in the reader by the right style.

His difficulties were enormous. Like all believers in a transcendent reality, he is forced to describe one world in imagery gathered from another, and must similarly describe spiritual states and feelings in physical terms. This is particularly important at the opening of the book, where it is vital to win the imaginative sympathy of the reader. I must quote freely from the early paragraphs in order to demonstrate the full force of Jefferies' rhythmical prose:

In the glow of youth there were times every now and then when I felt the necessity of a strong inspiration of soul-thought. My heart was dusty, parched for want of the rain of deep feeling; my mind arid and dry, for there is a dust which settles on the heart as well as that which falls on a ledge. It is injurious to the mind as well as to the body to be always in one place and always surrounded by the same circumstances. A species of thick clothing slowly grows about the mind, the pores are choked, little habits become a part of existence, and by degrees the mind is inclosed in a husk. When this began to form I felt eager to escape from it, to throw it off like heavy clothing, to drink deeply once more at the fresh fountains of life. An inspiration—a long deep breath of the pure air of thought—could alone give health to the heart.

There was a hill to which I used to resort at such periods. The labour of

10. Letter to C. J. Longman dated June 22, 1883, and reproduced in the Preface to the Second Edition. Quoted from the Uniform edition of *The Story of My Heart* (London: Eyre & Spottiswoode, 1949), p. xviii–xix.

walking three miles to it, all the while gradually ascending, seemed to clear my blood of the heaviness accumulated at home. On a warm summer day the slow continued rise required continual effort, which carried away the sense of oppression. The familiar everyday scene was soon out of sight; I came to other trees, meadows, and fields; I began to breathe a new air and to have a fresher aspiration. (*SH*, 19)

This extract yields a number of instances of metaphor being used to connect the spiritual and physical worlds. We may notice "the dust which settles on the heart," "the rain of deep feeling," "to drink deeply at the fresh fountains of life," "the pure air of thought." Later in the same chapter, we get numerous other examples, including "a wider horizon of feeling," "the lips of my soul," "the unattainable flower of the sky."

What we notice about these images is, of course, that they are all drawn from nature. This is both aesthetically and intellectually appropriate. Jefferies is describing his pilgrimage to the Downs; his writing is imaginatively effective because he fuses the physical and mental landscapes into one. But we should also notice that by describing his inner thoughts in terms of the outer reality he can gain two effects at the same time—three in fact, for the identification of the two worlds is an effect in itself. The very nature of his ideas makes this identification a positive requirement rather than a mere convenience. Jefferies is eager to emphasize that, despite his insistence on a "Beyond," there is really nothing remote or unnatural about his beliefs. We have already seen him describing his life-force as "ordinary and common as water" (which is itself another of these images), and in *The Story of My Heart* he claims that "things that have been miscalled supernatural appear to me simple, more natural than nature, than earth, than sea, or sun" (*SH*, 42). There can hardly be a more satisfactory way of demonstrating such a feeling than by describing his experiences in terms of natural images. This explains the appearance and the effectiveness of such sentences as the following: "As the brook ran winding through the meadow, so one thought ran winding through my days" (*SH*, 30); or the passage in which men and women are described as "beaten like seaweed against the solid walls of fact" (*SH*, 70–1). Moreover, as I have already shown, the tangible quality of the imagery is not merely a literary device but an essential element in the intellectual scheme.

As a specimen of prose style, *The Story of My Heart* differs in many respects from Jefferies' other work. This is understandable enough, for the subject-matter (though related) is itself different; but the prose remains a curious combination of the eloquently stylistic and the colloquially direct. The rhythms and periods are sometimes perfect, sometimes careless; the grammatical syntax is sometimes felicitous, sometimes clumsy. Yet there is no exact correlation between the parts which are particularly pleasing and those which are technically admirable. Critics tend to divide themselves into those who detect a dangerously florid style, and those who deny that Jefferies had a style at all. The truth lies, as usual, somewhere between these two extremes, but the latter group seem nearer the mark if the word "style" carries any sense of extrinsic decoration. Jefferies is not a stylist in the sense that, say, Gibbon or Pater may qualify for that title. At his best, the fusion between thought and expression is so successful that we fail to recognize that any "style" is involved. Thus we tend to notice his use of words only when he is working towards a particular conscious effect, or when by some mischance he *fails* to balance what he says with how he says it. Thus, it is the kind of writing that does not reveal its quality in short extracts, but gains impressiveness on acquaintance. As Mrs. Leavis has expressed it, "anyone in Bloomsbury can make a phrase, but Jefferies' effects are cumulative."[11]

Henry Miller has an interesting passage on his style, which is helpful even if we do not accept his general view of Jefferies as the grand iconoclast. Miller has been pointing out a resemblance to D. H. Lawrence:

There is not only a similarity of thought but of accent and rhythm. But then we find this same idiosyncrasy of speech, in English at any rate, whenever we come upon an original thinker. The iconoclast always exhorts us in short, staccato sentences. It is as if he were transmitting from a distant, higher station. It is an utterly different rhythm from that of the prophets, who are filled with woe and lamentation, with objurgation and malediction.[12]

This description is in the main sound. Jefferies' style is refreshingly free from the prophetic strain. The short sentences, perhaps the result of a non-literary directness, are none the less effective in conveying the ideas in as lucid a manner as possible. Indeed, it is by virtue of this unity of tone, rather than unity of style or structural orthodoxy, that the book makes any claim to artistic form.

11. Q. D. Leavis, "Lives and Works of Richard Jefferies," *Scrutiny*, VI (March 1938), 444.
12. Henry Miller, *The Books in My Life* (1952), p. 185.

But what, we may ask ourselves finally, is the all-round effect of *The Story of My Heart*? It will be as well, perhaps, to begin with the reservations. It would be foolish to deny that some of Jefferies' comments are naïve, others hopelessly impractical. This would not matter so much did not Jefferies lay so great an emphasis on the constructive nature of his proposals, and I refer particularly to his socio-political comments. At times his contempt for the small progress made by Man towards the ideal leads him to depreciate genuine achievement merely because other subjects, which Jefferies considers more important, have been neglected. He can in this cause employ the kind of Philistine argument which is the despair of any defender of the humanities. Thus he writes:

For instance, to go back as far as possible, the study and labour expended on Egyptian inscriptions and papyri, which contain nothing but doubtful, because laudatory history, invocations to idols, and similar matters: all these labours are in vain. Take a broom and sweep the papyri away into the dust. The Assyrian terra-cotta tablets, some recording fables, and some even sadder—contracts between men whose bodies were dust twenty centuries since—take a hammer and demolish them. Set a battery to beat down the pyramids, and a mind-battery to destroy the deadening influence of tradition. (*SH*, 89)

That Jefferies is in truth no Philistine may be shown by the sentence which immediately follows this passage: "The Greek statue lives to this day, and has the highest use of all, the use of true beauty." None the less, the contempt for history and research comes incongruously from the mouth of one whose early writings preserve so much of the tradition and history of his native county. One may sympathize with Jefferies' insistence that Man should look towards the future rather than the past, but there is no reason why this should be at the expense of the past. Jefferies has forgotten that the past just as much as the future has its fixed position in the "Eternal Now."

Again, there are the few curious sentences where this strange destructive instinct is applied to the animal world. There is the passage that so disturbed W. H. Hudson: "Give me an iron mace that I may crush the savage beast and hammer him down. A spear to thrust through with, so that I may feel the long blade enter and the push of the shaft." (*SH*, 82) It would not be difficult to make some very harsh psychological deductions from these passages; they might be interpreted as evidence of acute emotional frustration, or on the literary level as anticipations of the more unpleasant excesses of the Decadents. Such criticisms would be inappropriate because the passages in question account for so tiny a percentage of the whole output. It is true that they are lapses on Jefferies' part, though they are less disturbing when read in the context of his other writings, when they can be recognized as later (and generally unsuccessful) examples of the "blood-intimacy" already discussed with reference to *The Amateur Poacher*. Even if this is accepted only as a reason, not as an excuse, it must be granted that the passages are noteworthy because they stand out as exceptional, and generally unnecessary, elements in the general tenor of the work.

With this, however, the worst has been said, and it remains to characterize the effect which a reading of *The Story of My Heart* leaves upon a sympathetic reader. It is a sign of the vitality rather than the inconsistency of the book that readers have reacted to it in so many varying ways, and we may come to a better understanding of this vitality if we consider the various elements which previous commentators have stressed. The difference in emphasis is extreme, even with fundamental reactions. Thus Professor George Saintsbury maintained that "his philosophic background was not like Wordsworth's, clear and cheerful, but wholly vague and partly gloomy."[13] The inadequate generalization about Wordsworth may well put us on our guard against what I believe to be a similarly inadequate summing-up of Jefferies, but none the less we may be surprised and puzzled if we turn to an article by Mrs. D. E. Marshall, who claims that Jefferies "had a joy greatly in excess of the average person," and goes on to observe that "the most attractive and enduring gift he has is his sense of the newness and freshness of everything, . . . the enchanting rapture of existence."[14] Now it is clear enough that quotations could be found to bolster up both these views, but there is little doubt that Mrs. Marshall is much closer to the truth than Professor Saintsbury. It is a matter of what is primary and what is secondary in the work. "O beautiful human life!" wrote Jefferies, "Tears come in my eyes as I think of it. So beautiful, so inexpressibly beautiful!" (*SH*, 86) We may perhaps complain that such a passage reveals an excess of emotion, but there can be little

---

13. George Saintsbury, *A History of Nineteenth-Century Literature* (London: Macmillan, 1896), p. 397.

14. D. E. Marshall, "Richard Jefferies, 1848–1948," *Contemporary Review*, CLXXIV (Nov. 1948), 301, 302.

doubt of its sincerity. Jefferies does not hide himself away in an ivory tower in order to meditate over true beauty, and the gloom which Professor Saintsbury detects occurs in those passages where he is condemning the meanness and degradation which arise when the human ideal is ignored and denied. He is under no delusion about the poverty and misery of much of nineteenth-century England—he knew too much about rural conditions to be deceived into any form of Victorian complacency—but he looked to the future with hope and confidence that conditions would improve, and with them human happiness. That is why he insists in "The Pageant of Summer" that "I remain an optimist" (*LF*, 62).

Among other reactions one of the most interesting is that of Henry Miller, who, as I have said, sees Jefferies as the iconoclast *par excellence*. "Here is the man," he writes, "who speaks my inmost thoughts. He is the iconoclast I feel myself to be yet never fully reveal. He makes the utmost demands. He rejects, he scraps, he annihilates. What a seeker! What a daring seeker!"[15] Miller's approach to criticism is that of a creative writer, not of a professional critic. His judgments are therefore highly personal and subjective—legitimately so, for he is explicitly writing about the books in his life. It is not therefore surprising that we learn more in the chapter about Miller than we do about Jefferies. None the less, in the above extract Miller puts his finger on an important feature of Jefferies' writing. It is true that he makes the utmost demands; the political comment in the book arises directly out of an insistence on applying the principles he believes in to the world in general, irrespective of the consequences. The danger of such an approach as Miller's is that it stresses the destructive elements in Jefferies' thought to the detriment of the constructive ideas which are in many ways the more impressive. I am convinced that his chapter has some refreshing and valuable points to contribute, but it would be a mistake to accept this reaction as definitive.

As a counter-balance to Henry Miller's enthusiasm, the uncomfortable fascination of D. H. Lawrence may be cited. He provides the most interesting reaction of the various people who are ill at ease with the book. His comments are valuable, but by no means easy to appreciate. To separate the sentence "I don't like *The Story of My Heart*" from its context (a habit not uncommon in Jefferies criticism) is to mislead hopelessly, and it is

15. Miller, p. 177.

worthwhile to quote the whole piece. Lawrence is writing to Edward Garnett about a manuscript draft of his new novel, *The Trespasser*:

But this is a work one can't regard easily—I mean, at one's ease. It is so much oneself, one's naked self. I give myself away so much, and write what is my most palpitant, sensitive self, that I loathe the book, because it will betray me to a parcel of fools. Which is what any deeply personal or lyrical writer feels, I guess. I often think Stendhal must have writhed in torture every time he remembered *Le Rouge et le Noir* was public property: and Jefferies at *The Story of My Heart*. I don't like *The Story of My Heart*.[16]

The whole context seems to suggest that in the last sentence Lawrence is implying not so much that he considered the book bad as that it made him feel uncomfortable. After all, to be mentioned in the same breath as *Le Rouge et le Noir* is no small praise in itself. Lawrence's meaning, I think, is identical with that which he later expresses in *Aaron's Rod*: "When a man writes a letter to himself, it is a pity to post it to somebody else. Perhaps the same is true of a book."[17] Although we have no positive evidence that Lawrence knew any of Jefferies' other books, there can be little doubt, I think, that he was influenced by Jefferies. *The Trespasser* itself may be evidence that the influence was not always to the good, but Lawrence's later writings suggest that he did not renounce all he may have learnt from Jefferies. For our purposes, however, what is most interesting about the letter is its concentration on the "palpitant, sensitive self." This may seem obvious, but it is one of those obvious truths that can so easily be forgotten. It reminds us that *The Story of My Heart*, if it can be classi-fied at all, belongs to the small and motley group of writings which go under the title of Confessions. It is first and last personal; the "I" is the all important topic. This is of relevance because it recalls Miss Underhill's insistence that it was Jefferies' selfhood which prevented him from attain-ing to any advanced form of mystic reality. It also helps to remind us that the philosophical element in Jefferies can be exaggerated, that, for all its extension and application which it would be folly to deny, his is a personal rather than a public philosophy.

A full and sensitive reading of *The Story of My Heart* will hold all these strands in balance. It will recognize the faults, but, without condoning

16. D. H. Lawrence, *The Letters of D. H. Lawrence*, ed. Aldous Huxley (London: Heinemann, 1932), p. 21.
17. D. H. Lawrence, *Aaron's Rod* [1922] (London: Heinemann, 1952), p. 256.

them, will be careful not to give them an exaggerated place in the final judgment. Without a thorough understanding of this book, it is impossible to come to a really satisfactory appreciation of Jefferies' other works; to this extent *The Story of My Heart* is central to his whole achievement. But it has a wider application than this. It is a book on its own and can be judged on its own. It is the record of one man's struggle with problems of theological belief, social reform, and philosophical and scientific speculation. Perhaps Miller's phrase "a daring seeker" sums this up better than any other. Sometimes, of course, he proved too daring, but it is unnecessary to shield the blemishes. Edward Thomas provides an admirable comment which takes account of faults as well as virtues: "His lonely, retiring, and yet emphatic egoism made a hundred mistakes, narrow, ill-considered, splenetic, fatuous. He was big enough to take these risks, and he made his impression by his sympathies, his creation, not by his antipathies."[18] *The Story of My Heart*, despite all the necessary and often severe qualifications, remains an effective and impressive achievement. We cannot but admire the honesty and sincerity which caused Jefferies to publish a confession which, he must have known, was bound to be resented and misunderstood. He sets down the truth whether it may shock or irritate. He does not spare himself. We can say of the book, as Walt Whitman said of his own writings,

> This is no book;
> Who touches this, touches a man.

18. Thomas, p. 326.

v. The Romances:
Wood Magic, Bevis, and
After London

BEFORE DISCUSSING the two more or less conventional novels, *Greene Ferne Farm* and *The Dewy Morn*, and the daring experiment of *Amaryllis at the Fair*, we may consider the three remaining fictional works of Jefferies' maturity, *Wood Magic* (1881), *Bevis* (1882), and *After London: or Wild England* (1885), under the general term "romances." The first two are naturally linked by a common hero, Bevis, though they are so different in tone and intention that this superficial connection is somewhat misleading. But there are good reasons for considering all three books together. In all, Jefferies is concerned not only with the real world but with a dream-world; indeed, the latter is generally more important and more central than the former. But it is a dream-world which, in various significant ways, reflects everyday experience. Jefferies is not escaping into fantasy; instead he is bringing the world of imagination to the forefront and demonstrating its close connection with, and subtle influence upon, the so-called "real world." This connection is linked in all three books with the perennial theme of the "return to nature," which Jefferies presents with his characteristic precision and also with an admirable variety.

These three interrelated themes—the everyday world, the dream-world of the imagination, and the world of wild nature—are of course central to *The Story of My Heart*, and all three romances offer interesting parallels and comparisons to this central text in the study of Jefferies. In *Wood Magic* and *Bevis*, both written earlier, we get scattered thoughts and ideas that will find their true place in the later book. In *After London,* which was published two years after *The Story of My Heart,* some of the yearning intensity of the latter work acquires allegorical form. Moreover, in all three romances we are concerned with an imaginative projection of Jefferies' own personality. I shall show how the character of Felix Aquila in *After London* is really an extension of the Bevis of the earlier books; indeed, despite the future setting of *After London,* it would almost be possible to read these romances as a trilogy tracing the development of a single character—as a young child, as a growing youth, and as a man. An autobiographical element looms large in all Jefferies' work, whether fiction or non-fiction, but it is absolutely central here. None the less, at his most successful (and there can be little dispute that *Bevis* is easily the most accomplished of the three) he is able, as we shall see, to universalize his own personal vision, and so make it significant and valid for others.

Wood Magic is specifically a children's book, though this does not prevent Jefferies from writing into it principles and ideas worthy of adult attention. The hero is little "Sir" Bevis, who is remarkable for his ability to converse with the animals and birds which live in the vicinity of his farmhouse home. Nor is this gift of understanding confined to the animal kingdom; it extends to the plant realm, represented by the reed, and even to natural objects such as the wind and the brook. We are given no reason why Bevis, and Bevis alone, should possess such powers, though we may assume that his perfect relationship with nature has at least something to do with it. The book is a record of his role in the world of nature as an eager participant in the lives and adventures of wild creatures. The centre of attention is, then, not the real world but the animal world, though the connection between the two is considerable; indeed, they often seem indistinguishable. This is not because Jefferies is incapable of the imaginative effort necessary to conceive an entirely new world, but because he wishes to emphasize the essential similarities, to point out, in fact, that the everyday world is part of the world of nature. In *Wood Magic* the animal world is as a mirror through which the young Bevis may see life as it is.

For this is no sentimental story about a little boy amid the joys of nature. Indeed, the very first paragraph is enough to set our minds aright on that score:

One morning as little "Sir" Bevis (such was his pet name) was digging in the farmhouse garden, he saw a daisy, and throwing aside his spade, he sat down on the grass to pick the flower to pieces. He pulled the pink-tipped petals off one by one, and as they dropped they were lost. Next he gathered a bright dandelion, and squeezed the white juice from the hollow stem, which drying presently, left his fingers stained with brown spots. Then he drew forth a bennet from its sheath, and bit and sucked it till his teeth were green from the sap. (*WM*, 1)

Clearly, this is no Victorian mother's darling. Indeed, what impresses us about Bevis (and this is even more true of the later book) is the extreme fidelity with which he is portrayed. Jefferies has caught the truth of boyhood, and this includes the mischievousness and selfishness as well as the imagination and the charm. In this book, Bevis is only about seven or eight years of age, and he has not yet emerged as a particular personality, but we recognize the potential of the character who gives his name to the later book. Even here there are incidents which impress us by their subtle psychological truth. The following passage concerning Pan the spaniel is a good example:

In the midst of the noise out came Polly, the dairymaid, with a bone for Pan, which Bevis no sooner saw, than he asked her to let him give Pan his dinner. "Very well, dear", said Polly, and went in to finish her work. So Bevis took the bone, and Pan, all weary and sore from his thrashing, crept out from his tub to receive it; but Bevis put the bone on the grass (all the grass was worn bare where Pan could reach) just where the spaniel could smell it nicely but could not get it. Pan struggled and scratched, and howled, and scratched again, and tugged till his collar, buckled tightly now, choked him, and he gasped and panted, while Bevis, taking the remnant of his apple from his pocket, nibbled it and laughed with a face like an angel's for sweetness. (*WM*, 28)

The last phrase recalls the conventional angelic tradition only to contrast Bevis' reality. However much his adventures among animals and birds may savour of fantasy, Bevis himself is a very real child from a very real world.

There is a similarly refreshing lack of sentimentality and idealization about the presentation of Nature. This is no gentle wonderland; Jefferies, who knew the truth of the world of Nature so well, would never betray the truth even in a children's book—especially, perhaps, in a children's book. The natural world around the farmhouse is one in which the fact of death is ever present, and this is quickly brought home to the young mind of the hero. Thus, he discovers the weasel in a trap, and eventually releases it, despite the remonstrances of a passing mouse whose mate the weasel has killed. Later he hears other stories of the weasel's misdeeds. The hare tells him that, since his lucky escape, "the weasel has killed my son, the leveret, while he was sleeping, and sucked his blood" (*WM*, 40). There is a forceful directness about this, which is enhanced by a later speech: "I daresay this weasel will have me some day, and I do not care if he does, now my leveret is dead; and very soon his poor bones will be picked clean by the ants, and after the corn is carried the plough will bury them" (*WM*, 41). Bevis himself is responsible for some of the distress, as he learns when conversing with a swallow:

The swallow flew to and fro not far from Bevis, who watched it, and presently asked him to come closer. But the swallow said: "I shall not come any nearer, Bevis. Don't you remember what you did last year, sir? Don't you remember Bill, the carter's boy, put a ladder against the wall, and you climbed up the ladder, and put your paw, all brown and dirty, into my nest and took my eggs?" (*WM*, 13)

There is the scene, too, in which Bevis is tricked by the weasel into shooting the thrush with his home-made cannon. *Wood Magic* is perhaps a misleading title, though Jefferies naturally did not neglect the beauties and delights of the natural world which he, of all people, knew and loved. Rather, the magic lies in the variety, in the exquisite balance that Jefferies maintains between the beautiful and the cruel, the gentle and the violent.

The main narrative of the book is concerned with the political set-up of the local animal kingdom. King of the wild creatures is Kapchack, the magpie, who rules harshly and absolutely over an unwieldy state, whose individual members are continually warring among themselves and betraying each other as political traitors for reasons of private vendetta. The great rebel is Choo Hoo, the wood-pigeon, who has gathered an army of discontents on the outskirts of Kapchack's territory, and the plot concerns Choo Hoo's attempts to seize monarchical power. It is, then, a story of warfare, statecraft, and intrigue. The details of the narrative—the changes in political allegiance, the plots and counter-plots, actions and motives—are extremely complex and we need not elaborate upon them. What is significant is the book's nature and tone. In this enchanted animal-realm, Bevis is educated in the ways of the real world. The story is, in fact, an allegory of the world of men. "Allegory" is, perhaps, too grandiose a term, but it is appropriate in so far as there are obvious analogies between the animal state and human institutions, though the action is sufficiently generalized for no precise identifications to be possible. The disguise is at its thinnest in such passages as the following:

The rooks live under a limited monarchy; they had real kings of their own centuries since, but now their own king is only a name, a state fiction. Every single rook has a voice in the affairs of the nation (hence the tremendous clamour you may hear in their woods towards sunset when their assemblies are held), but the practical direction of their policy is entrusted to a circle or council of about ten of the older rooks, distinguished for their oratorical powers. These depute, again, one of their own number to Kapchack's court. (*WM*, 188)

At times this literary method leads to a lucid but dreamy naïveté, as when the reed explains to Bevis why the peace-loving majority are continually defeated and overruled by a minority of the evil-minded. If only they would agree among themselves and present a united front, he says, all would be well:

Then they could drive away the hawk, for there is only one hawk to ten thousand finches, and if they only marched shoulder to shoulder all together they could kill him with ease. They could smother the cat even, by all coming down at once upon her, or they could carry up a stone and drop on her head; and as for the crow, that old coward, if he saw them coming he would take wing at once. But as they cannot agree, the hawk, and the cat, and the crow do as they like. (*WM*, 72-3)

The matter is often over-simplified, but it is never trivial. Every action, every speech has meaning and application. The story includes within itself the matter of several parables; it is an enlarged Aesop's fable, though the moral is never pointed at the end, and it is ornamented, of course, with Jefferies' characteristic natural details.

But if *Wood Magic* were concerned merely with the animal battle, it would not be half the book it is; for the main interest, at least as far as adults are concerned, lies in the inspired lyrical passages which look forward, perhaps unexpectedly, to *The Story of My Heart*. *Wood Magic* is, I think, extremely important in the development of Jefferies' natural mysticism. We know from his notebooks that it was completed on November 3, 1880. That the ideas which were later to find their most direct expression in *The Story of My Heart* were very much in Jefferies' mind at this time

is evident, for the first crude notebook jottings were made at Pevensey at
the end of the same month. In *Wood Magic* it is as if Jefferies were ex-
perimenting with the expression of some of these ideas, and, as yet unsure
of himself, is hiding behind the fantasy of the childhood story.

The most eloquent of these passages are to be found in the last chapter,
"Sir Bevis and the Wind." The story of the birds and their great battle is
over, and Bevis has gone wandering on the Downs. As far as the mere
plot is concerned, the chapter is an excrescence, an irrelevance, but from
a more deeply artistic point of view, it is both vital and triumphant. It is
here that the young Bevis puts away childish things; it is a chapter that
transcends the rest of the book and raises the whole narrative to a higher
level of significance. The wind whispers to him, and he requests a story:

"I will try," said the wind; "but I have forgotten all my stories, because the
people never come to listen to me now."
"Why don't they come?" said Bevis.
"They are too busy," said the wind, sighing; "they are so very, very busy,
just like you were with Kapchack and his treasure and the war, and all the
rest of the business; they have so much to do, they have quite forsaken me."
"I will come to you," said Bevis. (*WM*, 372)

Thus the world of Kapchack and his kingdom is renounced at the close
of the book and we pass on to something more vital, something ultimate.
The wind appeals for a life of Nature in terms which remind us of the
famous closing paragraph of *The Amateur Poacher* (quoted on p. 78).
Bevis still persists in his childish questions—why? why? why?—but the
wind explains that he can only answer these questions himself, and only
by leading (in all its senses) a natural life:

"How can they know anything about the sun who are never out in the
sunshine, and never come up on the hills, or go into the wood? How can they
know anything about the stars who never stopped on the hills, or on the sea
all night? How can they know anything of such things who are shut up in
houses, dear, where I cannot come in?
Bevis, my love, if you want to know all about the sun, and the stars, and
everything, make haste and come to me, and I will tell you, dear. In the
morning, dear, get up as quick as you can, and drink me as I come down from
the hill. In the day go up on the hill, dear, and drink me again, and stay
there if you can till the stars shine out, and drink still more of me.
And by-and-by you will understand all about the sun, and the moon, and
the stars, and the earth which is so beautiful, Bevis. It is so beautiful, you can

hardly believe how beautiful it is. . . . If they say the earth is not beautiful, tell them they do not speak the truth." (*WM*, 374–5)

Extracted from the body of the book, the passages I have quoted may seem over-whimsical, but this is not the impression one receives in context. Childlike it is, but not childish, and there is a freshness and innocence about the writing which is the innocence of wisdom, not of ignorance. And it is this childlike message which draws Bevis across the threshold from childhood into boyhood. The boy who rides home on the carthorse in the final paragraph is, recognizably, the young hero of the opening chapter of the later and greater book.

Some years have passed between the close of *Wood Magic* and the opening of *Bevis: The Story of a Boy*. Bevis is now ten or twelve years of age. The setting is the same, except, of course, for the fact that the older boy can take in a far wider section of the surrounding country. He is now close friends with Mark, a boy of his own age who is only mentioned in passing in *Wood Magic*, and all the other characters remain—Polly the dairymaid, the Bailiff, Pan the spaniel, and Bevis' parents, though these two are still shadowy, distant characters whose participation in the plot is intentionally negligible. But despite all these resemblances, the book closest to *Bevis* in tone and subject-matter is not so much *Wood Magic* as the opening chapters of *The Amateur Poacher*.

The fancy and fantasy of *Wood Magic* are missing, but these are replaced by an imaginative realism which places the adventures of Bevis and Mark among the most vivid and credible evocations of boyhood in English literature. The book consists of a year in the lives of the two boys, and it divides itself into sections according to their various and ever changing interests. Together they sail a raft, explore the margins of the lake, make elaborate and sophisticated preparations to lead the lives of savages, arrange a battle, learn to swim and shoot and sail, and the climax of the book comes when they spend ten days living by themselves on an island in the lake. It is the great book of the outdoors, of a healthy and faithfully portrayed boys' world. Although the book is, I suspect, of more interest to adults than to boys, the wood has certainly not lost its magic.

I have already emphasized the unsentimental approach of *Wood Magic*; the point needs to be repeated here because it is even more true of *Bevis*. What most impresses us about the book is its modernity. Save for the details of dress and transport, it is difficult to believe that it was written eighty years ago. It would only be a platitude to say that boys have not changed during this time, but it is worthy of mention that Jefferies' methods of presenting them are in complete accord with modern taste. As before, Pan comes in for his share of ill-treatment, and an unobliging donkey is given harsh punishment. The passage is worth quoting at length:

So soon as John had gone, Mark looked at Bevis, and Bevis looked at Mark. Mark growled. Bevis stamped his feet.
   "Beast!" said Mark.
   "Wretch!" said Bevis.
   "You—you—you, Thing," said Mark; they ground their teeth, and glared at the animal. They led him all fearful to a tree, a little tree but stout enough; it was an ash, and it grew somewhat away from the hedge. They tied him firmly to the tree, and then they scourged this miserable citizen.
   All the times they had run in vain to catch him; all the times they had had to walk when they might have ridden one behind the other on his back; all his refusals to be tempted; all the wrongs they had endured at his heels boiled in their breasts. They broke their sticks upon his back, they cut new ones, and smashed them too, they hurled the fragments at him, and then got some more. They thrashed, thwacked, banged, thumped, poked, prodded, kicked, belaboured, bumped, and hit him, working themselves into a frenzy of rage.
   Mark fetched a pole to knock him the harder as it was heavy; Bevis crushed into the hedge, and brought out a dead log to hurl at him, a log he could but just lift and swung to throw with difficulty—the same Bevis who put an aspen leaf carefully under the fly to save it from drowning. The sky was blue, and the evening beautiful, but no one came to help the donkey. (B, 133–4)

It is but a short incident in a long book. It is not vital to the total scheme, and I can imagine certain people who would wish that Jefferies had never written it. But it is in passages such as this that the uncompromising truth of Jefferies' vision becomes apparent. He is intent on presenting both sides of boyhood, the callousness as well as the kindness, the strain of cruelty as well as the love and sympathy. The scene is as typical of the growing boy as the story of the fly and the aspen leaf, and it is a tribute to Jefferies' impartiality that he alludes to the one in the description of the other. Such a scene reminds us in its vividness and its psychological truth of the descriptions of the less savoury details of rural sport in *The Amateur Poacher* —the wringing of the rabbit's neck and the pheasant shooting. In passages such as these, the habit of Jefferies the reporter in presenting what he sees fully and faithfully is in complete accord with his artistic purpose.

Linked with this strain of callousness is the selfishness of the two boys. Bevis bullies the carter's boy into helping him launch his raft in the stream, but when the boy is nabbed by the bailiff who marches him back to his work, "Bevis and Mark were too full of the raft even to notice that their assistant had been haled off" (*B*, 31). This selfishness is especially charac-teristic of Bevis, who is the natural leader of the two and rarely thinks of his companion's rights or feelings. On one occasion, when digging a channel around an obstacle in the stream, they decide in their imagina-tions to be Greeks digging a canal through Mount Athos.

"And who are we then, if we are Greeks?"
"I am Alexander the Great."
"And who am I?"
"Oh, you—you are anybody."
"But I *must* be somebody," said Mark, "else it will not do."
"Well, you are : let me see—Pisistratus."
"Who was Pisistratus?"
"I don't know," said Bevis. "It doesn't matter in the least. Now dig."
(*B*, 42)

Similarly, a little later, they are discussing adventures in the jungle :

"Suppose I was shooting an elephant, and you did not hand me another gun quick, or another arrow; and suppose—"
"But *I* might be shooting the elephant," interrupted Mark, "and you could hand me the gun."
"Impossible," said Bevis; "I never heard anything so absurd. Of course it's the captain who always does everything; and if there was only one biscuit left, of course you would let me eat it, and lie down and die under a tree, so that I might go and reach the settlement."
"I *hate* dying under a tree," said Mark, "and you always want everything."
(*B*, 53-4)

It is this attitude, charming though it may be within the book, that Bevis must outgrow, and he does so. As in *Wood Magic*, we can see a definite development in the character of the hero from the beginning to the end of the book. The life in the open air has had its effect by the close; the educa-tion by Nature has been successful.

In fact education, and moreover self-education, is a major theme in the book. One of the reasons why the boys are left on their own for most of the time is because their parents, especially Bevis' "governor," realize that the best way to learn is to teach oneself. This is made explicit in two incidents, swimming and sailing. Seeing their determination to explore the lake, the "governor" rightly insists that they must first learn to swim, but he is careful to teach them only the basic essentials. "His object from the beginning," we are told, "had been so to teach them that they could teach themselves" (B, 107). It is the same when they are learning to sail. "He was almost as interested in their sailing as they were themselves, and had watched them from the bank of the New Sea concealed behind the trees. But he considered it best that they should teach themselves, and find out little by little where they were wrong" (B, 253). The same principle is implicit throughout the book. The two boys scorn to ask of the adults; they prefer to find out on their own, and the climax on the island is itself the perfect presentation of their claims to self-sufficiency.

In the quotations already made from the book, I have given some indication of its nature. Perhaps the best classification would be to call it an inverted adventure story. It contains all the ingredients of a conventional suspense tale—a fight, a shipwreck, life on an island, and a mysterious intruder—but the treatment which they receive is very different. In tone it is certainly not an adventure story. It comes closest to it in the course of the battle, with Bevis' hair-breadth scapes, but for the most part the adventure is confined to the imagination, fused with the real and the ordinary. The battle, for all its planning and strategy, is a relatively tame affair—"no one was hurt, and no one had even had much of a knock, except the larger boys, who could stand it" (B, 223). The shipwreck, though certainly a fact, turns out to be the reverse of romantic; "He [Bevis] could not quite suppress an inward feeling that shipwreck when one was quite alone was not altogether so splendid. It was so dull." (B, 203) When Bevis and Mark are on the island and they become aware of the "something," this too has its unsplendid aspects. Instead of revelling in the adventure, the two become really frightened, and the eventual explanation—the inquisitive cottage-girl, Loo, watching over them—comes as both a relief and a disappointment to the eager adventurers.

Mr. Guy Pocock has described the book as "a prose epic—the epic of boyhood,"[1] and it is certainly true that there are distinct heroic qualities about the book which need to be mentioned. It is worth noting, for instance, that there are over a dozen references to the *Odyssey* in the course of the book, and that Bevis is continually basing his own actions on the

1. Guy Pocock, Introduction to *Bevis* (Everyman ed.; London: Dent, 1930), p. 11.

adventures of Ulysses, "his favourite hero" (B, 164). When stuck on the
fallen hurdle beneath the cliff, Bevis asks himself: "What would Ulysses
have done?" (B, 187), and when they are living on the island, Bevis con-
sults the *Odyssey* in order to "read how Ulysses constructed his ship or
raft" (B, 327). This heroic quality in the book is nowhere more noticeable
than in the details. The battle which Bevis organizes is a schoolboy re-
construction of Pharsalia, with Bevis (inevitably) as Caesar, and their sailing boat is named the *Pinta* after one of the ships in Columbus' expedition. The favourite song of the two boys is "The Ballad of King Estmere,"
and this is more than a mere battle-song; Bevis reacts to the romance and
heroism of the situation. Another of the books which they take to the
island is *Don Quixote.*

Reference to Cervantes' comic epic is casual, but it provides a clue
to the precise nature of the story. For Quixote the romance lay entirely in
his own imagination, which persisted in investing the realities of everyday with a romantic glamour, and this is precisely the method of the two
boys. The great effect and charm of the book lie in the imaginative capaci-
ties of Bevis and Mark which transform a pleasant though unexceptional
stretch of countryside into a wonderland of magic and adventure. In truth,
it consisted of the immediate environs of an eighty-acre reservoir contain-
ing (in Jefferies' time) two small islands; a small stream flowed through
the reservoir, and a brook flowed into it. But in *Bevis* these are all transformed. The reservoir itself is called the New Sea, the two islands are
christened New Formosa (or the Magic Island) and Serendib, the stream
becomes the Mississippi, and the brook the Nile. On the horizon rise the
smooth contours of the Downs, but this is not good enough for them:

"What are those mountains?" asked Mark.
"The Himalayas, of course," said Bevis. (B, 89)

The flora and fauna are similarly rechristened to fit in with the new world.
The rabbits of the mainland become kangaroos, and the doves, parrots.
The whole transformation is achieved blatantly and completely, and there
is no loss of credibility:

"Oaks are banyans, aren't they?" said Mark. "They used to be, you know,"
remembering the exploration of the wood.
"Banyans," said Bevis.
"What are beeches?"

"Oh! teak."

"That's China; aren't we far from China?"

"Ask me presently when I've got my astrolabe." . . .

"Poplars?" said Mark in an interrogative tone.

"Palms, of course. You can see them miles away like palms in a desert."

"Pictures," said Mark. "Yes, that's it. You always see the sun going down, camels with long shadows, and palm trees. Then I suppose it's Africa."

"You must wait till we have taken an observation. We shall see too by the stars."

"Firs?" said Mark. "They're cedars, of course."

"Of course. Willows are blue gums."

"Then it's near Australia. I expect it is; because, don't you know, there were no animals in Australia except kangaroos, and there are none here at all. So it's that sort of country." (*B*, 304–5)

It is a world in which everything contains the possibility of mystery, and, moreover, everything can be explained by mystery, even though the real explanation is both evident and acknowledged. It is a state in which the mind can adapt at will to the dream and the reality, sometimes even accepting both at the same time. A nice example occurs during the early journey of exploration, when they come upon a structure of ash sticks by a path.

"It's a little house," said Mark, forgetting the quarrel. "Here's some of the straw on the ground; they thatch it in winter and crawl under." (It was about three feet high.)

"I don't know," said Bevis.

"I'm sure it is," said Mark. "They are little men, the savages who live here, they're pigmies, you know."

"So they are," said Bevis, quite convinced, and likewise forgetting his temper. "Of course they are, and that's why the path is so narrow. But I believe it's not a house, I mean not a house to live in. It's a place to worship at, where they have a fetish."

"I think it's a house," said Mark.

"Then where's the fireplace?" asked Bevis decidedly.

"No more there is a fireplace," said Mark thoughtfully. "It's a fetish-place."

Bevis went on again, leaving the framework behind. Across those bars the barley was thrown in autumn for the pheasants, which feed by darting up and down a single ear at a time; thus by keeping the barley off the ground there is less waste. *They knew this very well.* (*B*, 83–4 [my italics])

It will be seen that there are definite rules to the game. There must be a display of logic, however fanciful, to back up an opinion. If this is forthcoming the explanation is accepted for so long as it is convenient. And when it ceases to be convenient, it is quietly forgotten.

Bevis and Mark succeed in getting the best of both worlds. Their secret kingdom is both Africa and England; all the delights of a magic land are enjoyed within the quiet beauty of their native countryside. While the names are altered, and suitably fantastic explanations are pondered and adopted for the most commonplace occurrences, they continue to enjoy what remains a particularly English scene. Rabbits may become kangaroos, but they retain the essential characteristics of an English rabbit. The island, despite its new name, is a small islet in a Wiltshire reservoir, and the boys in their hearts would not have it otherwise.

"Everything," as Mark says in a profound understatement, "is somehow else" (B, 113). Gradually this imaginative ambivalence resolves itself into a dichotomy between "here" and "the other side." This latter phrase recurs at several points during the book and represents the real world from which all "magic" has been expelled. The concept first finds formulation in chapter xxxix when Bevis tells Mark a story. It concerns a traveller searching for a land that had no "other side." It is a typical boyish fantasy concerning lost valleys in Tibet and a hidden paradise (without an "other side") glimpsed through a narrow door. The traveller cannot himself get through the door, but "his mind . . . and soul had gone through" (B, 387), and although he fails ever afterwards to find his way back to the valley, the remembrance of the single vision is always with him:

He lived to be the oldest man there ever was, which was because he had breathed the delicious air. . . . Every night when he went to sleep he could hear some of the star flute music of the organ, and dreamed he could see it; but he could hear it plainly. At last he died and went to join his soul, which had travelled on down the footpath, you know, towards the opal sun. (B, 388)

It is an aspirational allegory which is more than a mere interlude. Reference to breathing "the delicious air" reminds us of the wind's exhortation in *Wood Magic*, and we remember that the young Jefferies-Bevis had his own vision of eternity (which has no "other side") on Liddington Hill, and never forgot the experience.

But the other side is real and, in this world, at any rate, cannot be escaped. Even in *Bevis* Jefferies cannot, and will not, suppress his concern for social conditions. When Loo is discovered to be the mysterious intruder on the island, she tells how she came to collect scraps for her baby brother who was ill and starving. Bevis is horrified. "Now Bevis had always been in contact with these folk, but yet he had never seen; you and I live in the midst of things, but never look beneath the surface. His face became quite white; he was thoroughly upset. It was his first glance at the hard road-side of life." (B, 459–60) It is not reading too much into the book to point out how Jefferies subtly manages the plot so that "the hard road-side of life," the other side at its most grim, is encountered on the island paradise, the magic land. The two worlds, of imagination and of hard economic fact, have met; indeed, they are inseparable. Once again, Nature has educated Bevis.

But Bevis' dream-world and the adult world of the imagination are not quite the same. The latter is an extension and a deepening of the former, and Bevis is to make the transition in the course of the book. Like the young Jefferies, Bevis was a dreamy youth for all his mischief and activity, and Jefferies, comprehensive as ever, does not ignore this aspect of boy-hood, though he links it, as later in *The Story of My Heart*, with intense physical activity. In the following passage, Bevis is swimming: "He did not see where he was going, his vision was lost in the ecstasy of motion; all his mind was concentrated in the full use of his limbs. The delicious delirium of strength—unconsciousness of reason, unlimited concious-ness of force—the joy of life itself filled him." (B, 324) The emphasis, as always, is on "life." In his notebooks, Jefferies headed most of his notes for *The Story of My Heart* and its projected sequel, "Sun-Life," a phrase which sums up perfectly his own brand of natural mysticism. And what education could prepare one more soundly for this ideal than the life recounted in *Bevis*? Time and time again, the health of the life is stressed: "the sunlight poured upon them, and the light air came along; they bathed in air and sunbeam, and gathered years of health like flowers from the field" (B, 126). It is the same when they return from their stay on the island: "In those days of running, racing, leaping, exploring, swimming, the skin nude to the sun, and wind and water, they built themselves up of steel, steel that would bear the hardest wear of the world" (B, 478–9).

Life is the key, in fact, to the "magic," as Bevis well knows:

"I wish we could get a magic writing. Then we could do anything, and we could know all the secrets."

"What secrets?"

"Why, all these things have secrets."

"All?"

"All," said Bevis, looking round and pointing with an arrow in his hand. "All the trees, and all the stones, and all the flowers—"

"And these?" said Mark, picking up a shell.

"Yes, once; but can't you see it's dead, and the secret, of course, is gone." (*B*, 62)

This aspect of childhood is given its fullest covering in the exquisite lyrical chapter "Bevis's Zodiac" where, during their stay on the island, Bevis leaves Mark one evening to go away by himself, and lies down beneath a tree to look up at the stars. It is the corresponding scene to the final chapter of *Wood Magic*. The fact that many passages are identical with sentences in *The Old House at Coate* proves that the tone, if not the occasion, is autobiographical. It emphasizes, as we might expect, the reality of both the physical and the spiritual. It is a natural mysticism closely linked, as in *The Story of My Heart*, with the sense of touch:

The sward on the path on which Bevis used to lie and gaze up in the summer evening was real and tangible; the earth under was real; and so too the elms, the oak, the ash trees, were real and tangible—things to be touched, and known to be. Now like these, the mind, stepping from the one to the other, knew and almost felt the stars to be real and not mere specks of light, but things that were there by day over the elms as well as by night, and not apparitions of the evening departing at the twittering of the swallows. They were real, and the touch of his mind felt to them. (*B*, 355)

But *Bevis*, it must be emphasized, is an extremely happy book, absorbing, natural, and full of humour. The subtlety of the humour in *Bevis* seems to have gone for the most part unnoticed, though it is extraordinary that anyone could read the book and still maintain (as many have done) that Jefferies lacks a sense of humour. Even in the passages I have already quoted, there is more than sufficient to refute such a charge. A single example must suffice here. Bevis and Mark are on an expedition in search of the New Sea (Coate reservoir):

"When shall we come to the New Sea again?" said Mark presently, as they were moving more slowly through the thicker growth.

"I cannot think," said Bevis. . . .

"Oh! I know, where's the compass?"

"How stupid!" said Bevis. "Of course it was in my pocket all the time."

He took it out, and as he lifted the brazen lid the white card swung to and fro with the vibration of his hand. . . .

"Now, which way was the sea?" said Mark, trying to think of the direction in which they had last seen it. "It was that side," he said, holding out his right hand; he faced Bevis.

"Yes, it was," said Bevis. "It was on the right hand, now that would be east" (to Mark), "so if we go east we must be right." (B, 85)

Jefferies does not lack a sense of humour because he refuses to underline the joke; on the contrary, he demonstrates it. Again, the humour is frequently linked with pathos. The happiness of childhood is never far from sadness, and Jefferies succeeds in maintaining an admirable balance between the two. The mood changes from sunlight to shadow like an April day, and the melancholy has its place alongside the laughter. The transition is easy, because Jefferies hardly ever stands between the reader and the experience; he reports faithfully and accurately. The above quotation well illustrates the naturalness not only of the characters, but of the dialogue. Bevis and Mark are real boys, and they speak the true boys' language. Although the book is not completely true to his own boyhood, it is close enough for Jefferies to be able to dramatize his own self-made adventures and present his own feelings, but at the same time to present a private world which is universally valid. The point can best be made by suggesting that the effectiveness of the book stems from the fact that it was written by an adult Bevis who had never allowed his vision to fade into the light of common day.

After London, or Wild England, published in 1885, is perhaps the most original and unexpected of all Jefferies' productions. As its title suggests, it is set in the dim future, and is indeed one of the first novels to use a future setting for creative imaginative purposes. The story itself, though sufficiently interesting to hold the attention, is nearly always secondary to our interest in the facts of the setting. The book is divided into two parts, the first, entitled "The Relapse into Barbarism," being an account by a historian of the future of the changes, both historical and geographical, between our own time and his. It is a meticulously detailed survey which gives evidence, as Edward Thomas has pointed out, of "an unsuspected strength of remorseless logic and restraint." [2]

Although this is in many respects a new venture for Jefferies, the alternative title will remind us that the device is a daring and successful method

2. Edward Thomas, *Richard Jefferies: His Life and Work* (1909), p. 256.

of viewing his more usual field from a new angle. For Jefferies sees the
future not as a development, but as a retrogression. Instead of the town
overwhelming the country, it is the country that has survived and destroyed
the town. London is no more; we are presented with a collection of scattered, isolated communities which have lost the inventions and sophistica-
tions of our own age, and seem to have most in common with pre-
Conquest England.

There are indications in the earlier books that this theme had interested
him for some time. In his essay "Downs" from *The Open Air*, for instance, he states that the downs were originally covered by woodland, and
speculates that "probably the trees would grow again were it not for sheep
and horses" (*OA*, 138). It is precisely this process which is described in
After London. And in *Wood Magic* the Brook imagines a time "when all
the hills are changed and the roads are covered with woods, and the
houses gone" (*WM*, 157). In *After London* this becomes a reality. A
sudden catastrophe deprives England of most of her population; the survivors are unable to maintain control, and Nature reassumes her sway.
Man returns to Nature not through any desire on his part, but because
Nature returns to him. Thus we may note that the theme of the return
to Nature plays an opposite role here to the one it played in the earlier
"romances." Here the world of Nature has become the everyday world.
Any "escape" is into a lost world of progress and sophistication.

The precise nature of the catastrophe is left deliberately vague. Just as
there is no explanation given in *Wood Magic* about how "Sir" Bevis
succeeded in learning the language of the animals and birds, so here we
are offered no pseudo-scientific explanation of the changes in the *status
quo*. This vagueness is not the result of any imaginative weakness on
Jefferies' part. On the contrary, it is an important part of the fictional
design. The narrative is told by a clear-minded and responsible chronicler
of a future time. He builds up a picture by means of empirical evidence
and the scanty written records, and to these is added the personal con-
jectures and theories of other scholars. (Jefferies even invents a philosophical historian named Silvester, author of *The Unknown Orb* and *The
Book of Natural Things*, whom the narrator considers and refutes at various points in the writing.) For the truth is that the historians themselves
are uncertain about what happened. They are forced to rely on conjecture
and hearsay—the first sentence beginning "The old men say their fathers

told them . . ." (*AL*, 3) is typical of this process. There are later references to "when the ancients [i.e., ourselves] departed" (*AL*, 10) and to "the conflagrations which consumed the towns" (*AL*, 14), but in spite of a few sceptical accounts of theories concerning changes in the water-level and "the passage of an enormous dark body through space" (*AL*, 15), we are never told what happened. We are merely referred to "the event."

As Jefferies is attempting something much more ambitious than the average modern science-fiction, however, this is unimportant. We are not concerned with what happened; we are only interested in the fact that something did happen. This "event" is a fictional hypothesis which we accept from the outset. It is the consequences of the event with which we are concerned, and these are worked out with admirable detail and subtlety:

All that seems certain is, that when the event took place, the immense crowds collected in cities were most affected, and that the richer and upper classes made use of their money to escape. Those left behind were mainly the lower and most ignorant, so far as the arts were concerned; those that dwelt in distant and outlying places; and those who lived by agriculture. These last, at that date, had fallen to such distress that they could not hire vessels to transport themselves. (*AL*, 15)

This last sentence shows us that Jefferies' usual and continual interests are still in evidence here. This is, in fact, a romance of the agricultural depression; country society has been deserted by the townsmen, and left to its fate.

The result is inevitable. With insufficient men to work the land, the roads and footpaths soon became impassable, and the fields are overgrown with weeds and shrubs. Later, rivers and streams get out of control and form extensive swamps. Eventually the towns and cities are overwhelmed, and England reverts to a prehistoric landscape of marsh and forest. Domesticated cattle become wild and take to the hills and woods. Even the more intelligent of the human survivors are incapable of maintaining "modern" discoveries, and such inventions as railways and the telegraph become things of the past. "These marvellous things are to us little more than fables of the giants and of the old gods that walked upon the earth, which were fables even to those whom we call the ancients" (*AL*, 17). Men become hunters again, and the more backward of them remain in this condition. They become the Bushmen and the Gipsies who are the continual enemies of the more advanced communities of agricultural folk which gradually form themselves and begin the quest for civilization once again.

Little by little, villages are formed, and after these, towns and even kingdoms. Inevitably rivalry and war begin. The Welsh, Scots, and Irish assert their independence, and we are quite obviously back in the Dark Ages once more. It is a world of injustice and cruelty not unlike Kapchack's animal kingdom in *Wood Magic*. We are told that "there is hardly a town where the slaves do not outnumber the free as ten to one. The laws are framed for the object of reducing the greater part of the people to servitude." (*AL*, 26) Jefferies' views concerning the future are interesting; they are obviously at the opposite pole from the over-simple optimism of Morris' *News From Nowhere* (which it predates by six years), but on the other hand they do not partake of the calculated evil of the inverted Utopias of Huxley and Orwell. Instead we see a new struggling civilization making the same tragic mistakes and blunders as the old. It is a vision (and this is crucial) not of evil but of ignorance. Again this is a deliberate part of Jefferies' creative scheme. Far from its showing a lack of invention, the conception of sameness and repetition is itself the invention. "It is all changed and just the same." I have already had occasion to quote this as Jefferies' central statement concerning the rural scene of his own time; it is equally appropriate as a comment on the view of history which underlies *After London*.

There is one considerable change, however, that has not yet been mentioned. This is the appearance of the great central Lake. It is allegedly caused by impediments to the eastward flow of the Thames and the westward flow of the Severn. Be that as it may, we are presented with a vast inland Lake which stretches from Bristol on the west to London on the east, with the White Horse range as its southern boundary, its northern boundary being left vague. This lake is the central feature of the book. Upon it the hero, Felix Aquila, sets off on his voyage of adventure and discovery, and it is during this voyage that he arrives quite unwittingly upon the stagnant and poisonous swamp which covers the site of London.

Felix is remarkable in that, while living in an age of barbarism, he has the outlook and sensitivity of an "ancient." In an age when learning is despised, he is a lover of learning; in an age when brute force is essential and respected, he is slender, shy, and retiring. He presents a perfect contrast to his athletic brother Oliver who was, Jefferies tells us, "as active and energetic as Felix was outwardly languid" (*AL*, 47). But there are certain aspects of his character which are particularly significant. Even as we read they strike a familiar ring:

This unbending independence and pride of spirit, together with scarce concealed contempt for others, had resulted in almost isolating him from the youth of his own age, and had caused him to be regarded with dislike by the elders. . . . Too quick to take offence where none was really intended, he fancied that many bore him ill-will who had scarcely given him a passing thought. He could not forgive the coarse jokes uttered upon his personal appearance by men of heavier build, who despised so slender a stripling. (*AL*, 42)

This extract hardly gives a fair description of Felix who is throughout a sympathetic character, but the details are so close to many that we know of Jefferies' own youth that it is difficult to escape the suspicion that it is an idealized self-portrait. This is confirmed by later touches, especially his solitary excursions into the wild country and the observation that "the mystery of existence had impressed him deeply while wandering alone in the forest" (*AL*, 101).

The passage describing his construction of a large canoe could have come straight out of *Bevis*, and when Oliver points out the difficulty of sailing downstream because "there's an old fir across the river down yonder, and a hollow willow has fallen in" (*AL*, 57), we are clearly dealing with a real incident also treated in the second chapter of *Bevis*. At this point we realize that *After London* is in fact a continuation of the earlier book on a new imaginative and vastly enlarged scale. The setting, we find, is no more nor less than a giant Coate farm, and the reservoir which in *Bevis* was imagined by the children to be a new sea is now extended to cover a vast section of the south of England.

I am contributing nothing new in making this identification. The point is sufficiently obvious to any careful reader, and it has been noted several times. It is surprising, though, that critics have not followed up the autobiographical possibilities of *After London*, for there are numerous ways in which discussion could be extended. One leads us into the intricacies of psychological criticism, and while at times this critical approach can be both dangerous and misleading, at other times it can be necessary and helpful. I believe *After London* to be a case in point. If *Bevis* was Jefferies' childhood not precisely as it was, but as he would like it to have been, so the present book seems to be a fictional and barely disguised representation of his unrealized ambitions and yearnings. After we have been introduced to Felix, and have recognized him as a self-portrait of the author, we are shown his dissatisfaction with his present life, his passionate and apparently hopeless love for Aurora Thyma, and his determination to achieve some elaborate quest to impress Aurora and to satisfy himself. Eventually he chooses his objective—the circumnavigation of the great Lake in a home-made canoe. He sets out, and his first adventure brings him to a town that is being besieged, and he is appalled by the incompetence of the besieging prince. He is heard criticizing, is arrested, and eventually brought to trial in front of the prince. He speaks out boldly, repeats his criticisms, and offers suggestions for improving the attack which amaze and impress the court. But he overreaches himself, suggests a revolutionary assault weapon which is beyond the imagination of his hearers, and is beaten out of the camp as a fool. Basically, it is a story of intelligence against ignorance, of brain power against brute force. Felix is the enlightened man of intelligence, who is humiliated and ridiculed by inferiors whose only weapon is tyrannic power. His next adventure is on the site of London to which he sails by a combination of accident and curiosity, and barely escapes from the poisonous and intricate swamp. Here it is a case of achievement in the teeth of difficulty, success where others stronger but less intelligent had failed, of triumph that assures his name in history and the admiration of the woman he loves. The third phase of his adventure relates his meeting with the shepherds. His canoe has been wrecked, and he is at the nadir of his fortunes. On meeting the shepherds, he tells them his adventures on the swamps of London, and they greet him as a superman, if not a god. In one fantastic paragraph he comes into his own:

Their manner towards him perceptibly altered. From the first they had been hospitable; they now became respectful, and even reverent. The elders and their chief, not to be distinguished by dress or ornament from the rest, treated him with ceremony and marked deference. The children were brought to see and even to touch him. So great was their amazement that any one should have escaped from these pestilential vapours, that they attributed it to divine interposition, and looked upon him with some of the awe of superstition. He was asked to stay with them altogether, and to take command of the tribe. (*AL*, 179–80)

At last intelligence is rewarded. He agrees to stay, but flatters the elders by refusing the command—another instance of his wisdom. Instead, he is accepted among them under the title of "Leader." Later he adds to his achievements. With the help of his skill and guile, he defeats their enemies almost single-handed, and later locates a hidden spring (according to the shepherds, miraculously) when their flocks are in desperate need of water. He is credited with supernatural powers, and Jefferies emphasizes that "in innumerable little ways Felix's superior knowledge had told upon them" (*AL*, 191).

But Felix has greater ambitions than being merely the wise man in a tribe of shepherds. Nearby he has discovered a beautiful lake (Coate reservoir once more, idealized this time in beauty rather than in size), where he determines to build a strong fortress, and a tower in which he will live with Aurora. Here he will remain as "Leader" of the shepherds in a world of happiness and content. Unfortunately, the shepherds dislike the idea of his leaving them, even temporarily to fetch Aurora, and they plan to keep him with them by force. But again "superior knowledge" triumphs; he eludes them, and the book ends as he is on his way to Thyma Castle and Aurora. We are left with the impression that he will be successful, that he and Aurora will return to the shepherds and live in the fortified tower, an oasis of culture and intelligence safe, thanks to knowledge and learning, in the midst of a barbarous world. Like Bevis before him, Felix educates himself, but he is not confined to the terms or real life, and develops from a thwarted youth into a triumphant superman.

It is difficult to believe that the connection between the romance on the one hand and Jefferies' own character and ambitions on the other is completely fortuitous. There are incidents throughout his biography which remind us not only of Felix's original situation but also of his pride and obstinacy. Throughout his work there runs a continued strain of ambition, a confident sense of the possible, which is ever thwarted by a realization of his physical weakness and his lack of undoubted literary success. So in *The Story of My Heart* he writes: "Let me be physically perfect, in shape, vigour, and movement. My frame, naturally slender, will not respond to labour, and increase in proportion to effort, nor will exposure harden a delicate skin. It disappoints me so far, but my spirit rises with the effort, and my thought opens." (*SH*, 83) The resemblance to Felix's situation can hardly be denied.

It is interesting to note that this mounting ambition, this determination to achieve success, is almost invariably expressed in Jefferies' writings by the image of a voyage. This is natural enough—the voyage archetype doubtless has a similar universal significance—but in Jefferies it is particularly strong. It occurs in *Bevis* in the boys' voyage and the continual references to the *Odyssey*. In the essay "Red Roofs of London" Jefferies writes: "In the hearts of most of us, there is always a desire for something beyond experience. Hardly any of us but have thought, Some day I will go on a long voyage; but the years go by, and still we have not sailed." (*OA*, 192) The image recurs several times in *The Story of My Heart*, as here: "There is an immense ocean over which the mind can sail, upon which the vessel of thought has not yet been launched. I hope to launch it." (*SH*, 46) But Felix Aquila refuses to let the years go by; he insists on sailing, and thereby achieves his object and reaps the reward of his intelligence. The success which he missed in life Jefferies portrays in romance. The whole is a presentation of Jefferies' own dream-world, an enlarged version of his true life at Coate.

After London is not one of his best books—partly because it is too close to the patterns of his own subconscious. In addition, the narrative of the second part is less successful than the imaginative description of the first, and suffers by comparison with John Collier's *Tom's A-Cold*, a novel to which it bears a close resemblance. *After London* leaves the reader with a sense of admiration, but also of bewilderment. The balance between the intense logical realism and the heights of romantic fantasy is impossible to maintain, for the significant reason that the romance is too close to life. But it is an important document in his biography as man and as artist, and deserves greater attention than it has generally received.

VI. Jefferies' Fiction

JEFFERIES' FICTION (excluding the romances already discussed) divides itself conveniently into two halves—the early novels (*The Scarlet Shawl, Restless Human Hearts,* and *World's End*) and the later works (*Greene Ferne Farm, The Dewy Morn,* and *Amaryllis at the Fair*). The division is not only chronological but critical, for the early novels have to be classed as juvenilia, and it is wholly on the later trio that Jefferies' achievement as a writer of fiction must be judged.

There is little point in discussing the early novels here, for they contain nothing of interest that is not presented more subtly and more clearly in the later work. When the early novels are ready today (which is seldom), it is because of Jefferies' authorship rather than for any intrinsic interest in the books themselves. A student of Victorian popular fiction would doubtless find them no worse, perhaps even a little better, than hundreds of other novels now utterly forgotten, though Jefferies found to his cost (he contributed towards their publication) that in a commercial sense they were by no means popular. Suffice it to say here that their interest lies in three themes which are to develop and mature in the later fiction—the contrast between the natural (or "Nature") and the artificial, the tentative presentation of Jefferies' ideal of womanhood, and his general concern for spiritual aspiration.

The chief weakness of these early novels was the imperfect relation between characters and plot. This being so, it was perhaps apt that Jefferies' subsequent writings—the country books—should concentrate upon presenting the ordinary workaday lives of the people he knew best set against a familiar and vividly realized background. Surprising as it may seem, it is in books such as *Round About a Great Estate* and *Hodge and His Masters*, where Jefferies uses artistic methods to throw light on contemporary problems and situations, that his evolution as a novelist can best be studied. It is interesting to note that both these books were published in 1880, and the same year sees the appearance of his first mature work of fiction, *Greene Ferne Farm*. We shall see that the continuity of subject and attitude is more significant than the change of genre.

Greene Ferne Farm is a traditional bucolic novel; its plot is simpler and less forced than those of the earlier stories, and it is fused more naturally with the background against which it is played. The setting is in fact the district in which Jefferies was born, and many of the places mentioned in the text can still be recognized. It is no coincidence that *Greene Ferne Farm* appeared under the same imprint as the country books—that of Smith Elder. Indeed, the first chapter—"Up to Church"—might easily be mistaken for an extract from *Hodge and His Masters*. Superficially it is a straightforward description of a village service on a Sunday in summer. We first see the farmers leaning on the churchyard wall discussing pigs and prices, then the children playing on a concealed, fallen gravestone, then the arrival of the Squire's party—all the variety and humour of the rural life. But this variety of description is by no means arbitrary; every detail adds to our understanding of the scene and the motives and attitudes of the people who compose it. We learn much from Jefferies' description of the entry of the congregation into the church:

Now it was possible to tell the rank of the congregation as they entered, by the length of time each kept his hat on after getting through the door. The shepherd or carter took off his hat the moment he set his hobnailed boot down on the stone flags with a clatter. The wheelwright who had a little money and a house of his own, wore his hat till he got to the font. So did the ale-house keeper, who had the grace to come to church. So did the small farmers. Ruck, who could write a cheque for a thousand pounds, never removed his till he arrived at the step that led down to the side-aisle. Hedges, who was higher in the rank of society, inasmuch as he had been born in the purple of farming, kept his on till he reached the first pillar. One of the semi-gentleman-farmers actually walked halfway to his pew-door wearing his hat, though the congregation were standing listening to Jabez and the choir get through the introductory chant. (*GFF*, 14–15)

The effect is complex. Jefferies writes accurately and precisely, and we may notice the ironic effect of the introduction of social, worldly matters into the spiritual surroundings. But over and above this we learn something of the rigid but accepted social structure, and understand the assumptions and beliefs that underlie the society as a whole.

The scene itself represents, as Squire Thorpe decides in the final paragraph of the chapter, "human life in little" (*GFF*, 26). There is the pathos of past memories accentuated by the memorial tablets within the church, the charm of young love as reflected in the exchanged glances of lover and beloved during the service, the grotesque humour represented by the sight of Jabez being chased across the churchyard by jeering choirboys after making an absent-minded mistake in the final hymn. The scene is a perfect setting for what is to follow.

The central theme is the love of Geoffrey Newton for Margaret Estcourt, daughter of the mistress of Greene Ferne Farm, and the keen but ultimately unsuccessful rivalry of Valentine Brown. There is also a sub-plot concerning the love of a rich but conscientious curate, Felix St. Bees, for Margaret's friend May Fisher, granddaughter of the miserly miller, Andrew Fisher. With the exception of Andrew Fisher these characters are commonplace, and have obvious prototypes in the earlier novels. Margaret, for instance, is described as "simply very near the ideal of a fair young English girl, in the full glow of youth and with all its exquisite bloom" (*GFF*, 23). It is scarcely a striking portrait. Again, there is little differentiation between the characters of Geoffrey and Valentine. The significant improvement in the novel lies not in the characters themselves but in the way their story is integrated with the setting. We may cite two particular instances. In the fourth chapter the society of Greene Ferne Farm has decided to go haymaking to counteract a local strike of the agricultural labourers, and both the rivals for Margaret's love are eager to show off their physical prowess. What begins as a half-serious escapade becomes an exhibition of bitterness and ill feeling. Similarly a nutting expedition is marred by the two rivals earnestly striving to outdo each other in pulling down branches for Margaret to pick. Not only are these scenes credible and appropriate, but they prepare us for the climax of the novel in the tenth chapter, "A Fray." Geoffrey and Valentine are out shooting, but soon go their own ways. Geoffrey accidentally slips and his gun goes off, the bullet passing close to Valentine who, supposing that the shot was meant for him, returns fire. Soon both are blazing away as if on a battle-field. Jefferies comments: "Circumstances suddenly threw them as it were a thousand years back in civilization on the original savage instincts of man" (*GFF*, 249–50). It is an odd, almost grotesque scene which none the less succeeds because we are obliged to accept it as psychologically possible.

It would be true to say, however, that the plot of the novel is of less interest and importance than the general background. It is a novel of extreme contrasts and meaningful juxtapositions. For example, that portion of the plot which contains the death of old Andrew Fisher includes a number of effectively grotesque incidents. Felix St. Bees, the curate, is riding over to the Warren, when he comes upon several workmen who have uncovered a skeleton. At the scene of the discovery he finds the fragment of a Roman trumpet on which is inscribed the one word *Gaudeamus*—"let us rejoice"—and as he continues on his way, St. Bees moralizes on the theme of impermanence. On arriving at his destination he finds Fisher dead in his chair, and the place rifled by two dishonest servant-women who have even stolen the seal-ring from his dead finger and the watch from his fob. When St. Bees goes to a neighbouring shepherd's home to tell of Fisher's death, the news is greeted almost with joy ("Dead! be *he* dead? Missis [to his wife within], missis! The Ould Un have got measter at last" [*GFF*, 230]), whereupon *Gaudeamus* takes on a tragically ironic meaning. And the whole sequence of events is juxtaposed with the extreme beauty of the autumn evening which is in striking contrast to the scene upon which the setting sun is shining.

Greene Ferne Farm is of special literary interest because, despite certain original and experimental aspects to be discussed, it stands firmly in the centre of the rural novel tradition. In many respects it is reminiscent of Hardy's novels; I say "reminiscent" because the most obvious analogies are with Hardy's earlier books which had already been published, and which (though we have no direct proof that Jefferies had read them) may well have influenced the basic structure of the novel. Mr. J. W. Blench has written:

The comparison of this early work with Hardy's *Under the Greenwood Tree* will suggest itself to most readers. Both are short, both follow the revolutions of the seasons as the story progresses, both touch on passing rustic customs, and both end with a country marriage feast. However, although Hardy's is somewhat the more technically polished work, it is less rich in themes.[1]

We may also notice an organizing resemblance to *Far from the Madding Crowd*; both novels concentrate even in their chapter headings on the importance of the relation between plot and background. So Hardy has such chapters as "The Sheep-washing," "The Great Barn and the Sheep-shearers," and "Hiving the Bees"; *Greene Ferne Farm* has "The Nether Millstone," "A-Nutting," "Gleaning." Such titles do not merely indicate the location of the incidents but have a specific bearing upon the development of the plot.

But *Greene Ferne Farm* looks not only back but forward—forward to *The White Peacock* and *The Trespasser* of D. H. Lawrence. Its resemblance to the first of these lies particularly in the division of the *dramatis personae* between the rustic and the sophisticated, and the consequent juxtapositions of genuine rural life with detailed pictures of artificial pastoral. Although Mrs. Estcourt is a farmer, the society of Greene Ferne Farm and the Manor is not primarily rural, though it is not conceived, like its equivalent in *The White Peacock*, as fatally out of contact with the land. The farming community, represented by such characters as Ruck and Hedges, is aware of the difference in approach:

"What's that long chap [Geoffrey] doing at Squire's? He 'as been to Australia."
" 'A be goin' to larn farming."
"Larn farming!" Intense contempt. (*GFF*, 7)

In the haymaking scene Geoffrey and Valentine recite verses concerned, seriously and flippantly, with country life, and the scene looks forward to Lawrence's chapter, "Pastorals and Peonies." *The Trespasser* is anticipated in the scene where Geoffrey and Margaret are forced to spend the night on the Downs. The account of the sunrise, and Geoffrey's emotions on observing it, are of the same rather high-pitched sensitivity as Lawrence's novel, and look forward also, in Jefferies' own writings, to the more disciplined aspiration of Felise in *The Dewy Morn*.

Despite certain conventionalities of character and structure, *Greene Ferne Farm* remains fresh and often original. There is probably no other

1. J. W. Blench, "The Novels of Richard Jefferies," *Cambridge Journal*, VII (March 1954), 367.

novel, for instance, that evokes so elaborately the varied sounds of the
rural year. The first chapter opens to the "Ding-ding-dill! Dill-ding dill!"
of the cracked church bell, and closes with the " 'Cuckoo-cuckoo!' from
the bird on the elm below the hill" (GFF, 1, 25). The second chapter
begins with the "baa-baa!" of young lambs followed by the "crake-crake!"
of the corncrake, then the "coo-coo-coo!" of the doves and the "jug-jug-
jug!" of the nightingale (GFF, 28, 31, 35). The list could be extended, and
there is a significant twist towards the end of the novel when one paragraph opens: "Puff-puff! puff-puff! hum-m-m! The sound of the distant
ploughing engine came humming in the still air" (GFF, 245). So the age
of mechanism makes its contribution to the rural chorus, and is in its turn
absorbed into the country scene.

The book is not primarily a social novel, but Jefferies is too much a
realist to exclude from his narrative the discussion of social problems and
grievances. Squire Thorpe is a kindly, if reactionary, landowner who is
harassed by increasing duties and responsibilities and who declares himself to be "perfectly sick of science and superphosphates, shorthorns and
steam-tackle" (GFF, 240); but he genuinely loves the land and is represented as a decided improvement on some of his ancestors. The farmers in
the book seem prosperous enough—it represents the pre-depression
countryside still enjoying the material rewards of the "high farming"
period—though we are told that some of Mrs. Estcourt's less fortunate
neighbours were unable to meet the demands for higher wages. Jefferies
notes here the significant movement in the farming class towards the
social standards of the landowners, and makes a discontented labourer
remark: "I minds when farmers' daughters was Molly and Marjory, and
no vine Miss about it" (GFF, 203). There is too the labourers' strike in
the novel, and Jefferies writes about their general condition: "It was the
high wages paid in the factories and workshops there [i.e., in Kingsbury,
Jefferies' name for Swindon in this novel] that made the agricultural
labourers discontented; many walked miles daily to and fro to receive
them. There was unfortunately a reverse side to the medal, for the over-
crowded town had become notorious for disease, drunkenness, and misery."
(GFF, 72) It is upon this reverse side to the medal that Jefferies concentrates most of his brief but outspoken social comment. He paints a dismal
picture of a sick ex-shepherd visited in wretched lodgings in Kingsbury
by Geoffrey and St. Bees, who assures them that "I should get better

among the trees" (*GFF*, 80). Jefferies comments that "Geoffrey, who had been to Australia, found he was mistaken in thinking that he had seen the world. There were things here, close to the sweet fields of lovely England, not to be surpassed in the darkest corners of the earth." (*GFF*, 74–5) It is this kind of concern that justifies Mr. Blench's remark quoted above that *Greene Ferne Farm* is richer in themes than *Under the Greenwood Tree*, though Hardy's novel, of course, has other compensations.

The book is clearly not a major achievement, but it has numerous virtues and becomes more impressive at every rereading. Less ambitious than the two fictional works to follow, its attempt to achieve artistic form by means of juxtaposition of themes and moods is sufficiently original to merit attention. *The Dewy Morn* and *Amaryllis at the Fair* are more experimental, but there is more than enough skill and subtlety displayed here to dispose of the common misapprehension that Jefferies lacked the necessary qualities for a serious novelist. The difficulty with these novels is not that they fail to satisfy the more conventional requirements of Victorian fiction, but that they are attempting to break new ground. This becomes even more evident in the last two works.

A notebook entry for the spring of 1878 reads as follows: "Atalanta. Take a classic name: heroine so interesting as to be far more interesting than the plot." (*N*, 32) This note is generally taken to be a first step towards the conception of Felise, heroine of *The Dewy Morn*, and indeed an early version of the novel, now lost, was written in the same year. It is certainly true that, while writing the book as we know it in 1883, Jefferies had this same idea in mind. Thus at the beginning of August he writes: "Felise, a strong character—follow her line, work her out, and there is the book at once without anything else" (*N*, 142), and a month later: "The reader should be so much interested, in love with the heroine, that every little thing she does is pleasant to read of" (*N*, 146). In the finished book, too, the classic name lingers on in simile, and we are told how "she ran as swiftly as Atalanta" (*DM*, I, 90). The later name, Felise, seems to have been borrowed, as Edward Thomas pointed out, from a name-poem in Swinburne's *Poems and Ballads*, and it may well have suggested itself by way of the same writer's *Atalanta in Calydon*.

Certainly the Hellenic references within the novel are all-important. The classic names were eventually abandoned (the hero, Martial Barnard, was originally to be called Adonis!), but the essential Greek tone remains, especially with regard to Felise. Just as the incident in which she runs with the harriers reminds us of Atalanta, so the scene in which Barnard sees her bathing in the pool recalls the story of Diana and Actaeon, though without, of course, the tragic results. Even the tunic in which she bathes "might have been worn by a Grecian maiden" (*DM*, I, 99). In her simplicity, her perfect integration with nature, her combination of strength and beauty, Felise embodies the Greek ideal which is, for Jefferies, perfection. The book opens with her climbing the Downs to see the sunrise, following Jefferies' own habit, but following also the traditional custom of ancient days:

Of old, old time the classic women in the "Violet Land" of Greece went out to the sunrise, and, singing to Apollo, the sun, prayed that their hearts might be satisfied, and their homes secured; by the fountain they asked of the water that the highest aspirations of their souls might be fulfilled; of the earth they asked an abundance for those whom they loved. . . . Felise asked the same as many a deep-breasted maiden in the days of Apollo and Aphrodite. (*DM*, I, 28–9)

We recognize in Felise many of the qualities which have appeared, with less vitality, in earlier portraits—in the Heloise of *Restless Human Hearts* or the Cicely of *Round About a Great Estate*. But the character of Felise is an advance artistically in that her spiritual aspiration is channelled into areas that allow her to become the active centre of a novel of ideas. Jefferies describes her feelings at the opening of the book as follows: "Her whole existence was quivering with love; this intensity of life was love. She was gathering from sunlight, azure sky and grassy fields, from dewy hills and all the morning, an immense strength to love." (*DM*, I, 8–9) During the course of the novel Felise's "strength to love," learnt and derived from nature, expands to include her love for a particular man, Barnard, and her general love for humanity, represented by her sincere and positive sympathy for the rural poor. Felise succeeds in being "the book at once without anything else" because her love is all-embracing, and includes within itself all the themes with which the novel treats. She thus becomes the core of the novel, a central figure who dominates the plot. This is not to deny that there are exterior pressures brought to bear—indeed, it is part of the Classical make-up of the story that Fate, specifically labelled

Sophoclean, takes a hand in events—but the novel as a whole has an organic motivation which the earlier fiction noticeably lacked.

Jefferies communicates the complex nature of Felise's character in the same way that he describes the contemporary agricultural situation : he presents us with a series of "aspects." The opening chapters concentrate upon the spiritual element. There is a rather chilly intensity about the whole scene on the Downs, which is heightened by a lush prose. But Jefferies adds some individualized, human features that set Felise off from the "classic women" of his Greek ideal. Thus she cannot resist touching whatever she sees, and the trait is picked up later in the novel :

An ash-branch stood out to bar her path. She stopped and touched it, and counted the leaves on the sprays; they were all uneven. . . .

Her white hand wandered presently among more blue veronica flowering on the slope of the bank. She did not gather—she touched only, and went on. She touched, too, the tips of some brake, freshly-green, and rising rapidly now day by day. . . .

There was honeysuckle on the hedge above the bank, too far to reach. She took a hawthorn leaf, felt it, and dropped it; then pulled a bennet, or grass-stalk, and dropped that; then pulled a rush, and left it. A lover might have tracked her easily by the footprints on the dewy grass—by the rush thrown down, and by the white handkerchief which she had carried in her hand and unconsciously dropped. (*DM*, I, 3-4)

It is characteristic of Felise that she fails to achieve her prime object through sheer carelessness : "She had started in time to see the sun rise, from [the Down's] summit, but had idled and dallied with flowers and green boughs on the way, and lost the sunrise" (*DM*, I, 9). Her casual, careless qualities temper her effect as representative of feminine perfection.

The next scene emphasizes her physical strength and health. Felise is seen bathing in a private pool and dreaming on its verge. There is a mass of physical detail, but Jefferies' innocent frankness saves it, I think, from the indecorous. Edward Thomas writes : "It is sensuous, without the bold fleshliness of Shakespeare's 'Venus and Adonis,' without the headiness of Keats' 'Eve of St. Agnes,' and without Pater's languor. . . . Of shame there is no touch, in Jefferies or in his reader."[2] And again he adds an individual detail which influences and qualifies our response. On her way to the pool, she pauses and considers her position with regard to Barnard; she determines to force herself upon his attention, and plans possible

2. Edward Thomas, *Richard Jefferies: His Life and Work* (1909), p. 237.

stratagems to encourage their paths to cross. The point is stressed after the rich (perhaps over-rich) description of her lounging on the grass by the bathing pool; our image of perfect womanhood is jolted by her practical determination—"she was thinking how to accomplish her resolution" (*DM*, I, 110). Her methods of implementing this resolution add a further dimension to her character, and there is a charming, individualized naïveté about her attempts to gain her end. Felise is repeatedly revealed within the novel as an individual as well as a type. Edward Thomas made the point when he wrote: "Jefferies is not merely interested in her, but pours out her passion by an intense imaginative act in which she absorbs him, yet retains her individuality; she is virginal, like few heroines, entirely uncorrupted by the author. She is the girl of 'Love in the Valley' seen by a different lover."[3] We may admit that Amaryllis in Jefferies' final fictional work is his most successful female creation because she is less consciously (though not, I think, less truly) a model of Jefferies' convictions, but Felise admirably fulfils her function within the novel, which is to link in one person the human and the ideal. Like the Venus Accroupie in the Louvre, Felise was "an ideal indeed, but real and human" (*FH*, 290). In *The Dewy Morn* these qualities are intentionally indivisible.

It should not be thought, however, that because Jefferies insists on the supremacy of the heroine over the plot the latter is either slight or unimportant. On the contrary, it is well told and carefully constructed, and it will be worth while considering it in some detail to demonstrate Jefferies' gifts for human presentation and significant creation.

Early one spring morning, as we have seen, Felise climbs the Downs to see the sunrise, and to strengthen her capacity for an as yet uncommitted "love"; "she loved," we are told, "before she had seen the object of her love" (*DM*, I, 26). But the object of her love soon appears on horseback in the person of Martial Barnard who is one of the local tenant-farmers. Felise holds him in conversation, and the way in which she conveys her tenderness towards him by the gentle stroking of his horse Ruy is an effect worthy of Lawrence. For a single moment their eyes meet, and it becomes an eternal moment never to be forgotten. But for Barnard it is not love at first sight, or—at least—he does not realize his love at first sight. He has been in love before, but the engagement was broken off when the agricultural depression affected his financial position, and he was delivered

3. Thomas, p. 228.

from a liaison of which he was beginning to tire. Henceforth he sets his mind against love, and the novel concerns the power of Felise's positive love and practical cunning gradually but surely conquering Barnard's negative intellectual decision.

Felise lives with her uncle, Mr. Goring, who owns one of the few pieces of property in the district not in the possession of the local squire, Cornleigh Cornleigh. Goring has a philosophical nature and strong Radical opinions, and he is respected by the local inhabitants as an upholder of public right against the tyranny of the Cornleigh estate. One of his enemies is Robert Godwin, steward of the estate, who is chiefly responsible for the harsh dictatorial rule. It transpires that Godwin, a character totally lacking in imagination and, as Jefferies puts it, "without any redeeming trait" (*DM*, II, 35), is secretly in love with Felise, though he realizes from the start that this love is futile. Barnard is forced to sell his horse Ruy to Godwin to pay his debts, and Felise buys it back for him with her own money, and returns it anonymously. Hereby Godwin realizes her love for Barnard and, in a daring and successful scene of psychological masochism, contrives their meeting on his own grounds so that he may torture himself by observing the growth of their love.

Mary Shaw, Felise's maid, is in love with an agricultural labourer, Abner Brown. Felise discovers that Brown's parents are due to be evicted from their tied-cottage because they are too old for work, and she appeals, unsuccessfully, to both Godwin and Cornleigh to allow them to stay. Mary Shaw later throws herself into the mill-pond, and Barnard, passing at the time, jumps in to save her. The attempt is almost fatal, but Barnard is strengthened by thoughts of Felise until help comes. None the less, Mary Shaw dies a few hours later, but not before giving birth to a child. It transpires that the reason for her suicide was a law of the Cornleigh estate whereby the whole family of any girl having an illegitimate baby is automatically evicted from their home.

The agricultural depression worsens, and Barnard, forced to resell Ruy to Godwin, decides to give up his farm. At this same time, there is a public meeting at which Cornleigh is to be honoured for his alleged services to the community in twenty-five years' parliamentary work (though in all this time he has never opened his mouth in the House). Barnard causes a sensation by making a speech in which he bitterly attacks Cornleigh, Godwin, and the whole system by which the local inhabitants

—labourers, farmers, and merchant-class alike—are at the mercy of the landowning class. At this point Felise's love for Barnard fuses with her other concern—the rights of the poor—which he is championing.

Meanwhile Godwin, believing that Felise must be Barnard's mistress, plans an insane revenge. Attacking Felise in the fields one day, he ties her to the ground and attempts to mutilate her beauty under the hoofs of the horse Ruy. Fortunately Barnard arrives at this moment and shoots Ruy, and the sight of Felise in danger finally persuades him that he loves her. After a violent scene, Godwin goes off and shoots himself (at the very spot where he had attacked Felise, where the body of the horse still lies), and Felise marries Barnard after a scheme is arranged whereby he will oppose Cornleigh at the next election as an independent on the side of reform.

I have narrated the plot in some detail in order to show how skilfully Jefferies has woven the different themes into a whole. It will be noticed, for instance, what an important part is played by the horse in the structure of the novel; he is in his life the unconscious cause of misunderstanding, and in his death finally brings the lovers together. The three rural estates are firmly represented by Cornleigh the landowner, Barnard the tenant-farmer, and Abner Brown the labourer. Mr. Goring is an example of the dying class of independent yeomen, and Felise's qualities of love, beauty, strength, and sympathy cut across all class barriers. Again, the bitterness of Barnard's first lover, Rosa Wood, towards Felise is balanced by God-win's bitterness towards Barnard for which Felise is responsible. There are many examples of artistic balance in the novel. On one occasion, at the opening of the book, Barnard finds the handkerchief that Felise had dropped, just before Ruy is going to tread on it, and this looks forward to the climax when he sees Ruy about to step on Felise herself. Again, Robert Godwin's suicide balances and, to some extent, atones for Mary Shaw's. The novel ends one morning after the marriage with Felise looking out of their bedroom window towards the Downs and the sunrise, the plot thereby coming full circle.

At first it is somewhat difficult to acclimatize oneself to the rich variety of tone. The opening chapter, taking us as it does to the rarefied air at the top of the Downs, seems at a far remove from the bustling reality of the political meeting at Maasbury; the pastoral idyll of Felise's bathing and the love scene in Goring's garden may at first sight seem artificial, the more so since they are juxtaposed with the tragic rural realities of the Browns' eviction and Mary Shaw's suicide. If we read Jefferies properly, however, we shall realize that his essential truth lies in this very juxtaposition of contrasting attitudes. Here at last the differing aspects of the countryside meet between two covers, and we must accept both. On occasions the actual circumstances of the juxtaposition make the point. In her determination to see and win Barnard, Felise pays a visit to his home. This is a crucial point in the love theme, and it is as she is returning that she calls in at the house of Abner Brown and hears the cruel news of the eviction. Just as Bevis first discovered the harsh realities of peasant existence on his "magic" island, so Felise makes a similar discovery when her essentially Romantic love is at its strongest, when she seems furthest away from hard facts.

Similarly, the scenes of the death of Mary Shaw and Godwin's attempt on Felise may seem falsely melodramatic, but in reality are not so. Such scenes of violence do occur in life, and Jefferies includes such circumstances to complete his picture. In fact, each incident is well motivated and psychologically acceptable. Jefferies' aim is truth, and he will not sacrifice it by obeying the needs of "artistry" or by falsifying character. After Godwin shoots himself, Jefferies comments: "Artistically speaking, Robert Godwin ought not to have committed suicide; he should have removed himself in some other way—he might have gone off to America, or disappeared. He rather spoils the narrative, giving a cold deadly sensation to the finale; but he really could not help it—it was his nature." (*DM*, II, 318–19) We may well object to the interpolation of this kind of author's comment, but it does clarify Jefferies' aims and beliefs. Having finally abandoned the burden of a conventional, external plot, he insists on his characters behaving according to their "nature," irrespective of general notions of plot-pattern. His own patterning is achieved with effect, not with formal story. (We never hear what becomes of Mary Shaw's baby, nor even the fate of the Browns.) The process is carried still further, as we shall see, in *Amaryllis at the Fair*.

During the course of the novel, the spiritually inclined Felise learns the important lesson that "if we cannot reach to ideal things, at least we can do much, nearer to earth" (*DM*, I, 34). I have already called the book a social novel, and it is interesting to see how Jefferies, who perfected his own version of the creatively artistic social essay, weaves a propagandist theme into his novel. His aim was to draw attention to the abuses of the property system in the depressed years of the early eighties. He specifically attacks the tied-cottage system and the inhumanity of the Poor Law, and as enthusiastically defends the newly-introduced Ballot Act which was coming under attack from certain quarters. The novel was timely in that it was published in the year the agricultural labourers obtained the suffrage, and the ending looks forward to the first election in which they will cast their votes.

The difficulty with any social novel is its relation to art. If the emphasis is on the social comment, it tends to become a documentary, and the plot is lost in a wealth of description and statistics. If, on the other hand, there is a definite story, the social comment is distorted by the particular (and therefore often untypical) nature of the characters, such as the stock melodramatic types of wicked squire and seduced but innocent maiden. Jefferies avoids both extremes by confining his social comment to particular scenes in the novel which are sufficiently connected with the main story to be acceptable, yet not sufficiently "central" to divert attention from the main plot. Thus the problem of the tied-cottage is introduced when Felise, hearing of the Browns' trouble, takes up the case and escorts old Abner Brown to the magistrate's court to plead with Cornleigh. Apart from its intrinsic interest, we accept this because, as Jefferies says, the reader is so interested in Felise that "every little thing she does is interesting to read of." The defence of the Ballot Act and the general attack on contemporary landowners is put into the mouth of Barnard at the public meeting, and here he is not only speaking his mind but demonstrating by his courage and integrity that he is worthy of Felise.

Nor does Jefferies make the mistake of painting one side completely black and the other completely white. Godwin, though unpleasant, is scrupulously honest, and extremely efficient. He is certainly no Iago-like villain: "I do not think that he intended to be harsh in his dealings with his fellows. It was simply an absolute want of imagination." (*DM*, I, 214) It is the same with Cornleigh. The trouble is not that he is a villain, but that he is an nonentity. Conversely, the sympathetic characters are by no means without faults. Jefferies does not excuse Mary Shaw for having an illegitimate baby, though he does not condemn her either. And old Abner

Brown is not grateful to Felise for doing her best in his case after the unsuccessful appeal to Cornleigh:

In his cottage old Abner was complaining to his wife of Felise's interference and bad management. He was sure he should have got on all right if he had seen the Squire by himself, but she spoilt everything. "Hur would keep talking," he said. "Hur kept on talk, talk, talk." The truth being that he could say nothing for himself, and Felise had explained everything. (*DM*, II, 110)

Jefferies does not altogether condemn this attitude—"For one act of kindness in eighty years, why should they feel grateful?"—but he is forced to add: "A little experience of their ways is sufficient to destroy the interest of the kindest-hearted" (*DM*, II, 111). Even the tenant-farmers come under criticism for not taking a stand against Cornleigh's tyranny, for taking a short- rather than a long-term view. Jefferies also criticizes the labouring classes by implication when he shows how they resent the fact that young Abner Brown earns better wages (under Mr. Goring) than themselves. Because of these minor critical details, we are all the more prepared to accept (and sympathize with) his analysis of the general situation.

The Dewy Morn is a sturdy, humane novel, and it comes down to us as a fitting monument to Jefferies' foresight and sympathetic awareness. Predominantly, it is an advanced novel pointing towards the future, but there are hints too of a more reactionary outlook which should not pass unnoticed. Indeed, this is often most obvious on those occasions when he seems most progressive. Thus his criticism of the Cornleigh estate comes very close to being an attack on the centrality of any form of government. The large "estate" almost develops into a small "state" and, despite his earlier belief that agriculture could only be successful on a large scale, here he is clearly against the centralization of land into large areas because of the exaggerated power that it gives to individuals—especially if the individuals happen to be of the Cornleigh type. There are times, too, when he demonstrates the reactionary's suspicion of the new: "All the improvements which had straitened the old town, depriving it of its pleasant appearance and of its ancient freedom, sprang from Mrs. Cornleigh Cornleigh" (*DM*, II, 51). Cornleigh himself suffers by comparison with his grandfather, who used his power to good effect. Even in Barnard's bitter criticisms of the *status quo* there is as much looking back as forward. "There is nothing sturdy or independent about the British farmer of our day," he says (*DM*, II, 129), and the remark carries implicit reference to a past golden age when the yeomen of England showed the mettle of their pasture. In the very fabric of the novel, the rural traditions and customs stand firm against modern pressures, and Jefferies only criticizes what has become perverted or obsolete; the dead wood must be cut away, but only that the living green may be preserved and strengthened.

The novel is by no means without faults; there are irrelevant digressions, irritating personal comments, and an occasional repetitiveness which strikes a false chord. But such faults are venial, and they are set off by Jefferies' obvious artistic seriousness. Writing in *Scrutiny*, Mrs. Leavis has praised the book in the highest terms: "In *The Dewy Morn* he goes further than any Victorian novelist towards the modern novel—I mean the novel that seems to have significance for us other than as a mirror of manners and morals; I should describe it as one of the few real novels between *Wuthering Heights* and *Sons and Lovers*."[4] This provocative statement refers, I think, to Jefferies' striving towards a plot which is not so much an artistically planned story as an organic whole in which the relationships between the parts are fundamental, though not superficially obvious. A similar point is made (significantly from the same general critical standpoint) by G. D. Klingopulos, who has stressed Jefferies' contribution to "the social deepening of the novel," and a realization of "the moral importance of the underlying, ageless, agricultural pattern."[5] The relation between rural reality and literary art was a problem which dogged Jefferies throughout his writing life, and *The Dewy Morn* represents his most successful attempt to interfuse them. By the time we get to *Amaryllis at the Fair* Jefferies has left any attempt at conventional literary art far behind, with the result that it is meaningless to describe the book as a novel at all. Even in *The Dewy Morn* the difficulties are visible. A notebook entry during its composition reminds him "to go by central incidents" (*N*, 146), and in one of the digressions in the novel itself, where he compares the arts of the novelist and the dramatist, he asks: "Could not you let me write my scenes one after the other, and supply the con-

---

4. Q. D. Leavis "Lives and Works of Richard Jefferies," *Scrutiny*, VI (March 1938), 445.
5. G. D. Klingopulos, "The Literary Scene" in *Pelican Guide to English Literature, 6: From Dickens to Hardy*, ed. Boris Ford (Harmondsworth: Penguin Books, 1958), p. 111.

necting links for me out of your own imagination, as you do on the stage?" (*DM*, II, 175) He dislikes the pedestrian progress of the conventional novel by which the reader is led up to and away from all the important scenes and climaxes. To Jefferies this was an impediment for the true creative artist whose aim was to present reality in its highest manifestation. These doubts and dissatisfactions lead us directly to *Amaryllis at the Fair*.

Amaryllis at the Fair has met with extremely varied critical reactions. Edward Garnett described it as "one of the very few later-day novels of English country life that are worth putting on one's shelf,"[6] and Mrs. Leavis has not hesitated to term it "a masterpiece."[7] On the other hand, David Garnett, though admiring much of the book, called it "a complete failure as a novel,"[8] and along with *Greene Ferne Farm* and *The Dewy Morn* it has been labelled as a failure by several critics including Forrest Reid and, more recently, Peter Coveney. The difficulty can be traced, I believe, not so much to Jefferies' limitations as to the inability of critics to adjust themselves to a bold and original experiment in fiction. It must be admitted, however, that Jefferies did nothing to assist them. The title page of the first edition bears the description "a novel," but it is evident from private correspondence that this was the publisher's decision, not the author's. In a letter to George Bentley, who first considered the manuscript, Jefferies wrote:

I originally intended this book to form a series of scenes from country life and so proposed to call it *Scenes from Country Life*; a title of course suggested by the famous *Scenes from Clerical Life*. The idea of calling it a novel was secondary and in fact it is quite immaterial to me whether (supposing you should like it) you publish it as *Scenes* or as a novel—just as you think best. (*FF*, 42)

We are now in a position to follow Jefferies' clue. To consider the book as an orthodox novel is, I suggest, to play down its strengths and draw attention to its weaknesses. We shall do better to judge it impartially on its own merits.

It will be as well to begin by outlining the action of the book, for this

6. Edward Garnett, *Friday Nights: Literary Criticism and Appreciations* (1922), p. 164.
7. Leavis, 445.
8. David Garnett, Introduction to *After London* and *Amaryllis at the Fair* (Everyman ed. London: Dent, 1939), p. viii.

will reveal at least some of the causes of critical disagreement. It would be misleading to talk about a plot; the book consists of a series of pictures, in which we are given a detailed and moving description of life in the farmhouse at Coombe Oaks. We meet Farmer Iden, a sensitive, educated, intelligent but hopelessly impractical man who can think but cannot act, and is hamstrung by his deep sense of perfection—"Iden was like the great engineer who could never build a bridge, because he knew so well how a bridge ought to be built" (*AF*, 342). We meet Mrs. Iden, hard and dis- illusioned, once a kindly woman but now forced into the role of shrew by the worries of debt and loss. And between them is Amaryllis, poised between girlhood and womanhood, artistic and headstrong, affectionate and generous, trying desperately to please and so to unite her father and mother. On Lady-Day she goes down to the fair in Woolhorton, the nearby town, and visits her grandfather (nicknamed Lord Lardy-Cake and The Behemoth by the locals) who expects his family to gather round him on that day. With him she visits the manor house of the Pamments, but runs away when she considers herself being treated by the heir of the house as a half-an-hour's amusement. Later, we see her working in an attic, nostalgic and meditative, trying unsuccessfully to increase the family's declining income by selling drawings. At last, when the novel is three- quarters through, two new characters appear—Alere Flamma, artist, a relative of Mrs. Iden's, bringing a breath of Fleet Street into the country farmhouse, and Amadis Iden, pale and convalescent, "from Iden Court, over the Downs" (*AF*, 308), and, what is more, "unable to earn a shilling" (*AF*, 343). By the last page Amaryllis and Amadis are falling in love, and they are left together. That is all.

Such a scheme lays itself open to obvious criticisms, but instead of condemning the book for presenting an isolated series of incidents rather than a developing and organic plot, we shall do well to ask ourselves why Jefferies constructed it as he did. A writer with whom he naturally invites comparison, for reasons of subject-matter and contemporaneity, is Thomas Hardy, and a brief contrast between the two will draw attention to Jefferies' peculiar qualities. It may be noted that Jefferies' admirers often compare the two to Hardy's disadvantage. Thus Edward Garnett wrote: "In the respect of the artistic naturalness of its homely picture, the book is very superior to, say, 'The Mayor of Casterbridge,' where we are conscious that the author has been at work arranging and rearranging his charming studies and impressions of the old-world people of Casterbridge into the pattern of an exciting plot."[9] And David Garnett, for all his qualification, considers Iden "the greatest portrait of a countryman in English literature"[10]—a surprise to many who would expect Henchard to be awarded that title.

The essential differences between the two creations is obvious enough. When we first meet Iden, he is planting potatoes, and Amaryllis is watching him:

She watched him stooping till his back was an arch; in fact, he had stooped so much that now he could not stand upright, though still in the prime of life; if he stood up and stretched himself, still his back was bowed at the shoulders. He worked so hard—ever since she could remember she had seen him working like this; he was up in the morning while it was yet dark tending the cattle; sometimes he was up all night with them, wind or weather made no difference. Other people stopped indoors if it rained much, but it made no difference to her father, nor did the deep snow or the sharp frosts. Always at work, and he could talk so cleverly, too, and knew everything, and yet they were so short of money. (*AF*, 206)

This is the real Iden, the complete Iden. He has always been like this ("Ever since she could remember she had seen him like this") and he always will be. We see more of Iden—the well-known fourth chapter where he dozes after dinner and the mice come out and climb up his trouser-leg, and the exquisite scene where he paddles alone at evening in the dew-wet grass—but these details are etched in to the basic portrait which has been fixed from the start.

Henchard, of course, is planned on very different lines. Our first sight of him as a drunken and then repentant hay trusser presents only the seed from which the potential Henchard can grow. The novel as a whole is concerned with the development of his character over a period of time, his rise to mayor and his eventual decline until the wheel has come full circle and he is hay trusser once more. Hardy's distinction lies in his ability to present the whole life of the man, to show him in different moods and at different stages in his life and fortunes, and yet to convince us that the Henchard of the close of the novel is a recognizable and credible development from the Henchard of the beginning. By contrast, Jefferies presents Iden as a fully realized character from the start. He is

9. Edward Garnett, p. 169.   10. David Garnett, p. viii.

arrested at the moment in which we first see him (the whole action is limited to a single spring) and Jefferies deliberately avoids presenting any kind of organic development. The artistic schemes behind the two portraits could hardly be more different.

There can be no doubt, I think, that Jefferies was aiming at a conscious effect here, and a further clue can be gained from a passage on the last page of the book:

I shall leave Amaryllis and Amadis in their Interlude in Heaven. Let the Play of Human Life, with its sorrows and its Dread, pause awhile; let Care go aside behind the wings, let Debt and Poverty unrobe, let Age stand upright, let Time stop still (oh, Miracle! as the Sun did in the Vale of Ajalon). Let us leave our lovers in the Interlude in Heaven. (*AF*, 344)

It must be emphasized at once that the above passage should not be considered as a typical example of Jefferies' style, which is generally far less contrived and rhetorical, and far more natural and direct. But what is significant about the passage is its concern for the "Interlude in Heaven," and its exhortation to "let Time stop still." Here, as so often in Jefferies' work, a knowledge of his personal philosophical ideas is desirable for true appreciation. The passage invites us to consider to what extent the book is affected by Jefferies' ideas about Time and Eternity as expressed in *The Story of My Heart*.

There, in a well-known passage, Jefferies had written:

I cannot understand time. It is eternity now. I am in the midst of it. It is about me in the sunshine; I am in it, as the butterfly floats in the light-laden air. Nothing has to come; it is now. Now is eternity; now is the immortal life. Here this moment, by this tumulus, on earth, now; I exist in it. The years, the centuries, the cycles are absolutely nothing; it is only a moment since this tumulus was raised; in a thousand years more it will still be only a moment. To the soul there is no past and no future; all is and will be ever, in now. (*SH*, 41)

The connection with *Amaryllis at the Fair*, though not immediately obvious, is yet, I am convinced, vital. Jefferies believed that in supreme moments of perception one could experience an "Eternal Now" in which past, present, and future became fused, and full reality (in the Platonic sense) was achieved. One deduction from this would be that artistically human reality is best presented not as a development in time but as a fixed state outside time, and this is, I believe, what Jefferies has attempted in *Amaryllis at the Fair*. It is therefore impossible to discuss or criticize the book by the same standards that we use with traditional novels; it will be more satisfactory to attempt a general commentary on what Jefferies has given us, and then judge the effectiveness of what has been achieved.

It is well known that *Amaryllis at the Fair* is in many ways autobiographical: Mr. and Mrs. Iden are Jefferies' parents, Alere Flamma is his uncle Fred Gyde, Grandfather Iden is his own grandfather, while Amaryllis faces the same difficulties and disappointments that Jefferies faced himself. Coombe Oaks is the Coate Farmhouse of his childhood, which the historical and agricultural developments of the period had altered beyond recall. (It is perhaps relevant to remember here that by the time the book was written Jefferies' father had been forced to sell the house at Coate and give up farming.) But Jefferies has turned what might have been mere nostalgia into something subtler, and far more artistically significant. He has fixed in a permanent record the whole ethos of his childhood, of a vanished age and way of life, condensing it into four or five days chosen apparently at random but in fact designed to reflect back and forth upon each other in order to present a significant cross-section of experience. Thus the unity of the book depends not upon the development of a particular plot to a satisfactory conclusion, but upon the relevance of the particular moments that he has chosen to portray.

It may seem at this point as if we have become involved in a fatal contradiction. I have claimed that the moments which Jefferies portrays form an artistic structure which is fixed eternally outside time, and which has no temporal development within it. Yet the moments themselves (by the very fact that they are *moments*) are, or at least were, in time. The point is that these incidents have a double significance and can be considered from a temporal and an eternal viewpoint, in the same way that we can imagine the Jefferies of *The Story of My Heart* being conscious of the passing of time while in the very act of denying the reality of the concept. Critically, it can be said with equal truth that *Amaryllis at the Fair* takes place in an Eternal Now, and that it is a book about the past. Whatever philosophical difficulties, or even absurdities, this may entail, it remains a paradox that is artistically fruitful. Jefferies gains many of his subtlest effects by maintaining a balance between the temporal and non-temporal approaches to his matter. An examination of the book with such a balance in mind will reveal it as a carefully organized structure.

It begins with Amaryllis finding the first daffodil of Spring, and Jefferies comments:

There had been daffodils in that spot at least a century, opening every March to the dry winds that shrivel up the brown dead leaves of winter, and carry them out from the bushes under the trees, sending them across the meadow— fleeing like a routed army before the bayonets of the east. Every spring for a century at least the daffodils had bloomed there. (*AF*, 201–2)

But Amaryllis does not stay to "think of the century" but turns the corner of the house and comes into contact with the cold east wind, and Jefferies adds: "The wind had blown thus round that corner every March for a century" (*AF*, 202). In this way, he establishes a firm rhythm linking the human protagonists with the rhythms and cycles of nature. (A similar link is established in the opening pages of D. H. Lawrence's *The Rainbow*.) It is a world, we notice, in which the present is very like the past, and the future shows no signs, at least on the non-human level, of being any different. At the same time a situation is created which can be interpreted and appreciated from what I have called the temporal and the non-temporal points of view. The individual daffodil exists at a moment in time, which its subsequent fate (Mrs. Iden tramples it underfoot in a fit of temper) makes sufficiently clear. But the immortality enjoyed by the species, the annual reappearance of the daffodils at the same place in the same season, gives a sense of continuity and permanence to the scene. Although the action takes place at a particular moment, we can imagine it as occurring in any spring. It would have concerned a different Amaryllis and a different daffodil, but the place, the season, the reaction would all have been the same. It is in this sense that I maintain that we can see the incident occurring at a definite moment in the past, yet see it also as a part of the Eternal Now.

A farmhouse like Coombe Oaks is naturally bound to the rhythms of the earth by necessary ties. Such ties are part of the data of the book, but they are thrown into relief by various devices, such as the flower motif that seems to run throughout the narrative. Amaryllis herself provides a connection, for her name means daffodil, and the fate of the daffodil in the first chapter dramatically prefigures her own situation. She is delighted by wild flowers; she gathers them season by season to decorate her bleak and bare attic:

From the woods she brought the delicate primrose opening on the mossy bank among the grey ash-stoles; the first tender green leaflet of hawthorn coming before the swallow; the garden crocus from the grass of the garden; the first green spikelet from the sward of the meadow; the beautiful white wild violets gathered in the sunlit April morning while the nightingales sang. (*AF*, 304)

Here again a definite rhythm is achieved. A similar but subtler effect is gained in the scene where Amaryllis reads to her grandfather. Pressed flowers and leaves which flourished years before lie between the pages of the ancient books:

Among the yellow pages, pressed flat, and still as fresh as if gathered yesterday, Amaryllis found bright petals and coloured autumn leaves. For it was one of the old man's ways to carry home such of these that pleased him and to place them in his books. This had been done for half a century, and many of the flower petals and leaves in the grey old works of bygone authors had been there a generation. . . . The old and grey, and withered man gathered the brightest of petals for his old and grey, and forgotten books. (*AF*, 249)

The effect here is complex indeed. These leaves and flowers provide a meaningful contrast with the living flowers which are mentioned and described throughout the narrative. There is the ironical touch that they are "still as fresh as if gathered yesterday" and so are better preserved than the "old and grey, and withered man" who gathered them. Moreover, I do not think we are reading too much into the passage if we observe that the leaves and petals are preserved and fixed in the pages of the book just as Jefferies has fixed and preserved his childhood days at Coate in the narrative itself.

But this rhythm does not consist merely of a seasonal link between the men and the land. The human life of Coombe Oaks has a ritual of its own which is as constant and inevitable as the natural background against which it is played. The scenes which illustrate this carefully ordered way of life have Iden as the central figure. Most obvious is the scene at the dinner table where even the order of mouthfuls is strictly regulated:

First he ate a piece of the dark brown mutton, this was immediately followed by a portion of floury potato, next by a portion of swede tops, and then, lest a too savoury taste should remain in the mouth, he took a fragment of bread, as it were to sweeten and cleanse his teeth. Finally came a draught of strong ale, and after a brief moment the same ingredients were mixed in the same order as before. His dinner was thus eaten in a certain order, and with a kind of rhythm, duly exciting each particular flavour like a rhyme in its proper position, and duly putting it out with its correct successor. . . . Organization was the chief characteristic of his mind—his very dinner was organized and well planned, and any break or disturbance was not so much an annoyance in itself as destructive of a clever design, like a stick thrust through the web of a geometrical spider. (*AF*, 213)

When dinner is over the daily ritual continues. Iden's picking up his newspaper is a signal for Mrs. Iden and Amaryllis to retire, and he proceeds to take his after-dinner nap. Again the constant repetition of the same actions is emphasized. He takes up his accustomed position with the side of his head resting against the wainscot of the wall:

Just where his head touched it the wainscot had been worn away by the daily pressure, leaving a round spot. The wood was there exposed—a round spot, an inch or two in diameter, being completely bare of varnish. So many nods—the attrition of thirty years and more of nodding—had gradually ground away the coat with which the painter had originally covered the wood. It even looked a little hollow—a little depressed—as if his head had scooped out a shallow crater; but this was probably an illusion, the eye being deceived by the difference in colour between the wood and the varnish around it. (*AF*, 216)

In this case Jefferies takes care to draw attention himself to the potentialities of the image. To Mrs. Iden it is "a mark of devotion . . . to the god of Sleep," though Jefferies comments that the "god of Thought" would have been more accurate (*AF*, 216). But it is much more than this; it is "a cross on which a heart had been tortured for the third of a century" and also represents "the unhappiness, the misfortunes, the Nemesis of two hundred years" (*AF*, 217). Here we may notice yet again the insistence on temporal continuity. This tiny, closely observed detail gradually broadens out until it has become a symbol of both continuity and decay, and is relevant at both the temporal and non-temporal levels. It is the result of a continuous action in an apparently unchanging world—"the attrition of thirty years and more of nodding"—but just as it developed and manifested itself gradually in time, so it bears witness to a slow but continual decline in the fortunes of the farm and its inhabitants. It is only by pondering the implications of such pictures as these (for Jefferies seldom analyses them himself) that we begin to appreciate the subtlety, and the effectiveness, of his art.

Jefferies is quite explicit about his aim in the book. "I have set myself the task," he writes, "to describe a bit of human life exactly as it really is"

(*AF*, 272). This sentence in itself explains his refusal to construct a well-knit plot, which he felt would detract from any realism achieved. "I have read such a lot of silly novels with plots," he wrote in a notebook while *Amaryllis at the Fair* was being planned (*N*, 201). Most of all, his aim prevents a satisfactory or artistically neat ending. Jefferies stresses this point in another important notebook entry:

It is customary with comedists to make things end happily for at least a pair of their friends the characters. We all know so well the dread of poverty that we are not contented unless a pair are well provided at the finish with the good things of life. But this is not always the case in truth, after much pain and suffering, struggle and disappointment, most of us are still unprovided for. And so I must leave Amaryl. still working, watching, yet full of hope. (*N*, 201)

As a seeker after truth, Jefferies was inevitably attracted towards the imperfect and the unfinished, towards what the purists might call "the inartistic." This is a natural outcome of his philosophical ideas. It is clear from *The Story of My Heart* that he saw the world as governed throughout by a neutral Chance (which must not be mistaken for a hostile Fate), and the same outlook is present in *Amaryllis at the Fair* where he discourses on "the Turkish manner":

How crookedly things are managed in this world!

It is the modern fashion to laugh at the East, and despise the Turks and all their ways, making Grand Viziers of barbers, and setting waiters in high places, with the utmost contempt for anything reasonable—all so incongruous and chance-ruled. In truth, all things in our very midst go on in the Turkish manner; crooked men are set in straight places, and straight people in crooked places, just the same as if we had all been dropped promiscuously out of a bag and shook down together on the earth to work out our lives, quite irrespective of our abilities and natures. Such an utter jumble! (*AF*, 239)

So it must be to the end. Amaryllis ought (by the rules of art) to have found a better lover than the kindly but penniless Amadis, and the future ought to promise more than decline and poverty as the Idens slip rung by rung down the social and economic ladder, but it is not to be. Amaryllis and Amadis are happy together in their "Interlude in Heaven," but their future is precarious, and the impression with which we are left is hardly one of optimism. And the earlier image is here repeated: "Could any blundering Sultan in the fatalistic East have put things together for them with more utter contempt of fitness? It is all in the Turkish manner, you see." (*AF*, 343) The romance-names of Amadis and Amaryllis are ironic comments on their situation and prospects.

The insistence upon truth and reality will, of course, have a profound effect not only upon the "matter" of the book, but also upon the characters presented. In spite of the title, the most vivid portrait in the book is Iden, and the contrasts in his character are presented by juxtaposing the thoughts of Mrs. Iden, who is infuriated by his set ways and lack of success, and those of Amaryllis, who loves him for his tenacity and his knowledge, for both his strength and his weakness. Iden is a complex but real character of whom Jefferies was justly proud, but the publishers to whom he first submitted the manuscript questioned the consistency of the portrait; Jefferies replied that it was drawn from life. A distinction must be drawn here between consistency and reality. As Jefferies himself notes, "nothing is consistent that is human" (*AF*, 219). Iden is not a conventional hero acting within a consistent artistic organization; he is a living person.

In his portrait of Amaryllis, Jefferies maintains a skilful balance between the individual and the typical. She bears certain resemblances to Jefferies' earlier heroines, but she is never, as they sometimes are, an explicit model of his feminine ideal. Here again the reason lies in the fact that the book is not a novel, and so Amaryllis is not a novel-heroine. Indeed, Jefferies goes to great lengths to prevent her from being an orthodox heroine. He seems to be particularly conscious here of his idealizing tendency; at one point Amaryllis is shopping at Woolhorton and buys some bloaters as a treat for her mother, and he comments: "A lady whose hand smells of bloaters is not, I hope, too ideal" (*AF*, 284). Moreover he is careful, through subtle touches which we barely notice, to portray her failings as well as her virtues. The scene in Pamment House is a case in point. Grandfather Iden's sycophantic attitude to the young squire annoys her, and we can sympathize; she is a rebel, a republican, and again we can sympathize. But it cannot be denied that her behaviour towards Raleigh Pamment is uncalled for and rude. He may be treating her condescendingly as a temporary amusement, but Jefferies is careful to impress upon us that he behaved politely and courteously. "Now there was nothing in Raleigh's manner to give offence—on the contrary he had been singularly pleasant, respectfully pleasant" (*AF*, 277). When, to her grandfather's extreme annoyance, she dashes out of the picture gallery, Raleigh runs after her and overtakes her, but he "pressed the lock and the door swung open—he could easily have detained her there, but he did not" (*AF*, 277). The scene deepens our understanding of the characters of both the protagonists. On another occasion, hearing a creditor at the door arguing with her mother, Amaryllis "tore downstairs, flushed with passion" and roughly ejected him (*AF*, 294). Yet the man, for all his curtness, had right and reason on his side. Even her kinder actions are not always blameless: her motives for tolerating her grandfather (the hope of reconciling him to her father) are hardly less materialistic than those of the flattering relations whom she despises. Hers is an effective portrait because of her deficiencies as well as her virtues; like Felise, she is humanized by her venial faults.

Finally, there is Grandfather Iden who, next to Iden himself, is the subtlest character in the book. For the most part he appears to Amaryllis and the reader as a "hideous old monster" (*AF*, 256), yet the scene where he enters the room to meet his relatives and passes from chair to chair finding at last that the chair of his son (Iden) is empty, is perhaps the most moving moment in the book:

Amaryllis did not exactly watch him, but of course knew what he was about, when suddenly there was a dead silence. . . .

Dead, ominous silence. You could almost hear the cat licking his paw under the table.

Amaryllis looked, and saw the old man leaning with both hands on the back of his son's empty chair.

He seemed to cling to it as if it was a spar floating on the barren ocean of life and death into which his withered old body was sinking.

Perhaps he really would have clung like that to his son had but his son come to him, and borne a little, and for a little while, with his ways.

A sorrowful thing to see—the old man of ninety clinging to the back of his son's empty chair. His great grey tottery hat seemed about to tumble on the floor—his back bowed a little more—and he groaned deeply, three times. (*AF*, 257)

To obtain a complete view of Grandfather Iden, we must juxtapose this passage with that in which he makes the sycophantic bow to Raleigh Pamment and so stirs up Amaryllis' republican blood. Here is a triumphant vindication of Jefferies' method; we feel that no carefully developed study in the tradition of the novel proper could have equalled the truth of this portrayal.

In this discussion of *Amaryllis at the Fair*, I have concentrated upon those features which relate most clearly and significantly to the rest of Jefferies' work. This approach legitimately emphasizes the book's artistic merits; it is only fair to admit, however, that other features, somewhat less relevant to my purpose, reveal strengths as well as weaknesses. I have said little about Jefferies' style which varies, here as in his other work, between the imaginatively rich and the carelessly awkward. Then there are the "digressions" (sometimes continuing for chapters at a time, like the account of Alere's regular way of life) which can be explained but seldom excused, and the occasions when Jefferies interrupts with personal comment or reminiscence. Sometimes these interruptions are effective, but too often, especially towards the close of the book, the thought becomes naïve and the style turgid. But although these faults must be admitted, they do not seriously damage the whole picture—what Edward Garnett calls the book's "spiritual unity."[11] These rough edges in Jefferies' works are, as we have seen, connected with his artistic theory, and they are an integral part of his creative power. More important is the general tone of the whole, which provides a compelling mixture of vivid life and languid melancholy.

11. Edward Garnett, p. 173.

VII. The Final Essays

IN JEFFERIES' ESSAYS, which represent his most characteristic and distinguished work, there may be discerned a gradual, but no less clear progression. We have already noted the early, factual articles which he contributed to such periodicals as *Fraser's Magazine* and the *Live Stock Journal*. Occasionally there were signs that he was introducing a deeper, more artistic strain into his writing, and studies such as "John Smith's Shanty" gave promise of higher things. But the significant change in his essays comes between *Nature Near London* (1883), the product of his natural observation at and near Surbiton, and the essays collected as *The Life of the Fields* (1884). It can hardly be a coincidence that the fourteen months that separated the publication of these volumes had seen the appearance of *The Story of My Heart*.

The Story of My Heart is a dramatic new departure, for Jefferies makes it clear that he is no longer satisfied with confining his attention to external nature. Henceforth he attempts to explore beyond nature, to search for some hidden inner reality to which the whole rich variety of empirical phenomena conforms. The point is made clearly and eloquently in the late essay, "Nature and Books":

I sit on the thrown timber under the trees and meditate, and I want something more : I want the soul of the flowers.

The bee and the butterfly take their pollen and their honey, and the strange moths so curiously coloured, like the curious colouring of the owls, come to them by night, and they turn towards the sun and live their little day, and their petals fall, and where is the soul when the body decays? I want the inner meaning and the understanding of the wild flowers in the meadow. (*FH*, 49)

Henceforward, observation takes second place to thought, and description gives way to meditation. The study of nature for its own sake is now found to be inadequate. The older Jefferies has recalled Bevis' "secret," the alchemic life-force which distinguishes the living organism from the dead shell. For the rest of his short life Jefferies will pursue this inscrutable will-o'-the-wisp through the treacherous no-man's-land of natural mysticism and eclectic philosophy. The result, thanks to his intellectual honesty and consummate ease of style, is a score of essays which ensure him a worthy and permanent position among Victorian prose writers. The two extremes in Jefferies' personality here become fused. The factual precision of the earlier writing blends with the idealistic intensity of *The Story of My Heart*. The resultant essays avoid the excesses of either ingredient.

An essay which most conveniently illustrates the fruitful connections between the individual strands of Jefferies' thought is "Nature in the Louvre." Written about the same time as *The Story of My Heart*, it is in many ways an unexpected essay to come from Jefferies' pen, though it is safe to forecast that, had he lived, we should have had more writings of this kind. It was not, however, a kind likely to appeal to the Victorian reading public, and the fate of the essay is significant. It was refused, albeit reluctantly, when Jefferies offered it to *Longman's Magazine*. Returning the manuscript, C. J. Longman wrote: "I am sorry to say that I do not find the enclosed quite suited to my magazine. I don't think the general public care much about statues—have a vague impression that they are improper."[1] "Nature in the Louvre" was finally printed in the *Magazine of Art*, but not until September 1887, by which time Jefferies was dead.

He begins by describing how he first entered the collection of sculpture in the Louvre knowing only that the famous Venus de Milo was in the collection. Almost immediately, however, he was confronted by "a statue in the sense in which I understand the word—the beautiful made tangible in human form" (*FH*, 289). This turns out to be the comparatively neglected Venus Accroupie or Crouching Venus. Jefferies proceeds to describe it from all angles, and (a considerably more difficult task) to express in words the effect it had upon his mind. It is at this point that he compares it favourably with the Venus de Medici:

1. Quoted by Samuel J. Looker in his notes to *The Story of My Heart*, p. 132.

Hers is not the polished beauty of the Venus de Medici, whose very fingers have no joints. The typical Venus is fined down from the full growth of human shape to fit the artist's conception of what beauty should be. Her frame is rounded; her limbs are rounded; her neck is rounded; the least possible appearance of fulness is removed; any line that is not in exact accordance with a strict canon is worked out—in short, an ideal is produced, but humanity is obliterated. . . . But here is a woman perfect as a woman, with the love of children in her breast, her back bent for their delight. An ideal indeed, but real and human. Her form has its full growth of wide hips, deep torso, broad shoulders. Nothing has been repressed or fined down to a canon of art or luxury. A heart beats within her bosom; she is love. (FH, 290)

Jefferies sees the difference between the two statues as the difference "between that which expresses a noble idea, and that which is dexterously conventional" (FH, 293). What, we may ask, is this noble idea, this prime requirement for Jefferies in all great art? As far as the Venus Accroupie is concerned, it seems to be that vital combination of body and soul, of the physical and the spiritual, which is so important an argument in The Story of My Heart. At its highest achievement, the art of sculpture can combine the physical ideal of the nude with the supreme spiritual qualities of imagination and aspiration. In other words, the genius of the artist creates in a statue a tangible symbol ("the beautiful made tangible in human form") of this connection between soul and body. The artist's vision is thus communicated to the spectator, who thereupon attains to the aspiration which is cognate with prayer. We can understand, then, why in The Story of My Heart Jefferies laments so strongly the rarity of good sculpture:

I have seen so little good statuary, it is a regret to me; still, that I have is beyond all other art. Fragments here, a bust yonder, the broken pieces brought from Greece, copies, plaster casts, a memory of an Aphrodite, of a Persephone, of an Apollo, that is all; but even drawings of statuary will raise the prayer. These statues were like myself full of a thought, for ever about to burst forth as a bud, yet silent in the same attiude. Give me to live the soul-life they express. The smallest fragment of marble carved in the shape of the human arm will wake the desire I felt in my hill prayer. (SH, 32)

The simile of the bud and the reference to the hill prayer help to remind us of the fact upon which we have not yet commented—that the essay is called "Nature in the Louvre." I have already suggested that the essay is in some ways unexpected from Jefferies, but if we care to examine it, we shall find that it is an extension, not a denial, of the more usual method. Jefferies' attitude to nature does not remain constant and static through-out his writing life; instead it develops and deepens. At length it reaches a position in which the very word "Nature" has changed in meaning from something predominantly rural to something which is mainly ethical and philosophical. Jefferies notes that the statue appears to him even more beautiful at a third visit than it did at first sight. The reason he gives for this is so central to his thought that it must be quoted at length:

Pondering upon the causes of this increasing interest, I began to see that one reason was because it recalled to my memory the loveliness of nature. Old days which I had spent wandering among deep meadows and by green woods came back to me. In such days the fancy had often occurred to me that, besides the loveliness of leaves and flowers, there must be some secret influence drawing me on as a hand might beckon. . . . I was now sitting in a gallery of stone, with cold marbles, cold floors, cold light from the windows. Without there were only houses, the city of Paris—a city above all other cities farthest from woods and meads. Here, nevertheless, there came back to me this old thought born in the midst of flowers and wind-rustled leaves, and I saw that with it the statue before me was in concord. The living original of this work was the human impersonation of the secret influence which had beckoned me on in the forest and by running streams. She expressed in loveliness of form the colour and light of sunny days; she expressed the deep aspiring desire of the soul for the perfection of the frame in which it is encased, for the perfection of its own existence. (FH, 297–8)

It is important to realize that Jefferies' enthusiasm for Greek and Roman sculpture is not an isolated matter; it is clear that his appreciation of the natural world and his delight in the best in Classical art are related parts of a single process. There are several links to be noted here. Jefferies' ideal of womanhood, which we have seen presented in his fiction, is identical with the "Nature" that he finds in the Louvre. When creating fictional heroines, Jefferies may be viewed as a Pygmalion bringing life and move-ment to the Venus Accroupie, and it is not an accident that most of them are likened from time to time to antique statues or praised as worthy models for a sculptor's chisel.

Moreover, he seems to have imagined himself facing the same artistic problems as the sculptor of the Venus Accroupie. Words may not be as tangible as stone, but Jefferies strove that his best prose should manifest the same qualities as the statue, that it should be ideal but at the same time real and human, that it should "indicate a glowing life" (*FH*, 295). Gazing at the natural beauty of the Venus Accroupie, he exclaims:

Here is the difference between genius and talent. Talent has lined the walls with a hundred clever things, and could line miles of surface; genius gives but one example, and the clever things are silenced. Here is the difference between that which expresses a noble idea, and that which is dexterously conventional. The one single idea dominates the whole. Here is the difference, again, between the secret of the heart, the aspiration of the soul, and that which is only the workmanship of a studio ancient or modern. (*FH*, 293)

The important sentence here is "the one single idea dominates the whole," for this is also true of the best of Jefferies' essays, and it is something which was not a noticeable feature of his earlier writing. Henceforth, however, we encounter a new artistry which is conscious of imposing an acceptable, satisfying unity on the material. Moreover the emphasis comes to rest on what Jefferies here calls "the secret of the heart, the aspiration of the soul," and this takes first place over the generous variety of nature in Jefferies' hierarchy of values.

The new strengthening and deepening of his approach may be readily seen with reference to the essay which for me represents Jefferies at his greatest—"A Roman Brook." It is appropriate to choose this essay for comment, because Jefferies had treated the subject on two earlier occasions, and it becomes, as it were, a case-book of his literary progress. The locality described was situated within two miles of Coate Farmhouse, and Jefferies had given a brief, journalistic account of it in his "History of Swindon" (*Jefferies' Land*):

Somewhat more than a mile from Lower Wanborough, near Stratton St. Margaret, is a place known as Wanborough Nythe. This may have been once a Roman station, the site of which was upon Covenham Farm, near to the edge of the Nythe brook. Numerous remnants of the Roman occupation have been found here—chiefly coins. . . . (*JL*, 115)

This is neither better nor worse than the average guide-book; it gives the broad facts, and that is all. In *The Gamekeeper at Home*, an incident which occurred at the spot is recounted:

Skeletons are found in all manner of places. I recollect seeing one dug out from the bank of a brook within two feet of the stream. The place was perhaps in the olden time covered with forest . . . and therefore more concealed than at present. Or, possibly, the stream, in the slow passage of centuries, may have worn its way far from its original bed. (*GH*, 52)

Again the treatment is commonplace, though the antiquarian discovery is given not merely as a historical record but as a matter of rural interest. In "A Roman Brook," however, the centre of attention is the brook itself. Jefferies has seen new possibilities in the old subject, and the plain facts become a mere starting-point from which the creative imagination can take wing. The detail and the antiquities are secondary to a presentation of the actual scene in all its beauty and reality:

The brook has forgotten me, but I have not forgotten the brook. Many faces have been mirrored since in the flowing water, many feet have waded in the sandy shallow. I wonder if anyone else can see it in a picture before the eyes as I can, bright, and vivid as trees suddenly shown at night by a great flash of lightning. All the leaves and branches and the birds at roost are visible during the flash. It is barely a second; it seems much longer. Memory, like the lightning, reveals the pictures in the mind. (*LF*, 53)

Here is the characteristic theme of personal reminiscence linked with that of the indifference of nature. The picture in the mind, sharp and momentarily fixed as in a lightning-flash, reminds us of the "eternal Now" of *The Story of My Heart* and the series of significant moments through which the intense reality of *Amaryllis at the Fair* is achieved. Again we realize that Jefferies' intention is to fix the fleeting moment, to catch on paper the vigour and movement of the natural scene. There follows a beautiful and detailed description of the surging life of the brook—fish, plants, birds, animals. "The life as it were of the meadows seemed to crowd down towards the brook in summer, to reach out and stretch towards the life-giving water" (*LF*, 54). The details are not, as in his earlier work, arbitrary. He is not attempting merely to convey the undisciplined richness of nature. Instead, every observation, every word, is as a single piece in a mosaic which, when complete, will perfectly recreate a significant "picture in the mind." Nor are the human inhabitants neglected, for Man is essentially a part of nature. The peasant girls come down to bathe, and the village children accompany them:

Always the little children came with them; they too loved the brook like the grass and birds. They wanted to see the fishes dart away and hide in the green flags: they flung daisies and buttercups into the stream to float and catch awhile at the flags, and float again and pass away, like the friends of our boyhood, out of sight. . . . All life loved the brook. (*LF*, 55)

Even within the picture, the theme of reminiscence, of recreating the vanished past, is not forgotten.

We are later told of the finding of Roman pottery and coins, and this too is brought into the artistic design, for here is a record of life centuries before even the lost "friends of our boyhood." And Jefferies' account of the Roman station is packed tight with significant interest:

Fifteen centuries before there had been a Roman station at the spot where the lane crossed the brook. There the centurions rested their troops after their weary march across the downs, for the lane, now bramble-grown and full of ruts, was then a Roman road. There were villas, and baths, and fortifications; these things you may read about in books. They are lost now in the hedges, under the flowering grass, in the ash copses, all forgotten in the lane, and along the footpath where the June roses will bloom after the apple blossom has dropped. (*LF*, 56–8)

"These things you may read about in books." As mere facts they are no longer of any interest to him, yet in his earlier work facts provided the main content. Here he is only concerned with the interaction of time and the timeless, of change and sameness, progress and retrogression. But it is in the last brilliant paragraph that all the pieces are fitted into the mosaic, and the recreation of the experience—a very simple but moving experience —is complete. The incident of the skeleton recurs not as a piece of rural gossip but as an organic component of the artistic mood. Despite the link of subject-matter, the Jefferies of *The Gamekeeper at Home* is unrecognizable:

The old man, seeing my interest in the fragments of pottery, wished to show me something of a different kind lately discovered. He led me to a spot where the brook was deep, and had somewhat undermined the edge. A horse trying to drink there had pushed a quantity of earth into the stream, and exposed a human skeleton lying within a few inches of the water. Then I looked up the stream and remembered the buttercups and tall grasses, the flowers that crowded down to the edge; I remembered the nests, and the dove cooing; the girls that came to dip, the children that cast their flowers to float away. The wind blew the loose apple bloom and it fell in showers of painted snow. Sweetly the greenfinches were calling in the trees: afar the voice of the cuckoo came over the oaks. By the side of the living water, the water that all things rejoiced

in, near to its gentle sound, and the sparkle of sunshine on it, had lain this
sorrowful thing. (*LF*, 58)

The skeleton is not merely a skeleton, not merely a Roman remain. Without being anything so definite or didactic as a symbol, it none the less
conveys that feeling of sadness amid joy, of death amid life, which gives
the whole essay its imaginative strength. The lightning-flash has revealed
its picture.

But the change from the earlier writings lies not only in increased richness of thought, but in the more subtle use of art which is especially
evident here. In this final paragraph, all the previous subjects recur—the
grasses, the flowers, dove, girls, and children—but these are shown to be
not merely random observations but integral parts of a finished design.
And this design, though made up of essentially natural objects, is just as
essentially an artificial design. For it is imposed from without, a considered artefact of the author's mind. Jefferies has realized that, admirable
as it is, the completely objective approach has severe and undesirable
limitations. He had implied this in the introduction to *Nature Near London* when he pointed out that "no two persons look at the same thing
with the same eyes" (*NNL*, iv). For Jefferies this was both his despair and
his glory, though he may not have been aware at this time of the full
implications of the remark as far as his own literary technique was concerned. Yet, as we shall see when we come to consider "My Old Village,"
it is this very problem—the relation between the subject seeing and the
object seen, together with the influence of the former upon the latter—
that underlies all his major work.

"A Roman Brook" is a short essay gathered with two others under the
general title "Bits of Oak Bark." One, "The Legend of a Gateway," is a
trivial and unsuccessful attempt at a supernatural short story, but the other,
"The Acorn-Gatherer," is of special interest for its use of simple but
successful patterns of imagery to strengthen the central theme. Here
Jefferies returns to a consideration of the human inhabitants of the countryside; like "One of the New Voters," it is an artistic presentation of a
rural problem, and Jefferies has succeeded in imposing a form upon his
material which brings home the facts of the case with particular effect.
The essay begins with the simplest of statements: "Black rooks, yellow oak

leaves, and a boy asleep at the foot of the tree" (*LF*, 43). Here Jefferies does not even allow a verb to disturb the stillness and serenity of the scene. But beneath this idyllic rural picture lies the harsh reality of human poverty and neglect. Jefferies describes the young acorn-gatherer closely, especially his frown, in fixed lines "like the grooves in the oak bark" (*LF*, 43). Thus Man is linked to nature, human flesh described in terms of the tree which provides his livelihood. By contrast we are told how "the happiest creatures in the world are the rooks at the acorns" (*LF*, 43), unlike the boy for whom acorns represent the bitterness of labour. An old woman arrives on the scene, and, finding the boy asleep, beats him with an ash-stick for his laziness. Again we notice the linking of Man with nature, human flesh in contact, this time, with ash. The scene is beautifully conveyed in terms of sound: "Caw! Caw! Thwack, thwack, bang, went the ash stick on the sleeping boy, heavily enough to have broken his bones" (*LF*, 44). Gradually we are told of the boy's history, how he was the illegitimate son of the old woman's daughter, how his mother was dead and his drunken father neglected him, and how he was brought up with heartless severity by his grandmother. One day he vanishes, and no one really cares when his body is recovered from a nearby canal. He had fallen into the water while fishing with an ash sapling, his legs having become entangled in the line; and so the wood that had been his punishment at work becomes the death of him at play. Jefferies makes the final and uncompromising comment:

This was the end; nor was he even remembered. Does any one sorrow for the rook, shot, and hung up as a scarecrow? The boy had been talked to, and held up as a scarecrow all his life: he was dead, and that is all. As for granny, she felt no twinge: she had done her duty. (*LF*, 47)

The whole effect of the story lies in the economy of reference and comment. It is told simply in terms of boy, rook, and wood, and despite the obvious opportunity for preaching or moralizing, Jefferies wisely leaves well alone; the mere hint is enough. The tale speaks for itself, and though slight, is perfect in its kind.

In "The Pageant of Summer," which is generally considered to be Jefferies' finest piece of work, we encounter his most impassioned attempt to pierce through to "the soul of the flowers." Here his outstanding qualities can be seen most clearly. He begins with a description not of the conventionally lovely or the brilliantly exotic, but of an ordinary hedge-row such as we would generally pass by with no more than a glance: "Green rushes, long and thick, standing up above the edge of the ditch, told the hour of the year as distinctly as the shadow on the dial the hour of the day. Green and thick and sappy to the touch, they felt like summer, soft and elastic, as if full of life, mere rushes though they were" (*LF*, 59). His intention is to convey the essence of the experience as well as the essence of the external scene. Summer is to be condensed on to the paper not as a dried flower is set in a herbarium, a dead museum-piece, but living and quick. Consequently the familiar and ordinary must be the centre of attention. Imaginative realism is linked with profound simplicity—"they felt like summer"—which adds up to what Richard Church, in an ex-cellent phrase from his *Memorial Lecture*, called Jefferies' "physical vision." [2]

This physical vision combines the subjective with the objective. Jefferies is presenting human reality rather than the reality of Nature. In these mature essays he is no longer the objective reporter, the faithful "camera" that he had been in the earlier books. "The Pageant of Summer" is a brilliant and accurate evocation not of the natural world but of the effect on the sensitive mind at the moment of experiencing the natural world. Again he is attempting to catch and preserve the fleeting moment as it passes, to fix the eternity which is about him in the sunshine.

There is no less natural observation in this essay than in the earlier, more straightforward work. There are passages on the rushes, on humble-bees, on bird-song and flower colour, which could hardly be equalled in, say, *Wild Life in a Southern County*. But there is more besides. Realizing that it is the human mind which, in a sense, creates order out of the prolific chaos of nature (Jefferies is especially conscious of what he calls "Nature's waste"), he penetrates the surface to discover the generalized but no less vivid reality. So he tries to locate and present the essence of summer:

Winter shows us Matter in its dead form, like the Primary rocks, like granite and basalt—clear but cold and frozen crystal. Summer shows us Matter chang-ing into life, sap rising from the earth through a million tubes, the alchemic power of light entering the solid oak; and see! it bursts forth in countless leaves.

2. Richard Church, *Richard Jefferies Centenary Memorial Lecture* (1948), p. 10.

Living things leap in the grass, living things drift upon the air, living things are coming forth to breathe in every hawthorn bush. No longer does the immense weight of Matter—the dead, the crystallized—press ponderously on the thinking mind. The whole office of Matter is to feed life—to feed the green rushes, and the roses that are about to be; to feed the swallows above, and us that wander beneath them. So much greater is this green and common rush than all the Alps. (*LF*, 61)

The passage raises many opportunities for commentary. We see how subtly he brings Man into the process in the penultimate sentence, firmly but unobtrusively stressing the constant underlying theme, Man's creative and positive relation to nature. We may also notice the selective artistry by which the generalized comment is referred back to the particularized rushes and roses from which it originally sprang; the stylistic unity by which the cumulative phrases commencing with the refrain "living things" imitate the central idea of the sap rising from the earth; and the paradoxical contrasts prominent throughout his work (whether as reporter or "mystic") between winter and summer, matter and spirit, life and death.

But it suggests, too, how the intellectual foundations of the essay give Jefferies' habit of random and apparently arbitrary detail (often called his cataloguing) a new interest and a new justification. In this varied and beautiful "pageant," a pageant not merely of summer but of life, there can be no irrelevant or unworthy players. Jefferies lists them faithfully and with love, and they pass across his pages effortlessly, inevitably—and at random. Dandelions, blackbird, kingfisher, buttercups, fern, meadowsweet, sedges—the list goes on and on, and at the end of the paragraph Jefferies comments: "As I write them, so these things come—not set in gradation, but like the broadcast flowers in the mowing-grass" (*LF*, 74). We accept this statement without question, not recognizing it as either an excuse or an explanation. There can be nothing out of place in summer's pageant: "Without the blackbird, in whose throat the sweetness of the green fields dwells, the days would be only partly summer. Without the violet all the bluebells and cowslips could not make a spring, and without the blackbird, even the nightingale would be but half welcome." (*LF*, 79–80) Jefferies' vision is a whole; eliminate the variety and the disorder, and there would be no summer and no pageant. What was once, in the country books, a new and refreshing non-literary device now gains an intellectual and artistic backing which invests it with new life and possibility.

It is a pageant in time and a pageant in eternity. The present, he says, reminds us of the past, reminds us of "how many other pageants of summer in old times" (*LF*, 76–7). And again: "All the days that have been before, all the heart-throbs, all our hopes lie in this opened bud" (*LF*, 77). Just as the world of nature in some mysterious, alchemical way draws life out of dead matter—"earth made into life," as he calls it in another of his simple, vivid phrases (*LF*, 62)—so Man draws from nature life, inspiration, and hope. In the magnificent final paragraph he conveys something of his hardly won faith:

I seem as if I could feel all the glowing life the sunshine gives and the south wind calls to being. The endless grass, the endless leaves, the immense strength of the oak expanding, the unalloyed joy of finch and blackbird; from all of them I receive a little. Each gives me something of the pure joy they gather for themselves. . . . Feeling with them, I receive some, at least, of their fulness of life. (*LF*, 80)

A pageant relies upon spectators, and this is no exception; what is more, it is able to convey to its watchers something of its power.

For sheer artistry, however, it is difficult to think of any essay to equal "Sunlight in a London Square," and the title is enough to remind us that Jefferies' interests were by no means confined to the rural scene. It is a tribute to his range that such an essay can rank among his finest achievements. He is, indeed, unique among our rural writers for his deep sensitivity to the city.

We have just been considering the pageant of summer in the country, and this essay does the same thing for the town. "There are days now and again," it begins, "when the summer broods in Trafalgar Square." Something of the effect experienced is conveyed to the reader in Jefferies' direct and limpid prose:

Not only from the sun—one point—but from the entire width of the visible blue the brilliant stream [of light] flows. Summer is enclosed between the banks of houses—all summer's glow and glory of exceeding brightness. The blue panel overhead has but a stray fleck of cloud, a Cupid drawn on the panel in pure white, but made indefinite by distance. The joyous swallows climb high into the illuminated air till the eye, daunted by the glow, can scarce detect their white breasts as they turn. (*LF*, 257)

Here once again Jefferies' selective imagination is at work. The scene in the square is conveyed with reference to three objects in the air above the square—first the sun, then the fleck of cloud, then the wheeling swallows. These are the first and most important images with which we are faced. Later, Jefferies describes the scene in detail, and goes on, as by now we might expect, to draw a generalized, meditative conclusion: "If the light shall thus come in, and of its mere loveliness overcome every aspect of dreariness, why shall not the light of thought, and hope—the light of the soul—overcome and sweep away the dust of our lives?" (*LF*, 259) But immediately he returns to the original images of sun, fleck of cloud, and swallow, though this time, with symphonic variation, he considers them in the reverse order:

I stood under the portico of the National Gallery in the shade looking south-wards, across the fountains and the lions, towards the green trees under the distant tower. Once a swallow sang in passing on the wing, garrulous still as in the time of old Rome and Augustan Virgil. . . . Away in the harvest field the reaper, pausing in his work, had glanced up at the one stray fleck of cloud in the sky, which to my fancy might be a Cupid on a blue panel, and seeing it smiled in the midst of the corn, wiping his blackened face, for he knew it meant dry weather. . . . It was a sign to him of continued sunshine and the prosperity of increased wages. The sun from whose fiery brilliance I escaped into the shadow was to him a welcome friend; his neck was bare to the fierceness of the sun. His heart was gladdened because the sky promised him permission to labour till the sinews of his fingers stiffened in their crooked shape (as they held the reaping hook), and he could hardly open them to grasp the loaf he had gained. (*LF*, 259–60)

The scene, and the three selected images, have set Jefferies thinking. His mind wanders, as ever, towards a future when the miseries of the world will be lessened, when all will be able to enjoy what he himself called "sun-life." We realize that the selected images were not arbitrarily chosen—each has a specific meaning and suggestion: "To look backwards with the swallow there is sadness, to-day with the fleck of cloud there is unrest; but forward, with the broad sunlight, there is hope" (*LF*, 260). And the essay ends on a characteristic note of hope, a plea that the light of the sun may enter into the lives of the future. Like D. H. Lawrence after him, Jefferies lamented the drabness of so many ordinary lives. "Sunlight in a London Square" is a plea for a Mediterranean colour, as realized in the paintings of the National Gallery—" a canvas painted under Italian skies, in glowing Spain, in bright Southern France" (*LF*, 260). And so we understand why this particular meditation is set in Trafalgar Square. Everything is right. The feeling for colour and artistic detail is inspired by the National Gallery, the feeling for humanity suggested by the jostling crowds, the recollection of the countryside conjured up by the swallow, cloud, and sun. Out of the chaos of sense-impressions, Jefferies' meditative mind has created order. Transferred to the printed page, this order takes on the satisfying and mature form of a finished work of art.

No serious discussion of Jefferies can afford to end without a consideration of his final dictated essay, "My Old Village." Not that it offers particular scope for general discussion of his typical artistic method; on the contrary, it is exceptional in its tone of ironic melancholy and casual reminiscence. At the same time it maintains a firm unity through the steady influence of Jefferies' own personality. One gains the impression that he is well aware of his approaching death, that he is speaking out calmly and finally in an easy but deliberate prose that carries a distinct authority. It was an appropriate, if obvious, gesture on Mrs. Jefferies' part to print this as the closing essay in the posthumous volume, *Field and Hedgerow*, for it is in many ways a summing up of his whole work. Just as we traced in *The Amateur Poacher* ideas and themes which look with confidence towards a creative future, so "My Old Village" contains within itself almost all the interests and attitudes which occupied Jefferies in his all-too-brief spell of literary production.

The opening is abrupt and dramatic; news of the death of an agricultural labourer whom he once knew well takes Jefferies' thoughts back to his native Coate:

"John Brown is dead," said an aged friend and visitor in answer to my inquiry for the strong labourer.

"Is he really dead?" I asked, for it seemed impossible.

"He is. He came home from his work in the evening as usual, and seemed to catch his foot in the threshold and fell forward on the floor. When they picked him up he was dead."

I remember the doorway; a raised piece of wood ran across it, as is commonly the case in country cottages, such as one might easily catch one's foot against if one did not notice it; but he knew that bit of wood well. The floor was of brick, hard to fall on and die. He must have come down over the crown of the hill, with his long slouching stride, as if his legs had been half pulled away from his body by his heavy boots in the furrows when a ploughboy. He must have turned up the steps in the bank to his cottage, and so, touching the threshold, ended. He is gone through the great doorway, and one pencil-mark is rubbed out. (*FH*, 348)

It is a melancholy opening, but a news of death which brings back all the half-forgotten details of a bygone life. The description of the rural cottage in the paragraph quoted is reminiscent of *The Gamekeeper at Home*, but the fact of death has suffused a human association over the bald detail. The floor, we are told bluntly, was of brick, and this is the directness of the early Jefferies, but it is also "hard to fall on and die," and this addition is enough to introduce a dignified simplicity into the whole passage. The last sentence is an instance of Jefferies' frequent, though by no means invariable, verbal sensitivity. He uses a dulled and pompous cliché, but the shift of emphasis in context (the *great* doorway in contrast to John Brown's little one) and the subsequent suggestion of pointlessness ("one pencil-mark is rubbed out") gives it new life and establishes an appropriate mood of homely yet not undignified grief.

There follows a short account of John Brown's life, with a description of how he used to frighten the boys by telling them local ghost-stories. But now, as Jefferies observes, times are changed: "The ghosts die as we grow older, they die and their places are taken by real ghosts" (*FH*, 351). These real ghosts are his memories of the dead, and in imagination he recreates his own village, Coate, as it was in his youth a quarter of a century before. With the casual remark, "houses grow to their owners" (*FH*, 352), he initiates a series of vivid portraits from the past, in which the connection between man and environment is woven into the stuff of his description. Thus we learn of the sly and secretive Job:

Job had a lot of shut-up rooms in his house and in his character, which never seemed to be opened to daylight. The eaves hung over and beetled like his brows, and he had a forelock, a regular antique forelock, which he used to touch with the greatest humility. There was a long bough of an elm hanging over one gable just like the forelock. His face was a blank, like the broad end wall of the cottage, which had no window. (*FH*, 352)

All this is told in the early manner, but with a new depth and feeling. There follows an account of the changes in the district that I have already had occasion to quote (see p. 22), and this gradually develops into a general meditative survey of the obliteration of his own past. In the following passage Jefferies rises to a new and noble eloquence:

I think I have heard that the oaks are down. They may be standing or down, it matters nothing to me; the leaves I last saw upon them are gone for ever-more, nor shall I ever see them come there again ruddy in spring. I would not see them again even if I could; they could never look again as they used to do. There are too many memories there. The happiest days become the saddest afterwards; let us never go back, lest we too die. (*FH*, 359)

The memories that he conjures for himself are painful enough; the reality would be unbearable. Jefferies knows that they cannot be as they once had been, because he cannot be as he once had been. Since he has changed, the landscape must also change with him. Again the problem of Man's relation to nature is raised in veiled form:

The brooks have ceased to run. There is no music now at the old hatch where we used to sit in danger of our lives, happy as kings, on the narrow bar over the deep water. The barred pike that used to come up in such numbers are no more among the flags. The perch used to drift down the stream, and then bring up again. The sun shone there for a very long time, and the water rippled and sang, and it always seemed to me that I could feel the rippling and the singing and the sparkling back through the centuries. The brook is dead, for when man goes nature ends. I dare say there is water there still but it is not the brook; the brook is gone like John Brown's soul. (*FH*, 360)

Gently, unobtrusively, Jefferies is returning to all his old themes, and it is as if, approaching death, he sees the old problems with a new clarity. "When man goes nature ends." Even in negation the two are linked. And Jefferies does not flinch from the difficulties; the last sentence is as close as he ever comes to a denial of conventional immortality.

The essay flows easily and inevitably. After more reminiscences and stories from the past, we are confronted with a story of a lost city in the desert, not unlike Bevis' story of the land that had no "other side." When travellers return from the city they have discovered, they find that they have been away not a month or two, as they had thought, but twenty years. In old age they set out once more in search of the lost paradise, but they can no longer find it, and they die in the desert. The story is recounted because it was one of the tales told in past days. At first sight it may seem a rambling digression, and Jefferies himself gives no indication that it is anything more, but we soon realize that it is in fact a parable of his own plight. Jefferies at the close of his life is searching back for his own lost paradise, wondering whether this too was not an illusion—a mirage of the desert. We notice, however, that he is searching back only in his imagination; he refuses the invitation to return to his native home, lest he find that the imagination and the facts do not tally :

I might find the trees look small, and the elms mere switches, and the fields shrunken, and the brooks dry, and no voice anywhere. Nothing but my own ghost to meet me by every hedge. I fear lest I should find myself more dead than all the rest. And verily I wish, could it be without injury to others, that the sand of the desert would rise and roll over and obliterate the place for ever and ever. (*FH*, 365)

This is the price of idealization. Just as *Bevis* was not Jefferies' childhood, but his childhood as it might have been, so perhaps the Wiltshire countryside which he has left behind him for ten years has been altered by his imagination out of all recognition. Consequently he renounces the fact in favour of the picture in the mind, and once again we notice the unifying effect of the metaphorical language : his fear of meeting his own ghost recalls John Brown's supernatural stories, and the "sand of the desert" points the connection with the tale of the lost city.

But the suspicion that he may have deceived himself still rankles, and in the final paragraph of the essay Jefferies imagines himself facing a band of sceptics who ask "Are you quite certain that such a village ever existed?" (*FH*, 365). He realizes, sadly but firmly, the weakness of his case:

I begin to think that my senses have deceived me. It is as they say. No one else seems to have seen the sparkle on the brook, or heard the music at the hatch, or to have felt back through the centuries; and when I try to describe these things to them they look at me with stolid incredulity. No one seems to understand how I got food from the clouds, nor what there was in the night, nor why it is not so good to look at it out of window. They turn their faces away from me, so that perhaps after all I was mistaken, and there never was any such place or any such meadows, and I was never there. (*FH*, 366)

It is as if Jefferies were acknowledging defeat, admitting a fault at the very foundations of his work. But the final sentence of all rises from the bedrock of faith that we invariably find even in his least optimistic writings; with a confident sarcasm he boldly reaffirms the original vision : "And perhaps in course of time I shall find out also, when I pass away physically, that as a matter of fact there never was any earth" (*FH*, 366).

I have quoted generously while considering this last essay, for only by so doing can anything like the full force of Jefferies' effects be appreciated. Most impressive is, I think, the emotional unity of the whole, reinforced as it is by the discipline of art and an enviable ease of style. Second only to this, however, is his ability to raise profound problems and make important statements without appearing to veer from an effortless simplicity. For the concern of the last paragraphs of "My Old Village" is a typical instance of the general concern which underlies his whole work. The early Jefferies—whom I have called Jefferies the reporter—was concerned with fact, with reproducing, without any distortion or elaboration, what was seen by the eye. But, as Thoreau has written, "there is no such thing as pure *objective* observation. Your observation, to be interesting, *i.e.,* to be significant, must be subjective." [3] Jefferies made a related discovery—that the eye was inadequate for the understanding of what truly is. It is only one of the five senses, and there was much, he realized, beyond the scope of all the senses combined. Only an imaginative treatment would convey some suggestion of the outer beams of the spectrum—what exists beyond nature, and what affects sight behind the eye. Jefferies' later work, whether in the lyrical outpourings of *The Story of My Heart,* the depths of insight in "The Pageant of Summer," or the carefully isolated moments of *Amaryllis at the Fair,* attempts to fuse the picture in the mind with the picture before the eye, to link the soul with the flowers. That phrase from "Nature and Books," "the soul of the flowers," demonstrates the importance of literary technique in forging this link, but ultimately the problem is deeper than this. At times the connection between the two worlds, the inner and outer landscapes, may seem so tenuous as to be non-existent. They may seem two distinct worlds, one of imagination, one of fact, as they seem to the sceptics at the close of "My Old Village." But the essential connection remains—Man. It is Man alone who can walk within the landscape of fact and at the same time create out of its varied elements a consistent and satisfying landscape of true reality in the mind. And it is Jefferies' success in this complex role that we celebrate. We call the region around Coate farmhouse "Jefferies' Land" not merely because it was the country about which he wrote but because, in a very real sense, it was the country that he himself created. He has taught

3. Odell Shepard (ed.), *The Heart of Thoreau's Journals* (Boston: Houghton Mifflin, 1927), p. 195.

us to view it as nearly as possible with his eyes which, we are ready to admit, are keener than our own. But it must be emphasized that Jefferies saw not merely with but through the eye, according to the Blakean distinction. It is not only that we see with Jefferies' eyes; what we see with and through them is his own personal vision. It is for this reason that we may talk of his "vision" in the double sense, because it is through creative vision that fact becomes reality.

And so, after a long and painful struggle, the junior reporter on the *North Wilts Herald* qualifies for a place in the distinguished company that have made a permanent contribution to English prose literature. Observation and creative vision combine. Jefferies transcended the limitations of the reporter because he learnt to feel as well as see, and this gives warmth and vitality to his prose; he might well have claimed with Wordsworth that "all my thoughts / Were steeped in feeling." By insisting that even the most commonplace of natural phenomena are "supernatural" and wonderful, he can acceptably combine the role of hardened realist with that of impassioned prose poet. For despite (perhaps, because of) his emphasis on truth and the real, there is always a suggestion in Jefferies of the ultimate mystery of nature that neither scientist nor observer nor even poet will ever fully comprehend. In the end even the most meticulous observer must admit that nature is unfathomable. Jefferies expresses the idea perfectly in "The Pageant of Summer": "There seems always a depth, somewhere, unexplored, a thicket that has not been seen through, a corner full of ferns, a quaint old hollow tree, which may give us something" (*LF*, 68). Bevis' "wood magic" remains.

Bibliography

A. WORKS OF JEFFERIES

1. Books and Pamphlets

This bibliography contains all Jefferies' published books and pamphlets, all books to which he contributed during his lifetime, and all Jefferies anthologies. The order follows chronology of publication (*see* p. 5).

Reporting, Editing, and Authorship. London: John Snow, 1873 (pamphlet).

Jack Brass, Emperor of England. London: T. Pettitt, 1873 (pamphlet).

A Memoir of the Goddards of North Wilts, Compiled from Ancient Records, Registers and Family Papers. London: Simmons and Botten, 1873.

The Scarlet Shawl: A Novel. London: Tinsley, 1874.

Restless Human Hearts. 3 vols. London: Tinsley, 1875.

Suez-cide!! Or How Miss Britannia Bought a Dirty Puddle and Lost Her Sugarplums. London: John Snow, 1876 (pamphlet).

World's End: A Story in Three Books. 3 vols. London: Tinsley, 1877.

The Gamekeeper at Home; or, Sketches of Natural History and Rural Life. London: Smith Elder, 1878.

Wild Life in a Southern County. London: Smith Elder, 1879 (an American reprint [1903, 1904] was retitled *An English Village*).

The Amateur Poacher. London: Smith Elder, 1879.

Greene Ferne Farm. London: Smith Elder, 1880.

Hodge and His Masters. 2 vols. London: Smith Elder, 1880 (one English reprint [1946] was retitled *A Classic of English Farming*).

Round About a Great Estate. London: Smith Elder, 1880.

Wood Magic: A Fable. 2 vols. London: Cassell, 1881 (an American abridgment [1899, 1900] was retitled *Sir Bevis: A Tale of the Fields*).

Bevis: The Story of a Boy. 3 vols. London: Sampson Low, 1882 (English abridgments [1937, 1940] were retitled *Bevis at Home* and *Bevis and Mark* respectively).

Nature Near London. London: Chatto & Windus, 1883.

Society Novellettes. By Various Authors. 2 vols. London: Vizetelly, 1883 (Jefferies contributed two short stories, "Kiss and Try" in volume I, "Out of the Season" in volume II. Volume I was reprinted in 1886 as *No Rose without a Thorn, and Other Tales*, volume II as *The Dove's Nest, and Other Tales*).

The Story of My Heart: My Autobiography. London : Longmans, 1883.

Red Deer. London : Longmans, 1884.

The Life of the Fields. London : Chatto & Windus, 1884.

The Dewy Morn. 2 vols. London : Bentley, 1884.

After London; or, Wild England. London : Cassell, 1885.

The Open Air. London : Chatto & Windus, 1885.

WHITE, GILBERT. *The Natural History of Selborne* [1789]. With an introduction by RICHARD JEFFERIES. London : Walter Scott, 1887.

Amaryllis at the Fair. London : Sampson Low, 1887.

Field and Hedgerow: Being the Last Essays of Richard Jefferies, Collected by His Widow. London : Longmans, 1889.

The Toilers of the Field. London : Longmans, 1892.

Thoughts from the Writings of Richard Jefferies. Selected by H. S. H. WAYLEN. London : Longmans, 1896 (anthology).

The Early Fiction of Richard Jefferies. Edited by GRACE TOPLIS. London: Simpkin, Marshall, 1896.

Jefferies' Land: A History of Swindon and Its Environs. Edited by GRACE TOPLIS. London : Simpkin, Marshall, 1896.

T.T.T. Wells : A. Young, 1896 (short story).

Jefferies' Nature Thoughts. Edited by THOMAS COKE WATKINS. Portland, Maine: T. Mosher, 1904 (anthology).

Passages from the Nature Writings of Richard Jefferies. Selected by A. H. HYATT. London : Chatto & Windus, 1905 (anthology; the third impression was issued as *The Pocket Richard Jefferies Anthology*, 1911).

The Hills and the Vale. With an introduction by EDWARD THOMAS. London: Duckworth, 1909.

Selections from Richard Jefferies. Made by F. W. TICKNER. London: Longmans, 1909 (anthology).

Out-of-Doors with Richard Jefferies. Edited by ERIC FITCH DAGLISH. London: Dent, 1935 (anthology).

Richard Jefferies: Selections of His Work, with Details of His Life and Circumstance, His Death and Immortality. Edited with an introduction by HENRY WILLIAMSON. London : Faber, 1937 (anthology).

Jefferies' England. Edited by SAMUEL J. LOOKER. London : Constable, 1937 (anthology).

Readings from Richard Jefferies. Edited by RONALD HOOK. London : Macmillan, 1940 (anthology).

The Nature Diaries and Notebooks of Richard Jefferies, with an Essay "A Tangle of Autumn," now printed for the first time. Edited by SAMUEL J. LOOKER. Billericay, Essex : Grey Walls Press, 1941 (not to be confused with the complete 1948 edition).

Jefferies' Countryside. Edited by Samuel J. Looker. London: Constable, 1944 (anthology).

Richard Jefferies' London. Edited by Samuel J. Looker. London: Lutterworth Press, 1944 (anthology).

A Richard Jefferies Anthology. Selected by George Pratt Insh. London: Collins, 1945.

The Spring of the Year. Edited by Samuel J. Looker. London: Lutterworth Press, 1946 (anthology).

Summer in the Woods. A selection from the works of Richard Jefferies, with four drawings by S. H. de Roos. Amsterdam: Type Foundry, 1947 (anthology).

The Essential Richard Jefferies. With an introduction by Malcolm Elwin. London: Jonathan Cape, 1948 (anthology).

The Jefferies Companion. Edited by Samuel J. Looker. London: Phoenix House, 1948 (anthology).

Beauty is Immortal (Felise of the Dewy Morn), with Some Hitherto Uncollected Essays and Manuscripts. Edited by Samuel J. Looker. Worthing: Aldridge Brothers, 1948.

The Old House at Coate, and Other Hitherto Unprinted Essays. Edited by Samuel J. Looker. London: Lutterworth Press, 1948.

The Nature Diaries and Note-Books of Richard Jefferies. Edited by Samuel J. Looker. London: Grey Walls Press, 1948.

Chronicles of the Hedges, and Other Essays. Edited by Samuel J. Looker. London: Phoenix House, 1948.

Field and Farm: Essays Now First Collected, with Some from MSS. Edited by Samuel J. Looker. London: Phoenix House, 1957.

2. Serializations

The dates of Jefferies' serial contributions to newspapers and magazines are given below. This supplements and completes the check-list of individual essays to follow. Where Jefferies later included in the published volume a paper not originally intended as part of the scheme, the entry (also listed with the essays) is given in parenthesis.

The Amateur Poacher, in *Pall Mall Gazette.* (1877: Nov. 16); 1879: March 1, 8, 14, 25, 29; April 3, 10, 16, 23, 26; May 6, 10, 17, 23, 31; June 10, 18, 21, 25; July 1, 5, 7.

The Gamekeeper at Home, in *Pall Mall Gazette.* (1877: Dec. 12, 14, 29); 1878: Jan. 4, 9, 12, 18, 22, 26, 31; Feb. 2, 8, 12, 16, 23; March 2, 12, 15, 19, 26, 28; April 1, 5, 9, 12, 17, 24.

Greene Ferne Farm, in *Time.* One chapter each month from April 1879 to February 1880.

Hodge and His Masters, in *Standard*. 1878 : Nov. 19, 26; Dec. 4, 12, 19, 25; 1879 : Jan. 2, 8, 17, 28; Feb. 4. (There follows a break in contributions.) 1879 : Aug. 16, 22, 26; Sept. 2, 8, 15, 23, 30; Oct. 7, 14, 21, 28; Nov. 4, 12, 18; Dec. (16), 26, 30; 1880 : Jan. 5, 12.

Round About a Great Estate, in *Pall Mall Gazette*. 1880 : Jan. 13, 19, 21, 24, 29; Feb. 5, 11, 14, 18, 24; March 2, 11, 17, 22, 29; April 2, 10, 14, 26, 28.

Wild Life in a Southern County, in *Pall Mall Gazette*. 1878 : May 9, 13, 17, 22, 28; June 1, 6, 11, 14, 19, 21, 27; July 1, 6, 10, 16, 19, 22, 27; Aug. 1, 6, 10, 13, 16, 21, 23, 26; Sept. 5, 7, 11, 14, 19, 21, 25, 30; Oct. 7, 12, 16, 19, 24, 28; Nov. 2, 9, 16, 25; Dec. 4.

3. Essays

Essay titles are listed alphabetically, followed by the place and date of first publication in newspaper or magazine, and finally the location in collected volumes. Where the first publication is posthumous, the entry is given in brackets.

"Acorn-Gatherer, The." *See* "Bits of Oak-Bark."

"After the County Franchise." *Longman's Magazine*, Feb. 1884. *The Hills and the Vale.*

"Agricultural 'Capital Account', The." *Live Stock Journal*, Sept. 7, 1877. Uncollected.

"Agricultural Heraldry." *Live Stock Journal*, Dec. 7, 1877. *Field and Farm.*

"Agricultural Labourer's Vote, The." *Pall Mall Gazette*, May 24, 1877. Uncollected. (This essay has not previously been claimed for Jefferies, but internal evidence—in particular, the Wiltshire references—is strongly in favour of its being his.)

"Agricultural Side of the Water Question, The." *Live Stock Journal*, April 5, 1878. Uncollected.

"Agriculture and the Water Congress." *Live Stock Journal*, May 31, 1878. Uncollected.

"America and the Meat Market." *Live Stock Journal*, Jan. 5, 1877. Uncollected.

"American Views on the Meat Traffic." *Live Stock Journal*, March 2, 1877. Uncollected.

"Among the Nuts." *Standard* (?). *Field and Hedgerow.*

"Anthills. Adders." *See* "Heathlands."

"April." *See* "Picture of April."

"April Gossip." *St. James's Gazette*, April 19, 1886. *Field and Hedgerow.*

"Art of Shooting, The" (editor's title). (*The Field*, March 15, 1947.) *Field and Farm.*

"At Coate Farm." *See* "The Cattle Shed at Coate."

"August Out-of-Doors." *Pall Mall Gazette*, Aug. 28, 1879. *Chronicles of the Hedges.*

" 'Autonomy' and What It Means." *Cassell's Family Magazine*, Feb. 1877. Uncollected.

"Autumn Fairs, The." *Live Stock Journal*, Oct. 19, 1877. Uncollected.

"Average of Beauty, The." (Besant lists this title [*The Eulogy of Richard Jefferies*, 124], but no essay of the name can be traced. He was most probably thinking of "Beauty in the Country.")

"Average Servant, The." *Cassell's Family Magazine*, Jan. 1878. Uncollected.

"Backwoods, The." Not published. *Beauty is Immortal.*

"Backwoods of London." *Globe*, Sept 21, 1877. *Chronicles of the Hedges.*

"Bad Harvests in Sussex." *The Times*, Sept. 21, 1881. *Chronicles of the Hedges.* (This paper is the final paragraph of "Some Uncultivated Country: Downs" as it first appeared in *The Times*. It was later omitted when the essay was collected under the title "Downs" in *The Open Air.*)

"Barn, A." *Standard*, Sept. 23, 1880. *Nature Near London.*

"Bathing Season, The." *Pall Mall Gazette*, July 28 and Aug. 8, 1884. *The Open Air.*

"Bath Show Yard, The." *Live Stock Journal*, June 15, 1877. Uncollected.

"Battle of 1866, The" (poem). *North Wilts Herald*, 1866. *The Early Fiction of Richard Jefferies* (Preface).

"Beatrice and the Centaur" (editor's title). Not published. Uncollected. (*See* Samuel J. Looker, "Jefferies Unpublished Manuscripts.")

"Beauty in the Country." Not published (?) *The Open Air.*

"Beauty of the Fields, The." *Magazine of Art*, 1882. *The Life of the Fields.* (Collected as Part I of the essay "Notes on Landscape Painting.")

"Beauty of the Trees, The" (editor's title). *See* "Fir, Larch, and Sycamore, Near London."

"Benediction of the Light, The" (editor's title). *See* "Thoughts in the Fields."

"Ben Tubbs Adventures." Not published. Uncollected. (*See* notes on sales in *Times Literary Supplement*, May 29, 1959. The MS. was sold at Hodgson's, 24 April 1959.)

"Bill-Hook, The." *See* "Chronicles of the Hedges."

"Bird Notes in June" (editor's title). Not published. *Field and Farm.*

"Birds Climbing the Air." *St. James's Gazette*, July 28, 1883. *The Life of the Fields.* (Published in *St. James's Gazette* under the title "Climbing the Air.")

"Birds of Spring." *Chambers' Journal*, March 1, 1884. *The Hills and the Vale.*

"Birds' Nests." *St. James's Gazette*, April 19, 1884. *Field and Hedgerow.*

"Bits of Oak-Bark." *Longman's Magazine*, March 1883. *The Life of the Fields.* (This overall title includes "The Acorn-Gatherer," "The Legend of a Gateway," and "A Roman Brook.")

"Both Sides of the Meat Question." *Live Stock Journal*, Feb. 9, 1877. Uncollected.

"Breeze on Beachy Head, The." *Standard*, Sept. 6, 1881. *Nature Near London.*
"Brook, A." *Standard*, Sept. 30, 1880. *Nature Near London.*
"Buckhurst Park." *Standard*, Aug. 19, 1886. *Field and Hedgerow.*
"By the Exe." *Standard*, Sept. 25, 1883. *The Life of the Fields.* (In the collected version, "The Otter in Somerset" [q.v.] is added to the original text, plus a new passage concerning otters near London.)
"Cattle Shed at Coate, The" (editor's title). (*Countrygoer*, Winter 1948.) *Field and Farm.* (This fragment should really form part of "The Old House at Coate" but was only discovered after that essay was published. Published in *Countrygoer* under the title "At Coate Farm.")
"Chaffinch, The." *See* "Chronicles of the Hedges."
"Changes in Country Habits." *Pall Mall Gazette*, Aug. 28, 1877. *Field and Farm.*
"Choosing a Gun." Not published. *The Hills and the Vale.* (Some of the matter was used in the final chapter of *The Amateur Poacher.*)
"Christmas : Then and Now." *Live Stock Journal Literary Supplement*, Dec. 21, 1877. *Field and Farm.*
"Chronicles of the Hedges." *Land*, Feb. 12, 19, 26; March 19; April 2, 23; May 14, 21, 1881. *Chronicles of the Hedges.* (This over-all title includes "The Bill-Hook," "The Chaffinch," and "The Meadow Gateway.")
"Clematis Lane." *Standard*, Sept. 12, 1883. *The Life of the Fields.*
"Climbing the Air." *See* "Birds Climbing the Air."
"Coming of Summer, The." (*Longman's Magazine*, Dec. 1891.) *The Toilers of the Field.*
"Contrasts Between Town and Country" (editor's title). Not published. *Chronicles of the Hedges.*
"Cost of Agricultural Labour in 1875, The." *Standard*, Oct. 1, 1875. Uncollected.
"Cottage Ideas." *Chambers' Journal*, May 8, 1886. *Field and Hedgerow.*
"Cottage Society and County Suffrage." *Pall Mall Gazette*, Nov. 6, 1877. *Field and Farm.*
"Country Curate, The." *Standard*, Dec. 16, 1879. Later incorporated into *Hodge and His Masters.*
"Country Literature." *Pall Mall Gazette*, Oct. 22, 29; Nov. 5, 22, 30, 1881. *The Life of the Fields.*
"Country Places." *Manchester Guardian* (?). *Field and Hedgerow.*
"Country Readers." *Pall Mall Gazette*, Dec. 22, 1877. *Field and Farm.*
"Countryside : Sussex, The." *Manchester Guardian* (?). *Field and Hedgerow.*
"Country Sunday, The." *Longman's Magazine*, June 1887. *Field and Hedgerow.*
"Crows, The." *Standard*, Nov. 12, 1880. *Nature Near London.*
"Dairy District, A." *Live Stock Journal*, Oct. 5, 1877. *Field and Farm.*
"Dairy Factory System, The." *Live Stock Journal*, Feb. 15, 1878. Uncollected.
"Danger to Dairymen, A." *Live Stock Journal*, Nov. 9, 1877. *Field and Farm.*

"Dangers of Hunting, The." *Live Stock Journal*, Jan. 12, 1877. Uncollected.

"Dawn, The." Not published. *The Hills and the Vale*.

"Decline of Breeding, The." *Live Stock Journal*, Jan. 4, 1878. Uncollected.

"Decline of Partridge Shooting." *Pall Mall Gazette*, Aug. 31, 1878. *Chronicles of the Hedges*.

"Defence of Sport, A." *National Review*, Aug. 1883. *Chronicles of the Hedges*. (Part of this essay, omitted from *Chronicles of the Hedges*, had already been published by Jefferies as "Sport and Science" in *The Life of the Fields*.)

"Dinner at the Farm." (*The Bryanston Miscellany*. Samuel J. Looker, "Jefferies Unpublished Manuscripts.") Uncollected.

"Ditch and the Pool, The" (editor's title). Not published. *Chronicles of the Hedges*.

"Domestic Rook, The." *Live Stock Journal*, Feb. 1, 1878. *Chronicles of the Hedges*.

"Downs." *The Times*, Sept. 21, 1881. *The Open Air*. (Published in *The Times* under the title "Some Uncultivated Country: Downs." *See also* "Bad Harvests in Sussex.")

"Dream of Landseer's Lions, A." Not published. Uncollected. (An early draft of "The Lions in Trafalgar Square." *See* Samuel J. Looker, "Jefferies Unpublished Manuscripts.")

"Early Autumn." *Pall Mall Gazette*, Oct. 20, 1879. *Chronicles of the Hedges*.

"Early in March." *Standard*, March 31, 1879. Uncollected. (This essay has hitherto escaped notice, but it is quite definitely by Jefferies, as may be proved by comparing it with passages from the *Notebooks*.)

"Earth Prayer, The" (poem, editor's title). Not published. *Chronicles of the Hedges*.

"Economic Value of Game, The." *Live Stock Journal*, Nov. 30, 1877. Uncollected.

"English Agricultural Chemists." *Live Stock Journal*, May 17, 24, 1878. Uncollected. (There is some doubt whether this essay is by Jefferies. *See* Looker's note in *Field and Farm*, 186.)

"English Animals Abroad." *Live Stock Journal*, April 20, 1877. *Field and Farm*.

"English Deerpark, An." (*Century Illustrated Magazine*, Oct. 1888.) *Field and Hedgerow*.

"English Homestead, An." *Fraser's Magazine*, Nov. 1876. *The Toilers of the Field*.

"Entered at Stationer's Hall." *Cassell's Family Magazine*, Oct. 1877. Uncollected.

"Essay on Instinct." Not published. Uncollected. (*See* Samuel J. Looker, "Jefferies Unpublished Manuscripts.")

"Extinct Race, An." (*Longman's Magazine*, June 1891.) *The Toilers of the*

Field. (In *Longman's Magazine* this fragment was included in Andrew Lang's miscellany, "At the Sign of the Ship.")

"Fallacy of Prices, The." *Live Stock Journal*, May 4, 1877. Uncollected.

"Farmer at Home, The." *Fraser's Magazine*, Aug. 1874. *The Toilers of the Field*.

"Farmer's Stores in London : An Opening for Young Agriculturists." *Live Stock Journal*, July 12, 1878. Uncollected.

"Farms Out of Cultivation." *The Times*, Sept. 3, 1881. *Field and Farm*.

"February Day in Stanmer Park, A." *St. James's Gazette*, Feb. 17, 1883. *Chronicles of the Hedges*.

"Fictitious Manure." *Live Stock Journal*, April 18, 1878. Uncollected.

"Field and Farm." *St. James's Gazette*, March 30, 1883. *Field and Farm*.

"Field-Faring Women." *Fraser's Magazine*, Sept. 1875. *The Toilers of the Field*.

"Field-Play, The." *Time*, Dec. 1883. *The Life of the Fields*. (This essay consists of two parts : "Uptill-a-Thorn" and "Rural Dynamite.")

"Field Sports in Art." *Art Journal*, 1885. *Field and Hedgerow*.

"Field Words and Ways." *Pall Mall Gazette*, Nov. 25, 1886. *Field and Hedgerow*.

"Fields in April, The." *Pall Mall Gazette*, May 2, 1879. *Chronicles of the Hedges*. (In *Chronicles of the Hedges* this essay forms Part 2 of "In the Fields. April.")

"Fields in May, The." *Pall Mall Gazette*, June 3, 1879. *Chronicles of the Hedges*.

"Fir, Larch, and Sycamore, Near London." (*The Field*, June 7, 1947.) *Chronicles of the Hedges*. (In *The Field* this fragment was entitled "The Beauty of the Trees." Both are editor's titles.)

"Flocks of Birds." *Standard*, Nov. 18, 1880. *Nature Near London*.

"Flowers of the Grass." Not published. *Chronicles of the Hedges*.

"Footpaths." *Standard*, Nov. 3, 1880. *Nature Near London*.

"Forest." *The Times*, Sept. 24, 1881. *The Open Air*. (Published in *The Times* under the title "Some Uncultivated Country : Forest.")

"Future of Country Society, The." *New Quarterly*, July 1877. Uncollected.

"Future of Farming, The." *Fraser's Magazine*, Dec. 1873. Uncollected.

"Future of the Dairy, The." *Live Stock Journal Almanack*, 1879. Uncollected.

"Game and Tenants' Leases." *Live Stock Journal*, Oct. 11, 1878. Uncollected.

"Game as Property." *Live Stock Journal*, March 8, 1878. *Field and Farm*.

"Game for Bicycles, A." Not published. Uncollected. (*See* Samuel J. Looker, "Jefferies Unpublished Manuscripts.")

"Game Question, The." *Live Stock Journal*, March 1, 1878. Uncollected.

"Gaudy as a Garden." *Graphic*, Aug. 26, 1876. *Chronicles of the Hedges*.

"Genesis of *The Story of My Heart*" (editor's title). Not published. *Field and Farm*.

"Getting to Market." *Live Stock Journal*, June 29, 1877. Uncollected.

" 'Gilt-Edged' Butter." *Live Stock Journal*, Nov. 23, 1877. Uncollected.

"Gold-Crested Wren, The." (*Longman's Magazine*, June 1891.) *The Toilers of the Field*. (In *Longman's Magazine* this fragment was included in Andrew Lang's miscellany "At the Sign of the Ship.")

"Golden Brown." *Pall Mall Gazette*, Aug. 27, 1884. *The Open Air*.

"Great Agricultural Opportunity, A." *Live Stock Journal*, Aug. 9, 1878. Uncollected.

"Great Agricultural Problem, A." *Fraser's Magazine*, March 1878. Uncollected.

"Great Grievance, A." *Live Stock Journal*, March 8, 1878. *Field and Farm*.

"Great Snow, The" (editor's title). (*The Field*, March 22, 1947.) *Beauty is Immortal*.

"Green Corn, The." *Good Words*, May 1883. *The Open Air*. (In *The Open Air* this essay becomes the last four paragraphs of "Out of Doors in February." *See also* "Vignettes from Nature.")

"Harvest Field, The." *Live Stock Journal*, Aug. 16, 1878. Uncollected.

"Haunt of the Hare, The." Not published (?). *The Open Air*.

"Haunts of the Lapwing." *Good Words*, Jan. and March 1883. *The Open Air*. (The second part of this essay also forms the first part of "Vignettes from Nature" [q.v.].)

"Hay Harvest Notes." *Live Stock Journal*, June 15, 1877. *Chronicles of the Hedges*.

"Haymaking by Artificial Heat." *Live Stock Journal*, July 5, 1878. Uncollected.

"Heart of England, The." Not published. Uncollected. (A fragment of a proposed book. *See* Samuel J. Looker, "Jefferies Unpublished Manuscripts.")

"Heathlands." *Standard*, Dec. 23, 1880. *Nature Near London*. (Published in the *Standard* under the title "Rural London : Anthills. Adders.")

"Hedge and the Smell of Hops, The" (editor's title). Not published. *Chronicles of the Hedges*.

"Hedge Miners." *Land*, Aug. 6, 1881. *Chronicles of the Hedges*.

"Hedgerow Sportsman, The." *St. James's Gazette*, Jan. 28, 1882. *Chronicles of the Hedges*.

"Henrique Beaumont" (short story). *North Wilts Herald*, July 21, 28; Aug. 4, 1866. *The Early Fiction of Richard Jefferies*.

"Herbs." *Standard*, Oct. 15, 1880. *Nature Near London*.

"High Pressure Agriculture." *Fraser's Magazine*, August 1876. Uncollected.

"History of Malmesbury." *North Wilts Herald*, April to Sept. 1867. Uncollected.

"History of Swindon and Its Environs." *North Wilts Herald*, Oct. 1867 to June 1868. *Jefferies' Land*.

"Horse as a Social Force, The." *Live Stock Journal*, July 20, 1877. *Field and Farm*.

"Horses in Relation to Art." *Magazine of Art*, 1878. *Beauty is Immortal*.

"Hours of Spring." *Longman's Magazine*, May 1886. *Field and Hedgerow*.

"House Martins." *Standard* (?). *Field and Hedgerow*.

"Hovering of the Kestrel, The." *St. James's Gazette*, Feb. 22, 1883. *The Life of the Fields.*

"How to Read Books." *Cassell's Family Magazine*, Aug. 1876. *Beauty is Immortal.*

"Hyperion" (editor's title). Not published. *Beauty is Immortal.*

"Idle Earth, The." (*Longman's Magazine*, Dec. 1894.) *The Hills and the Vale.*

"Improved Cars for Cattle." *Live Stock Journal*, June 28, 1878. Uncollected.

"In Brighton" (editor's title). Not published. *Beauty is Immortal.*

"Increasing Importance of Horse-Breeding." *Live Stock Journal*, July 13, 1877. Uncollected.

"Intermixed Agriculture." *Live Stock Journal*, Nov. 2, 1877. Uncollected.

"In the Fields: April." *St. James's Gazette*, April 20, 1881. *Chronicles of the Hedges.* (In *Chronicles of the Hedges* the essay "The Fields in April" is included as a second part under the same title.)

"In the Fields. March." *St. James's Gazette*, March 12, 1881. *Chronicles of the Hedges.*

"In the Hop-Gardens." *St. James's Gazette*, Sept. 23, 1880. *Chronicles of the Hedges.*

Introduction to Gilbert White's *Natural History of Selborne*. Camelot Classics, 1887. *The Spring of the Year.*

"January in the Sussex Woods." *Standard*, Jan. 22, 1884. *The Life of the Fields.* (In the *Standard* the title was "January in the Woods.")

"Jockeying Pheasant Preserves." *Live Stock Journal*, June 1, 1877. Uncollected.

"John Smith's Shanty." *Fraser's Magazine*, Feb. 1874. *The Toilers of the Field.*

"Joy of the Wind, The." Not published. *Chronicles of the Hedges.*

"July Grass, The." *Pall Mall Gazette*, July 24, 1886. *Field and Hedgerow.*

"Just Before Winter." *Chambers' Journal*, Dec. 18, 1886. *Field and Hedgerow.*

"Kilburn Show, The." *Pall Mall Gazette,* July 4, 1879. *Field Farm.*

"King of Acres, A." *Chambers' Journal*, Jan. 5, 12, 1884. *The Hills and the Vale.*

"Kiss and Try" (short story). *Society Novelettes*, I, 1883. Uncollected.

"Labourer and His Hire, The." *Live Stock Journal*, Aug. 30, 1878. Uncollected.

"Labourer's Daily Life, The." *Fraser's Magazine*, Nov. 1874; *The Toilers of the Field.*

"Larger Thought of London, The." Not published. *Chronicles of the Hedges.*

"Last of a London Trout, The." Not published. *The Old House at Coate.* (Not to be confused with "A London Trout.")

"Leafy November, A." *Pall Mall Gazette*, Nov. 25, 1879. *Chronicles of the Hedges.*

"Left Out in the Cold." *St. James's Gazette*, Dec. 30, 1884. *Field and Farm.*

"Legend of a Gateway, The." *See* "Bits of Oak-Bark."

"Leicester Square." Not published. *Chronicles of the Hedges.*

"Lesser Birds, The" (editor's title). *See* "Thoughts in the Fields."

"Lesson in Lent, A." *Live Stock Journal*, March 30, 1877. *Chronicles of the Hedges.*

"Less Stock, Less Wheat." *Live Stock Journal*, Oct. 26, 1877. Uncollected.

"Let Me Think." *Cassell's Family Magazine*, Oct. 1876. *Beauty is Immortal.*

"Life of the Soul, The" (editor's title). Not published. *The Old House at Coate.*

"Lions in Trafalgar Square, The." (*Longman's Magazine*, March 1892.) *The Toilers of the Field.*

"Locality and Nature." *Pall Mall Gazette*, Feb. 17, 1887. *Field and Hedgerow.*

"London Bridge Station." Not published. *Chronicles of the Hedges.*

"London Contrasts" (editor's title). Not published. *Chronicles of the Hedges.*

"London Mud" (editor's title). Not published. *Chronicles of the Hedges.*

"London Reflections." (*The Field*, Sept. 27, Oct. 4, 1947.) *Chronicles of the Hedges.* (This is Jefferies' over-all title for many untitled fragments later printed in *Chronicles of the Hedges*.)

"London Scents and Colours" (editor's title). Not published. *Chronicles of the Hedges.*

"London Selfishness" (editor's title). Not published. *Chronicles of the Hedges.*

"London Trout, A." *Standard* (?). *Nature Near London.*

"Lonely Common, The" (editor's title). Not published. *Field and Farm.*

"Machiavelli: A Study." (*Nineteenth Century and After*, Sept. 1948.) Uncollected.

"Magic of the Night." Not published. *Chronicles of the Hedges.*

"Magpie Fields." *Standard* (?). *Nature Near London.*

"Makers of Summer, The." *Chambers' Journal*, May 28, 1887. *Field and Hedgerow.*

"Manufacture of Milk, The." *Live Stock Journal*, Sept. 21, 1877. Uncollected.

"March Notes." *St. James's Gazette*, March 6, 1883. *Chronicles of the Hedges.*

"Marlborough Forest." *Graphic*, Oct. 23, 1875. *The Hills and the Vale.*

"Masked" (short story). *North Wilts Herald*, Oct. 13, 20, 27, 1866. *The Early Fiction of Richard Jefferies.*

"Meadow Gateway, The." *See* "Chronicles of the Hedges."

"Meadow Thoughts." *Graphic* (?). *The Life of the Fields.*

"Midsummer 1879." *Pall Mall Gazette*, July 12, 1879. *Chronicles of the Hedges.*

"Midsummer Hum, The." *Graphic*, July 15, 1876. *Chronicles of the Hedges.*

"Midsummer Pests." *Live Stock Journal*, June 22, 1877. *Chronicles of the Hedges.*

"Mind Under Water." *Graphic*, May 19, 1883. *The Life of the Fields.*

"Minor Sources of Income." *Live Stock Journal*, March 16, 1877. Uncollected.

"Minute Cultivation—A Silver Mine." *Live Stock Journal*, July 26, 1878. *Chronicles of the Hedges.*

"Mixed Days of May and December." *Pall Mall Gazette*, May 13, 1887. *Field and Hedgerow.*

"Modern Sporting Guns." *Pall Mall Gazette*, Nov. 17, 1879. *Chronicles of the Hedges.*

"Modern Thames, The." *Pall Mall Gazette*, Sept. 6, 1884. *The Open Air.* (The first part of the essay only was published in the *Pall Mall Gazette.* This was then entitled : "Our River : 1. Its Natural Denizens." Other writers contributed articles under the over-all title.)

"More About Butter." *Live Stock Journal*, Jan. 11, 1878. Uncollected.

"Mowers and Reapers : Recent Improvements." *Live Stock Journal*, April 26 and May 10, 1878. Uncollected.

"Mr. Mechi's Budget." *Live Stock Journal*, April 27, 1877. Uncollected.

"Mulberry Tree, The" (poem). *See* "The Tree of Life."

"My Chaffinch" (poem). *Pall Mall Gazette*, March 18, 1887. *Field and Hedgerow.*

"My Old Village." (*Longman's Magazine*, Oct. 1887.) *Field and Hedgerow.*

"Mystery of Offal, The." *Live Stock Journal*, April 12, 1878. Uncollected.

"Natural History of Beautiful Women, The." Not published. *Field and Farm* (appendix).

"Nature and Books." *Fortnightly Review*, May 1887. *Field and Hedgerow.*

"Nature and Eternity." (*Longman's Magazine*, May 1895.) *The Hills and the Vale.*

"Nature and the Gamekeeper." *St. James's Gazette*, March 13, 1883. *The Life of the Fields.*

"Nature in the Louvre." (*Magazine of Art*, Sept. 1887.) *Field and Hedgerow.*

"Nature Near Brighton." *Standard*, Aug. 28, 1883. *The Life of the Fields.*

"Nature on the Roof." *Chambers' Journal*, June 21, 1884. *The Open Air.*

"Neglected Pig, The." *Live Stock Journal*, Feb. 22, 1878. *Field and Farm.*

"Nightingale Road." *Standard*, Nov. 26, 1880. *Nature Near London.*

"Nightingales." *St. James's Gazette*, April 10, 1886. *Chronicles of the Hedges.*

"Noontide in the Meadow" (poem). Not published separately. *Greene Ferne Farm.* (Later printed separately as a poem by Samuel J. Looker in his notes to the Collector's ed. of *Field and Hedgerow*, 1948.)

"Notes on Landscape Painting." *Magazine of Art*, 1882. *The Life of the Fields.* (Only Part I of this essay was published in the *Magazine of Art* under the title "The Beauty of the Fields.")

"Novelty in Literature." Not published. Uncollected. (*See* Samuel J. Looker, "Jefferies Unpublished Manuscripts.")

"Nutty Autumn." *Standard*, Sept. 30, 1881. *Nature Near London.*

"Oak Bark." *See* "Thoughts in the Fields."

"October." (*The Bryanston Miscellany.* Samuel J. Looker, "Jefferies Unpublished Manuscripts.") Uncollected. (Extract from an early draft of *Bevis.*)

"Old House at Coate, The." Not published. *The Old House at Coate.*

"Old Keeper, The." Not published. *Field and Farm.*

"On Allotment Gardens." *New Quarterly*, April 1875. Uncollected.

"One of the New Voters." Not published (?). *The Open Air.*

"On the Downs." *Standard*, March 23, 1883. *The Hills and the Vale.*

"On the London Road." *Pall Mall Gazette*, April 2, 1885. *The Open Air.* (The title in the *Pall Mall Gazette* was "Scenes on the London Road.")

"Orchis Mascula." (*Longman's Magazine*, June 1891.) *The Toilers of the Field.* (In *Longman's Magazine* this fragment was included in Andrew Lang's miscellany "At the Sign of the Ship.")

"Otter in Somerset, The." *Manchester Guardian*, Aug. 27, 1883. *The Life of the Fields.* (In *The Life of the Fields* this essay, which has hitherto escaped notice in separate form, is incorporated into "By the Exe.")

"Our River : 1. Its Natural Denizens." *See* "The Modern Thames."

"Our Winter Food." *Live Stock Journal*, Sept. 14, 1877. Uncollected.

"Out of Doors in February." *Good Words*, Feb. 1882, May 1883. *The Open Air.* (The last four paragraphs appeared separately as "The Green Corn" on the later date. *See also* "Vignettes from Nature.")

"Out of the Season" (short story). *Society Novelettes*, II, 1883. Uncollected.

"Outside London." *Chambers' Journal*, Jan. 17, Feb. 21, 1885. *The Open Air.*

"Pageant of Summer, The." *Longman's Magazine*, June 1883. *The Life of the Fields.*

"Paradox : Slow Progress of Science, The" (editor's title). (*The Field*, July 19, 1947.) *Beauty is Immortal.* (Published in *The Field* under the title "Slow Progress of Science.")

"Parliamentary Measures Affecting the Grazier." *Live Stock Journal*, Feb. 23, 1877. Uncollected.

" 'Patent' Butter." *Live Stock Journal*, Feb. 8, 1878. Uncollected.

"Pasture and Stock." *Live Stock Journal*, March 23, 1877. Uncollected.

"Persecution of St. Partridge, The." *Live Stock Journal*, June 8, 1877. *Field and Farm.*

"Philosophy of Mayflies, The." (*The Field*, May 24, 1947.) *Field and Farm.*

"Piccadilly." Not published. *Chronicles of the Hedges.*

"Picture of April" (poem). *Pall Mall Gazette*, April 30, 1885. *Chronicles of the Hedges.* (The title in the *Pall Mall Gazette* was "April.")

"Picture of the Men and Women Living Upon the Land." Not published. Uncollected. (An early synopsis of *Hodge and His Masters. See* Samuel J. Looker, "Jefferies Unpublished Manuscripts.")

"Pictures in the National Gallery" (editor's title). Not published. *Chronicles of the Hedges.*

"Pigeons at the British Museum, The." *Pall Mall Gazette*, Jan. 11, 1884. *The Life of the Fields.*

"Pine Wood, The." *Standard*, Sept. 3, 1885. *The Open Air.*

"Place of Ambush, The" (editor's title). (*The Field*, April 26, 1947.) *Field and Farm.*

"Plainest City in Europe, The" (Paris). *Pall Mall Gazette*, Oct. 20, 1883. *The Life of the Fields.*

"Plea for Pheasant Shooting, A." *Live Stock Journal*, Sept. 28, 1877. Uncollected.

"Poaching as a Profession." *Pall Mall Gazette*, Dec. 12, 14, 1877. Later incorporated into *The Gamekeeper at Home*.

"Position of the Grazier, The." *Live Stock Journal*, Feb. 2, 1877. Uncollected.

"Power of the Farmers, The." *Fortnightly Review*, June 1874. Uncollected.

"Primrose Gold in Our Village." *Pall Mall Gazette*, June 8, 1887. *Field and Farm*.

"Producers and Consumers." *Live Stock Journal*, June 21, 1878. Uncollected.

"Professional Bird-Catcher, The." *St. James's Gazette*, Aug. 4, 1885. *Chronicles of the Hedges*.

"Profit from Rabbits." *Live Stock Journal*, Sept. 13, 1878. Uncollected.

"Protection of Hunting, The." *Live Stock Journal*, May 25, 1877. Uncollected.

"Protection of Nature, The" (editor's title). Not published. *Field and Farm*.

"Queen's New Subjects, The." *Cassell's Family Magazine*, Aug. 1877. Uncollected.

"Rabbits as Food." *Live Stock Journal*, Dec. 29, 1877. Uncollected.

"Rabbit Warrens and their Returns." *Live Stock Journal*, Jan. 4, 1878. *Field and Farm*.

"Railway Accidents Bill, A." *Fraser's Magazine*, May 1874. Uncollected.

"Rats, Mice and Game Preserves." *Live Stock Journal*, Sept. 27, 1878. Uncollected.

"Recapitulation" (poem, editor's title). Not published. *Chronicles of the Hedges*.

"Red Roofs of London." *Pall Mall Gazette* (?). *The Open Air*.

"Reorganizing the Meat Supply." *Live Stock Journal*, Jan. 26, 1877. *Field and Farm*.

"River, The." *Standard*, Sept. 10, 1880. *Nature Near London*.

"Roman Brook, A." *See* "Bits of Oak Bark."

"Rooks, The" (editor's title). Not published. *Chronicles of the Hedges*. (*See* "A Winter Scene.")

"Round a London Copse." *Standard*, Dec. 26, 1882. *Nature Near London*. (This essay contains passages which also occur in "The Spring of the Year" [q.v.].)

"Rural Dynamite." *See* "The Field Play."

"Rural London." An over-all title for most of the essays published later as *Nature Near London*. They are here listed under their separate titles.

"Sacrifice to Trout, The." *St. James's Gazette*, March 17, 1883. *The Life of the Fields*.

"Saint Guido." *English Illustrated Magazine*, Dec. 1884. *The Open Air*.

"Scarcity of Bacon Pigs, The." *Live Stock Journal*, July 19, 1878. Uncollected.

"Scenes on the London Road." *See* "On the London Road."

"Scientific Culture of Grasses and Clover." *Live Stock Journal*, Nov. 16, 1877. Uncollected.

"Seasons in Surrey : Tree and Bird Life in the Copse, The." Not published.
The Old House at Coate.

"Sea, Sky, and Down." *Standard*, Jan. 3, 1884. *The Life of the Fields.*

"Seed Inquisition, The." *Live Stock Journal*, Dec. 21, 1877. Uncollected.

"Selling by Rule of Thumb." *Live Stock Journal*, May 10, 1878. Uncollected.

Sermon on *Luke* xii, 52. Not published. Uncollected. (Listed in Hodgson's
Auction Catalogue for April 24, 1959.)

"Shipton Accident, The." *Fraser's Magazine*, Feb. 1875. Uncollected.

"Shooting." Not published. Uncollected. (*See* Samuel J. Looker, "Jefferies Unpublished Manuscripts.")

"Shooting a Rabbit." *Pall Mall Gazette*, June 25, 1880. *Chronicles of the
Hedges.*

"Shooting Poachers." *Pall Mall Gazette*, Dec. 13, 1884. *Chronicles of the
Hedges.*

"Shortest Day Scene, A." *St. James's Gazette*, Dec. 22, 1884. *Chronicles of the
Hedges.*

"Shorthorn in France, The." *Live Stock Journal*, June 7, 1878. Uncollected.

"Shorthorns on Arable Land." *Live Stock Journal*, April 13, 1877. Uncollected.

"Shrinking of the Scene in Winter." Not published. *Chronicles of the Hedges.*
(*See* "A Winter Scene.")

"Single Barrel Gun, The." *St. James's Gazette*, Dec. 19, 1884. *The Open Air.*

"Size of Farms, The." *New Quarterly*, Oct. 1874. Uncollected.

"Skating." Not published. *The Hills and the Vale.*

"Sleight-of-Hand Poaching." *Pall Mall Gazette*, Dec. 29, 1877. Later incorporated into *The Gamekeeper at Home.*

"Slow Progress of Science." *See* "The Paradox : Slow Progress of Science."

"Small Birds." *Pall Mall Gazette*, Dec. 30, 1878. *Chronicles of the Hedges.*

"Snipes and Moonlit Sport." *Pall Mall Gazette*, Nov. 16, 1877. Later incorporated in *The Amateur Poacher.*

"Sold by Auction." *St. James's Gazette*, Feb. 24, 1885. *Field and Farm.* (In the
St. James's Gazette the title was "To be Sold by Auction.")

"Some April Insects." *Pall Mall Gazette*, April 27, 1887. *Field and Hedgerow.*

"Some Triumphs of Poor Men." *Cassell's Family Magazine*, April 1877. *Beauty
is Immortal.*

"Some Uncultivated Country : Downs." *See* "Downs."

"Some Uncultivated Country : Forest." *See* "Forest."

"Southdown Shepherd, The." *Standard*, Aug. 31, 1881. *Nature Near London.*

"Spirit of Modern Agriculture, The." *New Quarterly*, July 1876. Uncollected.

"Sport and Science." *National Review*, Aug. 1883. *The Life of the Fields.* (*The
Life of the Fields* includes only part of the original essay whose full title
was "A Defence of Sport" [q.v.].)

"Spring Notes." *Pall Mall Gazette*, April 23, 1880. *Chronicles of the Hedges.*

"Spring of the Year, The." (*Longman's Magazine*, June 1894.) *The Hills and the Vale.* (This essay contains passages which had already appeared in "Round a London Copse" [q.v.].)

"Spring Prospects and Farm Work." *Live Stock Journal,* March 22, 1878. *Chronicles of the Hedges.*

"Squire and the Land, The" (editor's title). Not published. *The Old House at Coate.*

"Squire at Home, The." Not published. Uncollected. (*See* Samuel J. Looker, "Jefferies Unpublished Manuscripts.")

"Squire's Preserves, The" (editor's title). Not published. *Field and Farm.* (An unused section of *The Amateur Poacher.*)

"Stars Above the Elms, The" (editor's title). Not published. *Chronicles of the Hedges.*

"State of Farming, The." *St. James's Gazette,* Aug. 3, 5, 13, 1881. *Field and Farm.*

"Steam on Country Roads." *Standard,* Sept. 13, 1881. *Field and Hedgerow.* (Published in the *Standard* under the title "Steam on Common Roads." The essay was revised before book-publication.)

"Story of Furniture, The." *Cassell's Family Magazine,* June 1877. *Beauty is Immortal.*

"Story of Swindon, The." *Fraser's Magazine,* May 1875. *The Hills and the Vale.*

"Strand, The." Not published. *Chronicles of the Hedges.*

"Strange Story, A" (short story). *North Wilts Herald,* June 30, 1866. *The Early Fiction of Richard Jefferies.*

"Straw and Stock." *Live Stock Journal,* Oct. 12, 1877. Uncollected.

"Strength of the English" (editor's title). Not published. *The Old House at Coate.*

"Study of Stock, The." *Live Stock Journal,* May 11, 1877. *Chronicles of the Hedges.*

"Summer in Somerset." (*English Illustrated Magazine,* Oct. 1887.) *Field and Hedgerow.*

"Summer Meat Supply." *Live Stock Journal,* May 17, 1878. Uncollected.

"Summer Notes." *Pall Mall Gazette,* July 6, 1880. *Chronicles of the Hedges.*

"Sun and the Brook, The." *Knowledge,* Oct. 13, 1882. *The Hills and the Vale.*

"Sunlight in a London Square." *Pall Mall Gazette,* Sept. 7, 1883. *The Life of the Fields.*

"Sunny Brighton." *Longman's Magazine,* July 1884. *The Open Air.*

"Swallow Time." *Standard,* Aug. 3, 1886. *Field and Hedgerow.*

"Swindon : Its History and Antiquities." *Wilts Archaeological and Natural History Magazine,* March 1874. Uncollected.

"Tangle of Autumn, A." Not published. *Field and Farm.* (This essay had previously been printed in the 1941 edition of the *Notebooks.*)

"Thoughts in the Fields" (editor's title). (*The Field,* Sept. 13, 1947.) *Chronicles of the Hedges.* (This was the collective title used in *The Field* for fragments printed in *Chronicles of the Hedges* separately as "The Benediction of the Light," "The Lesser Birds," "Oak Bark," "Trees and Birds of the Wood," and "Wild Thyme of the Hills.")

"Thoughts on Cattle Feeding." *Live Stock Journal*, May 24, 1878. Uncollected.

"Thoughts on the Labour Question." (*Pall Mall Gazette*, Nov. 10, 1891.) *Field and Farm*.

"Three Centuries at Home." Not published. *The Old House at Coate*.

"Time of Year, The." *Pall Mall Gazette*, April 9, 1887. *Field and Hedgerow*.

"Tits and Trees" (editor's title). Not published. *Chronicles of the Hedges*. (*See* "A Winter Scene.")

"To a Fashionable Bonnet" (poem). *North Wilts Herald*, 1866. *The Early Fiction of Richard Jefferies* (Preface).

"To be Sold by Auction." *See* "Sold by Auction."

"To Brighton." *Standard*, Sept. 15, 1880. *Nature Near London*.

"Too Much 'Margin'." *Live Stock Journal*, Jan. 25, 1878. Uncollected.

"Training Schools for Servants." *Cassell's Family Magazine*, March 1878. Uncollected.

"Traits of the Olden Times." *North Wilts Herald*, 1866 (?). *The Early Fiction of Richard Jefferies*.

"Travelling Labour." *Live Stock Journal*, July 6, 1877. *Chronicles of the Hedges*.

"Tree of Life, The" (poem). (*Scots' Observer*, Nov. 8, 1890.) Reprinted by Samuel J. Looker in the 1941 edition of the *Notebooks* and in the notes to the Collector's edition of *Field and Hedgerow*, 1948. (Also known as "The Mulberry Tree.")

"Trees About Town." *Standard*, Sept. 28, 1881. *Nature Near London*.

"Trees and Birds of the Wood" (editor's title). *See* "Thoughts of the Fields."

"Trees in and Around London" (editor's title). Not published. *The Old House at Coate*.

"Trespass." *Live Stock Journal*, Aug. 24, 1877. *Chronicles of the Hedges*.

"True Approach to Nature, The" (editor's title). Not published. *Chronicles of the Hedges*.

"True Tale of the Wiltshire Labourer, A." Not published. *The Toilers of the Field*.

"T.T.T." (short story). *North Wilts Herald*, 1867. Printed separately in 1896. Otherwise uncollected.

"Twenty Years of Mechanical Farming." *Graphic*, Oct. 23, 1875. Uncollected. (There is some doubt whether this essay is by Jefferies. Salt lists it in the bibliography of the first edition of his *Richard Jefferies*, but he does not list "Marlborough Forest," definitely by Jefferies, that appeared in the same issue of the *Graphic*. He may have made a mistake. Internal evidence is inconclusive.

"Typical Prize Farm, A." *Live Stock Journal*, Aug. 23, 1878. Uncollected.

"Under the Acorns." *Chambers' Journal*, Oct. 18, 1884. *The Open Air*.

"Under the Snow." *Pall Mall Gazette*, Jan. 20, 1879. *Chronicles of the Hedges.*

"Under Tropical Rains." *Live Stock Journal*, Jan. 19, 1877. Uncollected.

"Unequal Agriculture." *Fraser's Magazine*, May 1877. *The Hills and the Vale.*

"Untutored Love." (*The Bryanston Miscellany.* Samuel J. Looker, "Jefferies Unpublished Manuscripts.") Uncollected.

"Uptill-a-Thorn." *See* "The Field Play."

"Utility of Birds." *Live Stock Journal*, Aug. 3, 1877. *Chronicles of the Hedges.*

"Value of Grass, The." *Live Stock Journal*, March 9, 1877. Uncollected.

"Value of Small Things, The." *Live Stock Journal*, Jan. 18, 1878. *Field and Farm.*

"Varied Sounds" (editor's title). Not published. *Chronicles of the Hedges.*

"Venice in the East End." *Pall Mall Gazette*, Nov. 5, 1883. *The Life of the Fields.*

"Vignettes from Nature." (*Longman's Magazine*, July 1895.) *The Hills and the Vale.* (The first part of this essay had already been printed as the second part of "Haunts of the Lapwing"; the second part consists of the essay "The Green Corn" which had already been assimilated into "Out of Doors in February.")

"Village Churches." *Graphic*, Dec. 4, 1875. *The Hills and the Vale.*

"Village Miners." *Gentleman's Magazine*, June 1883. *The Life of the Fields.*

"Village Organization." *New Quarterly*, Oct. 1875. *The Hills and the Vale.*

"Walks in the Wheat-fields." *English Illustrated Magazine*, July and August 1887. *Field and Hedgerow.*

"War, The." *Live Stock Journal*, May 18, 1877. Uncollected.

"Wasp-Flies or Hoverers" (editor's title). Not published. *Chronicles of the Hedges.*

"Water." *Live Stock Journal*, April 6, 1877. *Field and Farm.*

"Water-Colley, The." *Manchester Guardian*, Aug. 31, 1883. *The Life of the Fields.*

"Weeds and Waste." *Live Stock Journal*, Sept. 6, 1878. *Chronicles of the Hedges.*

"Wet Night in London, A." *Pall Mall Gazette*, Dec. 31, 1884. *The Open Air.*

"Wheatfields." *Standard*, Aug. 17, 1880. *Nature Near London.*

"Which is the Way?" *Cassell's Family Magazine*, Dec. 1876. Uncollected.

"Who Will Win? or, American Adventure." *North Wilts Herald*, Aug. 25; Sept. 1, 8, 15, 22, 29, 1866. *The Early Fiction of Richard Jefferies.*

"Wild Flowers." *Longman's Magazine*, July 1885. *The Open Air.*

"Wild Flowers and Wheat." *Pall Mall Gazette*, July 20, 1881. *Chronicles of the Hedges.*

"Wild Fowl and Small Birds." *Pall Mall Gazette*, April 18, 1877. *Chronicles of the Hedges.*

"Wild Thyme of the Hills, The" (editor's title). *See* "Thoughts in the Fields."

"Wiltshire Labourer, The." *Longman's Magazine*, Nov. 1883. *The Hills and the Vale.*

"Wiltshire Labourers." Letters to *The Times*, Nov. 12, 23, 27, 1872. *The Toilers of the Field.*

"Window-Seat in the Gun-Room, The." (*The Bryanston Miscellany*. Samuel J. Looker, "Jefferies Unpublished Manuscripts.") Uncollected. (Part of this fragment was used for "An English Deerpark.")

"Winds of Heaven." *Chambers' Journal*, Aug. 7, 1886. *Field and Hedgerow.*

"Winter Scene, A" (editor's title). Not published. *Field and Farm*. (This is a composite essay constructed out of various Jefferies fragments. It contains the notes, previously printed separately in *Chronicles of the Hedges*, of "The Rooks," "Shrinking of the Scene in Winter" and "Tits in the Trees.")

"Women in the Field." *Graphic*, Sept. 11, 1875. Uncollected.

"Woodlands." *Standard*, Aug. 25, 1880. *Nature Near London.*

B. Biography and Criticism

In presenting this bibliography of Jefferies scholarship, I have attempted a reasonable compromise between usefulness and completeness. At the end of his biography of Jefferies, Edward Thomas included what he described in a letter to Gordon Bottomley as "a monstrous bibliography for those who come after me." All subsequent critics must be grateful to Thomas' industry, but he included everything remotely connected with Jefferies, and to continue this comprehensive undertaking up to the present time would, I am convinced, prove more confusing than helpful. I have therefore omitted such items as formal obituaries, poems written about Jefferies, newspaper accounts of tablet unveilings, letters in provincial correspondence columns suggesting the forma-tion of Jefferies Clubs, etc.; but I have listed all books, pamphlets, and articles, however brief or derivative, that concern themselves with Jefferies' life or works. I also include review articles when they consider Jefferies' work in detail, and unpublished university theses, but introductions to individual reprints are not listed.

Anderson, A. H. "Richard Jefferies and Sussex," *Sussex County Magazine*, XI (Aug. 1937), 524–30.

Arkell, Reginald. *Richard Jefferies*. London: Rich & Cowan, 1933 (subse-quently reprinted under the title *Richard Jefferies and His Countryside*).

—— "Richard Jefferies at Coate," *Country Life*, CIII (June 18, 1948), 1224–5.

Avebury, Lord. "Richard Jefferies," in his *Essays and Addresses, 1900–1903*. London: Macmillan, 1903.

Bell, Julian. "A Neglected Master," *New Statesman and Nation*, Nov. 11, 1933, 596–600.

Besant, Walter. *The Eulogy of Richard Jefferies*. London: Chatto & Windus, 1888.

Blench, J. W. "The Novels of Richard Jefferies," *Cambridge Journal*, VII (March 1954), 361–77.

BRITTAIN, F. "Richard Jefferies," *Cambridge Review*, April 19, 1947.
—— "The Centenary of Richard Jefferies," *Cambridge Review*, May 22, 1948.
—— "Richard Jefferies and Others," *Cambridge Review*, Feb. 5, 1949.
BUCKE, R. M. "Richard Jefferies," in his *Cosmic Consciousness: A Study in the Evolution of the Human Mind*. Philadelphia : Innes & Sons, 1901.
BUGADA, FRANCO. "Richard Jefferies, 1848-1887." Unpublished doctoral dissertation presented to the University of Milan, 1958.
CASSERES, BENJAMIN DE. "Richard Jefferies : A Pagan Mystic," in his *Forty Immortals*. New York : Joseph Lawren, 1926.
CHURCH, L. F. "The Centenary of Richard Jefferies," *London Quarterly*, CLXXIII (Oct. 1948).
CHURCH, RICHARD. *Richard Jefferies Centenary Memorial Lecture*. Swindon: Borough Council, 1948.
—— "The Horizon of Richard Jefferies," *Picture Post*, XLI (Nov. 6, 1948), 11-13.
CLARKE, ARTHUR C. "A Link with Jefferies : Unpublished Letters written when he was engaged on *Red Deer*," *The Field*, May 1, 1948, 494.
CLUTTON-BROCK, ARTHUR. "A Neglected Romance" (*After London*), *The Speaker*, XIII (Nov. 4, 1905), 108-9.
COLERIDGE, GILBERT. "Richard Jefferies and the Unknown God," *Nineteenth Century and After*, LXXXVII (March 1920), 492-8.
COLLARD, LORNA KEELING. "Richard Jefferies," *Contemporary Review*, CXXXIV (Nov. 1928), 622-32.
COLLIN, CHRISTEN CHRISTIAN DREYER. "Richard Jefferies," in his *Studier og Portraeter*. Christiana : Det Norske Aktieforlag, 1901.
Countrygoer (Richard Jefferies Centenary Number), XII (Winter 1948).
COURTS, D. C. "Richard Jefferies : A Reinterpretation." Unpublished thesis submitted in connection with the M.A. degree, Birmingham University, 1958.
COVENEY, PETER. "Mark Twain and Richard Jefferies," in his *Poor Monkey: The Child in Literature*. London : Rockliff, 1957.
CRAWFURD, OSWALD. "Richard Jefferies : Field-Naturalist and Litterateur," *The Idler*, XIII (Oct. 1898), 289-301.
DALE, DARLEY. "Natural Mystics" (Jefferies and Thoreau), *American Catholic Quarterly Review*, XXXIX (Jan. 1914), 160-73.
DARTNELL, GEORGE E. "Richard Jefferies," *Wiltshire Archaeological and Natural History Magazine*, XXVII (June 1893), 69-99.
"Did Richard Jefferies Die a Christian? Reminiscences by People Who Knew Him," *Pall Mall Gazette*, Sept. 22, 1891.
DUNK, JAMES. "Jefferies' Great Prayer," *Great Thoughts*, July 1901, 251-2.
EDWARDES, TICKNER. "The Heart of Richard Jefferies," *Chichester Diocesan Gazette*, May and July 1921, 165-7, 229-31.
ELLWANGER, GEORGE H. "Afield with Jefferies," in his *Idyllists of the Countryside*. London : Bell, 1896.

FISHER, CHARLES. "A Study of Richard Jefferies," *Temple Bar*, CIX (Dec. 1896), 502–9.

FOERSTER, NORMAN. "The Vogue of Richard Jefferies," *PMLA*, XXVIII (1913), 530–8.

FOLEY, CAROLINE A. "Women in the Works of Richard Jefferies," *Scots Magazine*, VII (Feb. 1891), 218–31.

FREEMAN, CHARLES G. "Richard Jefferies at Surbiton," *Surbiton Times*, 1896.

FREEMAN, GARTH. "Richard Jefferies, 1848–1887." Unpublished thesis presented in connection with teacher's training diploma, Westminster College, Oxford, 1960.

GARNETT, EDWARD. "Richard Jefferies," *Universal Review*, II (Nov. 1888), 357–71.

——— "Richard Jefferies as a Novelist," *Academy*, LXIV (April 4, 1903), 348.

——— "Richard Jefferies' *Amaryllis at the Fair*" in his *Friday Nights: Literary Criticism and Appreciations* (first series). London : Jonathan Cape, 1922.

GAY, FRANCES J. "Jefferies Farm Situate at Coate in the Parish of Chiseldon in the County of Wiltshire," *Swindon Review*, 1955.

——— "Richard Jefferies 1848–1887," *Wiltshire Courier*, I (Oct. 1962), 24–5, 30.

GIBBS, HENRY. "Richard Jefferies, The English Genius," *Books Today*, XXX (Oct. 1948), 1–3.

GRAHAM, P. ANDERSON. "Round About Coate," *Scots Observer*, IV (Oct. 18, 1890), 564–5. (Not to be confused with Graham's article in the *Art Journal*.)

——— "The Magic of the Fields (Richard Jefferies)" in his *Nature in Books: Some Studies in Biography*. London : Methuen, 1891.

——— "Round About Coate," *Art Journal*, XLV (1893), 16–21. (Not to be confused with his *Scots Observer* article.)

GRAVETT, DAVID. *Richard Jefferies: The Prose Poet of the Countryside*. Worthing : Art Development Scheme, 1939 (pamphlet).

GREENWOOD, FREDERICK. "Richard Jefferies," *Scots Observer*, IV (Aug. 2, 1890), 275–7.

GRINSELL, L. V. "The Archaeological Contribution of Richard Jefferies," *Transactions of the Newbury District Field Club*, VIII (1940), 216–26.

[HALL, FANNY CATHERINE] ("Jefferies Luckett"). "The Forebears of Richard Jefferies," *Country Life*, XXIII (March 14, 1908), 373–6.

HALL, FANNY CATHERINE, and BOTT, FLORENCE E. *The Jefferies Family Tree, 1686–1925*. Bath : privately printed by the compilers, 1925 (pamphlet).

HARVIE, ARTHUR. "Richard Jefferies : The Tender Mercies of a Great Naturalist," *Humane Review*, II (July 1901), 162–76.

——— "The Summer Psalms of Richard Jefferies," *Inquirer*, CCCXLVII (Aug. 20, 1904).

HAWKINS, DESMOND. "Richard Jefferies, Countryman," *Home and Country*, XXX (Nov. 1948), 199.

HENLEY, W. E. "Jefferies" in his *Views and Reviews, Essays in Appreciation: Literature*. London : David Nutt, 1890.

HICKS, ERIC. "They Knew the River. XV : Richard Jefferies," *PLA Monthly* (Magazine of the Port of London Authority), CCXCVIII (Aug. 1950), 155–60.

"Homes and Haunts of Richard Jefferies," *Pall Mall Budget*, Aug. 25, 1892 (illustrations only).

HORSELL, AUDREY. "Reminiscences of Richard Jefferies," *The Countryman*, XIII (April 1936).

HOSTE, M. R. "Richard Jefferies," *Argosy*, LXXI (June 1900), 227–32.

HYDE, WILLIAM J. "Richard Jefferies and the Naturalistic Peasant," *Nineteenth Century Fiction*, XI (Dec. 1956), 207–17.

JACKSON, HOLBROOK. "Richard Jefferies" in his *All Manner of Folk: Interpretations and Studies*. London : Grant Richards, 1912.

[JEFFERIES, HAROLD.] "Richard Jefferies," *Montreal Gazette*, May 30, 1929.

JOHNS, THE REV. B. G. "Jefferies the Naturalist," *Sunday Magazine*, May 1894, 334–9.

JOLLIFFE, HAROLD. *A Catalogue of the Books in the Richard Jefferies Collection of the Swindon Public Libraries*. Swindon : Libraries, Museum, Arts, and Music Committee, 1948 (pamphlet).

JONES, J. B. *The Liddington-Barbury Memorial*. Swindon : Swindon Press, 1941 (pamphlet).

JONES, DR. SAMUEL A. *Richard Jefferies*. Ann Arbor, Michigan : Register Publishing Company, 1893 (pamphlet).

JUPP, W. H. "The Poet-Naturalists III : Richard Jefferies," *Great Thoughts*, IV (March 23 and 30, 1895), 400–2, 411–12.

KEITH, W. J. "Richard Jefferies and *The Story of My Heart*." Unpublished thesis presented in partial fulfilment of the requirements for the M.A. degree, University of Toronto, 1959.

"Landlords, Tenants, and Labourers" (review of *Hodge and His Masters*), *Edinburgh Review*, CLII (July 1880), 139–69.

LEAVIS, Q. D. "Lives and Works of Richard Jefferies," *Scrutiny*, VI (March 1938), 435–46.

LOCK, D. R. "Richard Jefferies as Prophet," *Catholic World*, CXLV (Oct. 1937), 76–83.

LOOKER, SAMUEL J. *To the Immortal Memory of Richard Jefferies*. Worthing: Art Development Scheme, 1939 (pamphlet).

—— "Bibliographical Discoveries in the Work of Richard Jefferies," *Notes and Queries*, Feb. 12, 1944, 91–2.

—— "Richard Jefferies (1848–1887)," *Country Journal*, I (Winter 1948), 10–14.

—— *The True Richard Jefferies: An Examination of the Misunderstandings of Malcolm Elwin in "The Essential Richard Jefferies."* Cheadle, Staffs: privately printed, 1949 (pamphlet).

—— "W. H. Hudson and Richard Jefferies," *Notes and Queries*, April 30, 1949, 195–6.

—— "Jefferies Unpublished Manuscripts" in Victor Bonham-Carter (ed.), *The Bryanston Miscellany*. Bryanston School, Dorset: privately printed, 1958.

—— (ed.). *Concerning Richard Jefferies, by Various Writers*. Worthing: Aldridge Brothers, 1944.

—— (ed.). *Richard Jefferies: A Tribute by Various Writers*. Worthing: Aldridge Brothers, 1946.

LUBBOCK, SIR J. L. *See* AVEBURY, LORD.

LUCKETT, JEFFERIES. *See* HALL, FANNY CATHERINE.

LYMINGTON, VISCOUNT. "Richard Jefferies and the Open Air," *National Review*, X (Oct. 1887), 242–50.

MARSHALL, D. E. "Richard Jefferies: 1848–1948," *Contemporary Review*, CLXXIV (Nov. 1948), 299–303.

MASSECK, C. J. *Richard Jefferies: Etude d'une Personalité*. Paris: Emile Larose, 1913.

MERCER, W. C. "G. M. Hopkins and Richard Jefferies," *Notes and Queries*, May 10, 1952, 217.

MILLER, HENRY. "The Story of My Heart" in his *The Books in My Life*. London: Peter Owen, 1952.

MULLEN, ALICE CLARKE. "Richard Jefferies," *Audubon Magazine*, L (Nov.-Dec., 1948), 366–71.

MUNTZ, IRVING. "Richard Jefferies as a Descriptive Writer," *Gentleman's Magazine*, CCLXXVII (Nov. 1894), 514–32.

NEWCOMBE, BERTHA. "Richard Jefferies and His Home in Wiltshire," *Sylvia's Journal*, March 1894, 192–8.

"Notes Relating to a Forged Edition of Jefferies' Pamphlet, *Suez-cide!!*" Untitled news-item in *The Clique* (Derby), June 3, 10, 17, 24; July 1, 29, 1893.

OSBORN, J. LEE. *Coate, the Birth-place of Jefferies, and Chiseldon Church*. Malmesbury: Abbey Press, 1913 (pamphlet).

PAYNE, L. G. "Richard Jefferies, 1848–1887," *London Naturalist*, XXVI (1946), 11–13.

"Pernicious Works of Richard Jefferies, The." Correspondence in *Pall Mall Gazette*, Sept. 18–21, 1891.

POPE, T. MICHAEL. "Richard Jefferies," *Academy*, LXXIV (March 28, 1908), 617–18.

PURVES, JAMES. Review of *The Story of My Heart* in *Academy*, Nov. 3, 1883, 294.

QUILLER-COUCH, ARTHUR. "Mr Quiller-Couch and Richard Jefferies," *Critic* (New York), XX (Oct. 21, 1893), 262.

REES, ARTHUR WELLESLEY. "The Interpretation of Nature," *Great Thoughts*, Sept. 3, 1898, 355–6.

"Richard Jefferies" by C. W. M., *Girl's Own Paper*, Dec. 21, 1889.

"Richard Jefferies," *Great Thoughts*, V (Dec. 20, 1890), 456–9.

"Richard Jefferies," *Murray's Magazine*, VIII (Sept. 1890), 421–5.

"Richard Jefferies," *Marlburian*, XXVII (Nov. 16, 1892), 161–2.

"Richard Jefferies," *Edinburgh Review*, CCX (July 1909), 221–43.

RICKETT, ARTHUR. "Richard Jefferies" in his *The Vagabond in Literature*. London : Dent, 1906.

ROBERTS, NESTA. "Here Lived Richard Jefferies," *Manchester Guardian*, Sept. 24, 1960.

ROGERS, E. J. "Richard Jefferies and Goethe," *John o' London's Weekly*, LVIII (Sept. 2, 1949), 549.

S[ALMON], A. L. "Richard Jefferies in London," *Academy*, June 10, 1905, 613–14.

—— "Richard Jefferies : An Attempt at Appreciation," in his *Literary Rambles in the West of England*. London : Chatto & Windus, 1906.

SALT, H. S. "The Story of a Heart," *Today*, IX (June, 1888), 163–8.

—— "The Gospel According to Richard Jefferies," *Pall Mall Gazette*, Nov. 15, 1888.

—— "Richard Jefferies," *Temple Bar*, XCII (June 1891), 215–24.

—— "The Conversion of Richard Jefferies," *National Reformer*, Oct. 18, 1891.

—— *Richard Jefferies: A Study*. London : Sonnenschein, 1894 (reprinted in 1905, without bibliography, under the title *Richard Jefferies: His Life and His Ideals*).

—— *The Faith of Richard Jefferies*. London : Rationalist Press, 1906 (pamphlet, reprinted from *Westminster Gazette*, CLXIV (Aug. 1905), 177–8).

—— "Thoreau and Jefferies" in his *Company I Have Kept*. London : Allen & Unwin, 1930.

SCOTT, G. FORRESTER. "Three Nature Writers" (Walton, White, Jefferies), *Bookman*, XXVI (June 1904), 84–8.

SEAL, GABRIEL. "Country Authors—6 : Richard Jefferies," *The Countryman*, LIII (Winter 1956), 693–9.

SHARP, ARTHUR. "The Sussex of Richard Jefferies," *Sussex County Magazine*, XXII (July 1948), 236–8.

STAFFORD, DARBY. "Richard Jefferies at Home," *Badminton Magazine*, Sept. 1901, 320–34.

—— "The Home and Haunts of Richard Jefferies," *English Illustrated Magazine*, XXXII (Feb. 1905), 431–7.

SYMONS, ARTHUR. "Richard Jefferies" in his *Studies in Two Literatures*. London : Martin Secker, 1924.

TAYLOR, G. R. STIRLING. "Richard Jefferies," *Nineteenth Century and After*, XCV (April and May 1924), 530–40, 686–96.

THOMAS, EDWARD. "The Fiction of Richard Jefferies," *Readers' Review*, I (July 1908), 83–5.

—— *Richard Jefferies: His Life and Work.* London : Hutchinson, 1909.

—— "Richard Jefferies and London," *Bookman,* XXXV (Feb. 1909), 215–19.

THOMAS, GILBERT. "Richard Jefferies" in his *Builders and Makers.* London: Epworth Press, 1944.

THORN, ARTHUR F. *Richard Jefferies and Civilisation.* London : Arthur Stockwell, 1914 (pamphlet, later incorporated into the next item).

—— *The Life Worship of Richard Jefferies.* London : Pioneer Press, 1920.

VAUGHAN, HERBERT M. "Richard Jefferies : Natural Historian of the English Countryside" in his *From Anne to Victoria: Fourteen Biographical Studies between 1702 and 1901.* London : Methuen, 1931.

VEITCH, J. L. *Richard Jefferies: The Man and His Work.* Salisbury : Bennett Brothers, 1894 (pamphlet, reprinted from *Salisbury and Winchester Journal,* Feb. 10, 1894.

WARREN, C. HENRY. "Richard Jefferies," *New English Review,* I (Sept. 1948), 25–31.

—— "Richard Jefferies," *Fortnightly Review,* Nov. 1948, 338–42.

WILLIAMSON, GEORGE. "The Eye of Richard Jefferies," *Literary Guide,* LXX (Aug. 1955), 18–9.

WILLIAMSON, HENRY. "Richard Jefferies," *Atlantic Monthly,* CLIX (June 1937), 681–8.

—— "A Wiltshire Lad," *Fortnightly Review,* CXLII (Aug. 1937), 178–86.

—— "Report on the Jefferies Centenary," *Adelphi,* XXV (Oct.-Dec. 1948).

—— "Some Nature Writers and Civilisation" (Jefferies and Hudson), in *Essays by Divers Hands* (Transactions of the Royal Society of Literature), XXX. Oxford : University Press, 1960.

WILLIS, FRED. *The Ideals of Richard Jefferies.* Privately printed (n.p.), 1914 (pamphlet).

WRIGHT, ALAN. "Richard Jefferies," *Girl's Own Paper,* Aug. 31, 1889, 757

WRIGHT, LUCIAN. *"The Story of My Heart,"* *University Magazine and Free Review,* X (May, 1898), 158–65.

As THIS BOOK goes to press, a new biography is announced, *Richard Jefferies, Man of the Fields,* by Samuel J. Looker and Crichton Porteous, to be published in 1965 by John Baker. This biography, incorporating much of the information compiled by the late Mr. Looker, will be of vital interest to all readers of the present study.

Index

Trafalgar Square, London, 162, 164